Life As It Ain't Yet:

MEDITATIONS FOR LIVING NOW

Richard N. Johnson

CBP PRESS
ST. LOUIS, MISSOURI

© 1988 CBP Press
All rights reserved. No part of this book may be reproduced without the publisher's written permission. Address:

CBP Press
Box 179
St. Louis, MO 63166

Unless otherwise indicated, all scripture quotations are from the Revised Standard Version of the Bible, copyrighted 1946, 1952, © 1971, 1973, by the Division of Christian Education of the National Council of Churches of Christ in the United States of America.

Library of Congress Cataloging-in-Publication Data

Johnson, Richard N.

  Life as it ain't yet : meditations for living now / by Richard N. Johnson.
    p. cm.
  ISBN 0-8272-2119-3 : $8.95
  1. Meditations.   I. Title.
BV4832.2.J618   1988   87-25865
242—dc19   CIP

Printed in the United States of America

Acknowledgements

Grateful acknowledgement is made to the following copyright holders for permission to use their copyrighted material:

The Christian Century Foundation. The lines from Amos Wilder's "Electric Chimes or Rams' Horns" are reprinted from the January 27, 1971 issue of the *Christian Century*. Wm. B. Eerdmans Publishing Co. for the quotations from Mary McDermott Shideler, *Consciousness of Battle*, Copyright 1970. Used by permission.
Harcourt Brace Jovanovich for permission to quote from "On the Atomic Bomb in *Poems*, by C. S. Lewis, Copyright (c) 1964 by The Executors of the Estate of C. S. Lewis. Reprinted by permission of Harcourt Brace Jovanovich, Inc. For a quotation from "Ash Wednesday" in *Collected Poems 1909-1962*, by T. S. Eliot, Copyright 1936 by Harcourt Brace Jovanovich, Inc., Copyright © 1963, 1964 by T. S. Eliot. Reprinted by permission of the publisher. And for a quotation from *All the King's Men*, Copyright 1946, 1974 by Robert Penn Warren. Reprinted by permission of Harcourt Brace Jovanovich, Inc.
John Knox Press for the quotation from Fred B. Craddock, *Philippians* from Interpretation, A Bible Commentary for Teaching and Preaching series, Copyright 1985, and for the quotation from Eduard Schweizer, *The Good News According to Mark*, Copyright 1977.
Macmillan Publishing Company for the six lines from W. B. Yeats, "The Second Coming," reprinted with permission of Macmillan Publishing Company from W. B. Yeats, *The Collected Poems of W. B. Yeats*, Copyright 1924 by Macmillan Publishing Company, renewed 1956 by Georgie Yeats.
Ellen C. Masters for the quotation of "Aner Clute," from Edgar Lee Masters, *Spoon River Anthology* (New York: Collier Macmillan, 1962) p. 77.
New American Library for the quotation from *Ma Rainey's Black Bottom* by August Wilson. Copyright (c) 1981, 1985 by August Wilson. Reprinted by arrangement with New American Library, New York, New York.
W. W. Norton and Co. for the quotation from Rollo May, *The Courage to Create*, Copyright 1975.
Phaidon Press Limited for the quotation from Elias Bredsdorff, *Hans Christian Anderson*, Copyright 1975.
Random House, Inc. and Alfred A. Knopf, Inc. for the quotation from Lillian Hellman, *My Mother, My Father and Me*, Copyright 1963 by Random House, for the lines from W. H. Auden, "Profile," *Collected Poems*, Copyright 1976 by Random House, the quotation from Paddy Chayefsky, *Gideon*, Copyright 1962 by Random House, and the quotation from *Markings* by Dag Hammarskjold, translated by Leif Sjoberg and W. H. Auden, Copyright 1964 by Alfred A. Knopf.
Simon and Schuster, Inc. for the quotation from Nikos Kazantzakis, *Report to Greco*, Copyright 1965, the quotations from Nikos Kazantzakis, *The Saviors of God*, Copyright 1960, and the quotation from Nikos Kazantzakis, *Zorba the Greek* copyright (c) 1953, 1981 by Simon and Schuster, Inc. Reprinted by permission of Simon and Schuster, Inc.

Templegate for the quotations from H. A. Williams, *The Joy of God* Copyright 1979 and *Tensions*, Copyright 1976.

Ticknor and Fields for a quotation from *The Enthusiast: A Life of Thornton Wilder*, by Gilbert A. Harrison, Copyright (c) 1983 by Gilbert A. Harrison. Reprinted by permission of Ticknor and Fields, a Houghton Mifflin Company.

Yankee Publishing Incorporated for the quotation from Clark Andrews, "To Us He was Always 'T. W.,'" *Yankee*, September, 1978, pp. 152-154. Reprinted with permission from Yankee Publishing.

Contents

Preface

For years, my wife and daughter have encouraged me (perhaps "hounded" me would be more accurate) to put some of my thoughts on paper for a book. This collection of meditations is a result of their persistence. I have to admit, though, that writing it this year was fun!

I believe lay people will find the meditations suitable for public reading in situations where brief devotions are needed. Fellow preachers preparing sermons are invited to borrow any ideas they can use. I would like to think that some will find profit in reading and pondering these in private.

Thanks to Hallie Denny, Sheron Rodgers, Faye Linn, and Carolyn McLemore for typing the manuscript. Special thanks to Michele Johnson and Virginia Johnson, who proofread the text, made numerous valuable suggestions, and edited out most of my "Okie."

Shalom,
Dick Johnson

To my parents

Norris and Ruth Johnson

Life's New Beginnings

□

Jumping into Life

It is said that once, when he was down on his luck, Harry Sinclair shot himself in the foot to collect insurance and make a fresh start.[1] If that's true, he jumped back into life on one foot.

While I neither condone nor condemn that way of jumping, God sent his Son into the world to call us to jump back into life from the deadliness into which we all sink from time to time for one reason or another. We are sometimes challenged to risk our lives, but more frequently we are dared to risk living. That is often more frightenening than risking our lives, and that is why people who are fully alive are so rare. The leap from deadliness back into life usually takes at least as much courage as it would to shoot oneself in the foot.

God is waiting to catch us with his "everlasting arms" (*Deuteronomy 33:27*). We are called to catch each other. We all have to do our own jumping, however. That is scary! When we are trying to work up the nerve to jump into a swimming pool, we may wonder about the temperature of the water. The water of true life may seem rather icy if we only stick in a toe, but it feels good once we're all the way in. So, on the count of three, let's all jump! One, two, three, . . .

O God, give us the courage to risk living! Amen.

When Should We Hope?

Most of us feel hopeful when things are going well, and we feel discouraged when they are going badly. It seems logical that we should. The great prophets of the Old Testament usually were the opposite. In good times, they were inclined to preach doom, for they could see the injustice and greed that often accompanied prosperity. Often when conditions hit rock bottom, they turned to hope, for they could see that new beginnings were then possible.

When the people of Judah felt secure, Jeremiah kept speaking of a foe from the North that would destroy the nation. When Babylon brought that destruction, carrying the leaders and many of the people into exile, leaving the earth of Palestine so scorched that real estate prices hit a record low, Jeremiah bought a field as a sign that eventually God would allow the people to begin again (*Jeremiah 32:6-44*). Off in exile, Ezekiel turned from doom to hope only after he heard that the temple in Jerusalem had been destroyed. He knew the destruction of the old temple would eventually make possible the building of a new and purer temple.

Centuries later, the death of God's Son on the cross brought new life to him and to all humankind. The hope of the resurrection is that God makes possible an endless supply of new beginnings, not only in the next life, but even now in this one.

O God, when we are down, raise us up! Amen.

□

Forgetting the Past

In most of our pasts there are both people and events that we would prefer to forget. Sometimes the more we try to free ourselves from their hold on us, the more they seem to tighten their grip on our lives. Hugh Leonard's play, *Da*, is the story of an Irishman's relationship to the father who adopted him. The play opens on the day of the old man's funeral. Through a series of flashbacks, the anger and guilt of that relationship unfold. The Irishman, Charlie, hopes Da's death will free him from the anger and guilt, and he trys to destroy everything that might remind him of it. At the end of the play, however, Da is still following right behind him.[2]

Paul wrote, "Therefore, if any one is in Christ, he is a new creation; the old has passed away, behold, the new has come" (*2 Corinthians 5:17*). God's love in Christ can do what usually we cannot do for ourselves. It can free us from our pasts, and make us new.

Of course, there is a sense in which we can never entirely escape our pasts as long as we and others remember. We wouldn't want to forget everything in them. God's love, however, can free us from all that is deadly in them—the guilt, the anger, and the bitterness. The resurrection faith proclaims that God's grace can break not only the power of physical death, but also the power of all the deadliness in this life, so that we can even now live lives that are really new.

O God, make us new! Amen.

Lighting Candles

Jesus said, "I am the light of the world; he who follows me will not walk in darkness, but will have the light of life" (*John 8:12*).

Clyde Reid tells of a dream he once had in which Jesus handed him a lighted candle. Clyde kept blowing out the candle. Jesus kept lighting it.[3]

We are always blowing out our own candles. Most of the worst things we do, though they may be directed at others, end by hurting us more than anyone else. Usually, we are our own worst enemies.

But God, in Jesus Christ, keeps relighting our candles. The resurrection faith means not only that there is a new beginning after this life, but also that there are unlimited opportunities for new beginnings in this one. Regardless of the harm we may do to ourselves, God opens the way for us to begin again.

O God, keep relighting our candles. Amen.

Expecting the Unexpected

Sholom Aleichem wrote that the Jews in the fictional village of Kasrilevka wouldn't believe in the existence of railroad trains. After all, none of them had ever seen one. One day a villager took a train to Moscow. They could no longer doubt that trains existed. However, they could not comprehend the speed of the trains, so when the villager told them it took less than an hour, they interpreted this to mean that he took the train that long and then went the rest of the way on foot![4] They were like the elderly man interviewed on television at the time of the second moon launch. When asked what he thought about it, he replied, "They ain't nobody goin' to no moon."

By this time, most of us are so used to technological wonders that little surprises us. In times of personal crisis, though, many of us tend to be as skeptical about our futures as the Jews in Kasrilevka and the elderly man were about trains and space travel. Most of the best things that happen to us do so unexpectedly. Since we can't anticipate what the new opportunities will be, it is hard for us to believe they will come. Even when the future seems closed, doors are apt to open to lead us back into life. To live in hope is to expect the unexpected. As Paul wrote, "Now hope that is seen is not hope. For who hopes for what he sees? But if we hope for what we do not see, we wait for it with patience" (*Romans 8:24-25*).

O God, help us to trust in what we do not see! Amen.

Living Now

Cleaning Houses

When I first knew them, our friends in a little village in the South of France lived in a tiny house with only a kitchen and two bedrooms. There was no indoor plumbing. Their circumstances changed, and they built a fine new house with many rooms and a magnificent bath. For some time, they continued to live in the kitchen, saying that they wanted to keep the rest of the house clean for special occasions. Even their lovely bath with indoor plumbing went unused. On our most recent trips to their village, I have noticed that finally they are living in the whole house.

Many of us never get around to living in the house we build with our lives. We seem to be waiting perpetually for special occasions that never come. We spend our lives cleaning houses we never take time to inhabit, or planning trips we never get around to taking, or making money to be able to do things that we never do, or . . . .

That shows the point of Jesus' announcement that, "The time is fulfilled, and the kingdom of God is at hand . . ." (*Mark 1:15*) or "in the midst of you" (*Luke 17:21*). Real life is here now for any who choose to live it. It can't be saved for special occasions. There may not be any! Amen.

O God, lead us to life now! Amen.

☐

☐

The Time to Live

I remember seeing an advertisement for a book several years ago titled *Is There Life Before Death?* We can all relate to that question. When we add together the time we waste in useless busyness, the time we spend chasing after goals that prove much less fulfilling than we expect, and the times we are simply too dull or insensitive to appreciate the importance of the life we are living, there isn't much time left for being really alive. We all miss a lot of life as we live it.

In Mark's Gospel, Jesus says that the time is right and the kingdom or rule of God is at hand (*1:15*). "The kingdom of God is in the midst of you," he says in Luke's Gospel (*17:21*). At a time when most religious people were missing a lot of life by putting all their efforts into remembering the past or speculating about the future, those words woke them up to the present. Our time to live this life is now. If only we had ears to hear and eyes to see!

Despite all of the life we let slip by and all the death there is in this life, those moments when we do wake up enough really to live are worth it all. We can only stand in gratitude before the one who gives it!

O God, Thank you for life and for the heart to live it, at least sometimes. Amen.

The Final Two Weeks

A Spanish teacher at Central State University received an anxious call from a co-ed one evening. The student's roommate had not attended class even once, and only two weeks remained in the semester. She wanted to know if there were any way the roommate could make up in those final two weeks all the work she had missed. The teacher replied, "Inform your roommate she has flunked the course." If one can do a semester's work in two weeks, there would be no need for semester-long classes. It takes a whole semester to do a semester course. Have you ever tried to learn a foreign language in two weeks?

We chuckle at the students' naivete in thinking there still might be a last-minute chance, yet sometimes we live as though we thought we could crowd all our dreams into our final two weeks. How many parents have wished, after it was too late, that they had spent more time with their children when they were growing up? How many opportunities have all of us missed by putting off until it was too late? We can't wait until the final two weeks to live. It takes a whole lifetime to live a life!

O God, raise us up before the last two weeks! Amen.

□

As Warm as They

Those who have done brass rubbings or visited the cathedrals of England know that many people are buried in the walls or floors of churches there. Evidently the most cherished burial sites, and therefore the most expensive, are those nearest the altar, while the cheaper ones are near the doors. Thus there is the following epitaph on a burial marker near the door of a church in Kingsbridge, Devon, England:

> Here I lie by the chancel door,
> Here lie I because I'm poor,
> The farther in, the more you pay,
> Here lie I as warm as they.[5]

An old Russian proverb goes, "Death carries a fat tsar on his shoulders as easily as a lean beggar."[6]

Freud claimed that in the unconscious part of our minds, none of us really believes he or she is going to die. Judging from some of the games we play in this life, I assume he was right.

Jesus told about a man who played a game of filling his barns with grain. The harvest was plentiful, so he pulled down his barns and built larger ones to make room for his crops. Thinking he had secured his life, he said to himself, "You have ample goods laid up for many years; take your ease, eat, drink, be merry." That very night, Jesus said, he died (*Luke 12:13-21*).

I suspect that if any of us realized fully how little time we have in this life, we would reorder our priorities. At least we wouldn't waste so much of our lives fretting about what might happen to us. We would all realize that, at some point, it will.

O God, help us to learn from death how to live! Amen.

Life as It Ain't Yet

"I don't want fake pictures. I want life as it is," Berney says in Lillian Hellman's *My Mother, My Father and Me.* To that his father replies, "Life as it is. A fine thing to want. Believe me, I'd take a little of what life ain't."[7] Son and father each have a point. If we are so caught up in our pursuit of better things to come that we can't enjoy life as it now is, we never get around to living. On the other hand, if we are so content with life as it is that we stop reaching out for what it might become, our lives begin to reek of the deadliness of stagnation. In both cases, we find ourselves among the ranks of the living dead.

I think that is the reason Jesus spoke of God's kingdom or rule as both present now and as yet to come. At times, he spoke of that kingdom as being very near: "The kingdom of God is at hand" (*Mark 1:15*). Having already begun his ministry, he said, "But if it is by the Spirit of God that I cast out demons, then the kingdom of God has come upon you" (*Matthew 12:28*). The kingdom is present already for his listeners: "The kingdom of God is in the midst of you" (*Luke 17:21*). At other times, Jesus spoke of the kingdom as still to come: "Truly, I say to you, I shall not drink again of the fruit of the vine until that day when I drink it new in the kingdom of God" (*Mark 14:25*).

Edward Schweizer puts it this way:

> The kingdom has both present and future aspects. Of course, that aspect of the kingdom of God is future, where men will have fellowship at table with Jesus in his glory, where death and pain will have been abolished, and where faith will have passed into sight.
>
> But the one who meets Jesus cannot continue to wait for the kingdom to appear sometime in the next ten to one thousand years. In the acts and words of Jesus the future kingdom has come upon him already.[8]

The life of God's kingdom or rule is here even now for those willing to enter it, but it is here only for those who yearn for its future fulfillment in him. Life in its fullness belongs to those who value both life as it is and as it ain't yet.

O God, we thank you for that life in you which now is, and is yet to come. Amen.

Living with
Open Eyes and Ears

□

Don't Blink

"Come now, don't go to sleep. Take deep breaths. You've only got 70 years. Keep turning your head in all directions. Don't blink." That is the advice Thornton Wilder gave three of his students on a trip to Europe.[9] Someone has said that the tragedy of man is not how much he suffers, but how much he misses. All of life is rich with God's gifts, but you have to keep turning your head in all directions to see them.

We all need goals in life to keep us going. Without them, we might never bother to get up in the morning. Even those I have reached, however, rarely have been as satisfying as the surprises along the way. The unexpected opportunities, the moments when somehow I have been able to touch the lives of other people or be touched by them, the chance glimpses of beauty or joy, or even the shared tears—those have been the sorts of things which have meant the most to me. We all need goals, but if we head toward them with our eyes so firmly fixed in their direction that we never turn our heads from side to side, we are apt to miss life's best surprises.

As C. S. Lewis said of the tragic road of history in a few lines of one of his poems:

> Narrow and long it stretches,
> Wretched for one who marches
> Eyes front. He never catches
> A glimpse of the fields each side, the happy orchards.[10]

O God, keep turning our heads with your surprises! Amen.

Seeing Clearly

Jesus once asked his disciples, "Having eyes do you not see, and having ears do you not hear?" (*Mark 8:18*). Sometimes the sighted are blind. Sometimes the blind see. There are different ways of seeing.

One evening, my wife and I were flying out of Chicago. The lights of the city had just come on. A group of conventioneers were on board the plane, flying back to their homes. One of them had a bullhorn. Pretending to be the pilot, he said, "Ladies and gentlemen, this is your captain speaking. We have just left O'Hare airport. If you will look out your left or right windows, you will see a vast panorama of light, color, and beauty. But, having been on the ground only a few minutes ago, you know it's just a dirty old city."

There are different ways of looking at the same situation. We can go through life looking at the dirt hidden beneath the beauty or at the beauty hidden by the dirt.

I suspect all of us catch glimpses, at least, of the hand of God in even the most ordinary events of our everyday lives. Unfortunately, we usually shut our eyes as quickly as those events appear, fearing that they are forbidden. To trust what we see, even when it disturbs and frightens us, is to see with the eyes of faith.

O God, open our eyes and ears! Amen.

Walking in the Day

When Picasso was told his portrait of Gertrude Stein did not look much like her, he replied, "Don't worry. It will." He knew that in time, the painting would help people see Gertrude Stein in a new way. One of the values of art is that it helps us see things in a way we haven't before.

A great artist helps us to see things that most of us miss. He gives us a new set of eyes so that we can see even ordinary things in a way we have never seen them before.

The same thing happens when God makes himself known to us. Through the eyes of faith, all of life looks different.

With his parables, Jesus helped us to see that God's kingdom or rule was already partly present in the most common, ordinary things of everyday life—mustard seeds, the growth of ears of grain, lost coins and lost sheep, and a father's extravagant forgiveness of a wayward son.

Jesus said, "If any one walks in the day, he does not stumble, because he sees the light of this world. But if any one walks in the night, he stumbles, because the light is not in him" (*John 11:9-10*). He also said, "I am the light of the world; he who follows me will not walk in darkness, but will have the light of life" (*John 8:12*).

O God, may we walk in your light that we may see! Amen.

□

Fleeting Glimpses

The Hebrew people believed that if anyone saw God face to face, he or she would die. Maybe if we saw our darkness exposed in the light of all that goodness, we would drop dead. Who knows? So when Moses asked to see God, God told him, "I will cover you with my hand until I have passed by; then I will take away my hand, and you shall see my back; but my face shall not be seen" (*Exodus 33:22-23*). Even Moses had only a rear view of the Almighty as he was going away. Christ appeared to two disciples on the road to Emmaus, and as soon as they recognized him, he "vanished out of their sight" (*Luke 24:31*).

It is just such fleeting glimpses of things divine that we are apt to have today in the midst of the ordinary events of our lives. Usually we are not quite certain that we have seen anything or of what has happened to us. Even Paul needed Ananias to explain to him what had blinded him on the Damascus road and what, in heaven's name, he should do about it (*Acts 9:10-19*).

We are used to dealing with things we can see over and over again, examine at our leisure, probe, dissect, count, and feed into computers. We aren't apt to pay much attention to fleeting glimpses. Dag Hammarskjold wrote:

> God does not die on the day when we cease to believe in a personal deity, but we die on the day when our lives cease to be illumined by the steady radiance, renewed daily, of a wonder, the source of which is beyond all reason.[11]

I don't know whether Hammarskjold got all the words exactly right when he tried to describe his glimpses of the divine. I doubt his mind was so small or his faith so petty that he attached much importance to simply getting the words right. When friends found his diary after his death, there was not a word in it about important achievements at the United Nations. It did not contain anything about the world-shaking events he had helped to shape as the U. N. General Secretary. It said nothing about the famous people with whom he was in daily contact. There were only some efforts to describe his fleeting glimpses of things divine. They were what seemed to matter most.

O God, help us to pay attention! Amen.

Myopia

My wife grew up in the South of France. She remembers when several motorists were killed after a bridge collapsed near her village. A man had been dredging and selling sand from the riverbed. He had removed too much near the pillars holding up the bridge, which was thought to be a contributing factor in the bridge's collapse. Among those killed was a motorcyclist. He was the sand dredger's own son!

Whenever we harm others, we harm our own selves. The more we are able to realize that all of us in this world are bound together as sons, daughters, sisters, brothers, and children of the one God, the more hope there will be for us all. "Do not rebuke an older man," reads the first letter to Timothy, "but exhort him as you would a father; treat younger men like brothers, older women like mothers, younger women like sisters . . ." (*1 Timothy 5:1*).

Our interests are bound together with those of others far more than we ever guess in our nearsightedness. In John Donne's famous words:

> No man is an *Iland*, intire of it selfe; every man is a peece of the *Continent*, a part of the *maine*; . . . any mans *death* diminishes *me*, because I am involved in *Mankinde*; and therefore never send to know for whom the *bell* tolls; It tolls for *thee*.[12]

O God, heal our myopia! Amen.

☐

Darkness Within

Jesus said, "The eye is the lamp of the body. So if your eye is sound, your whole body will be full of light; but if your eye is not sound, your whole body will be full of darkness. If the light in you is darkness, how great is that darkness!" (*Matthew 6:22, 23*). Usually the most intense darkness is not in the world but in ourselves.

The whole world is a miracle of God's grace. The bright light of that grace shines throughout our lives in it. The most common cause of moral and spiritual blindness is not the darkness of life, but our desire not to see. Some choose to see miracles only in special events at special times and places, so that they need not bother about God in the rest of life. Others choose not to see miracles at all. Sometimes we close our eyes to problems like suffering and injustice, for seeing might make us want to help. At other times we close our eyes to reasons for hope, for believing that there is no hope frees us from any need to keep trying. The light is always there, but too much of it is apt to hurt our eyes.

The light of God's grace has shown especially in the face of Christ, whom God sent "into the world, not to condemn the world, but that the world might be saved through him" (*John 3:17*). While God's purpose was not to condemn, that very act of grace became judgment for those who chose not to see. "And this is the judgment, that the light has come into the world, and men loved darkness rather than light, because their deeds were evil" (*John 3:19*).

The light of God's grace shines everywhere so brightly it may hurt our eyes. The darkness in us usually is the result of too much light outside.

O God, keep our eyes open, even when it hurts! Amen.

Six-Foot Rabbits and James Dean

Recently I saw an excellent performance of Ed Graczyk's play, *Come Back to the 5 and Dime, Jimmy Dean.* It especially interested me since I was an ardent fan of James Dean movies during my teenage years.

The play is about the members of a James Dean fan club who have built their lives on a series of illusions. Their illusions are dispelled during a reunion of the club, and the play ends, if not on a note of hope, at least on a note of relief that reality has been faced. One leaves the theater with the good feeling that, with the illusions gone, the club members can now get on with the business of rebuilding their lives.[13]

It is certainly a mistake to build our lives on illusions; that is what Jesus meant when he warned against building our lives on foundations of sand (*Matthew 7:26-27*). But while one part of me wants to say yes to the frequent modern plays about facing reality, another part wants to echo some words of Elwood P. Dowd in Mary Chase's play, *Harvey.* Dowd is the lovable character who imagines he has a six-foot rabbit for a friend. He tells a psychiatrist that he struggled with reality for years but finally conquered it.[14]

Although it sometimes takes a bit of both, the best way to deal with illusions is not to shatter them, but to replace them with some more solid hope. After all, there is a very fine line between facing reality and giving up in despair. The illusion that there is no hope is always very seductive; it relieves us of the need to keep on trying. It is the most dangerous of illusions, however, since it causes us to miss the unexpected opportunities that come along even when the future looks the most bleak. If we don't expect the unexpected, we are apt to miss it when it comes.

The best life, of course, is one that is free from both illusions and despair, but if I had to be stuck with one or the other, I'd take the six-foot rabbits and the legends of a living James Dean any day!

O God, help us to expect the unexpected! Amen.

Hoving Happenings

My fondest memories of New York City in the 1960s are of what people in the rest of the country perceive as hardships we had to endure there. I remember the incongruity of high piles of garbage in front of the most fashionable apartment buildings during the sanitation workers' strike, the sight of the Goodyear Blimp reminding us in huge neon letters not to flush our toilets more than once a day during the water shortage, and the ingenuity of New Yorkers in devising alternate means of transportation during a subway strike (A young man wore out eight pairs of skates to reach his office). I remember the great power outage, which transformed the whole city into a giant all-night party.

Our way of turning crises into celebrations was due in large measure to a very creative Commissioner of City Parks and Recreation, Thomas Hoving. He used almost any excuse to organize what people called "Hoving Happenings" in Central Park. He taught us that not only crises, but even the most trivial events, could become the occasion for "happenings."

It was a lesson I learned well. I am sometimes sad, occasionally afraid, sometimes discouraged, often angry. But I am rarely bored. One reason is that in order to keep coming up with things to say in sermons and meditations, I have to keep watching for "happenings." When we look for something, we see it. Although my job forces me to look, I believe I would look even if it did not, just as I keep taking slides when I travel, even though I rarely find a captive audience to view them. Taking slides forces us to see beauty we would otherwise miss. Watching for "happenings" helps even the smallest things to become significant.

When Jesus ate the last meal with his disciples, he took the most ordinary foods, bread and wine, and blessed them as sacraments of his presence. The whole world is God's. There is nothing in it which cannot become a "happening."

O God, may our lives be "happenings"! Amen

Listening

When people phone me to let me know of illnesses in our parish, far less than half of the reports are accurate in every detail. We only halfway listen to each other. Most of us are more eager to talk than to listen. Of course, preachers never have that problem, do they?

It is like that in our prayers as well. As nearly as I can tell, our usual prayers consist mostly of advice we give God about what he ought to do for us or for others or about how he ought to manage the universe. We are apt to do more talking than listening.

I doubt if it was that kind of prayer Paul had in mind when he gave the advice to "pray constantly" (*1 Thessalonians 5:17*). As much as we all like to talk, it would be difficult for most of us to have the time to spend every minute of every day talking to God, and I shouldn't think he would need that much advice anyway.

We can, however, listen constantly. We can be ever-attentive to the ordinary events of our lives in order to hear what God may be saying to us through them. Listening to our lives as we live them is the most important way of praying.

O God, open our ears! Amen.

□

The Miraculous Bucket

Nikos Kazantzakis said that, as a child, he loved cherries more than any other fruit. When he picked them, he would put them immediately into a bucket of water, in which their size would appear magnified. Of course, when he would take them out of the water, they would look small again. So, he wrote, "I closed my eyes, therefore, to avoid seeing them shrink, and thrust them—still monstrous, as I imagined—into my mouth."

That fantastic Greek author said that is how he continued to deal with reality, even as an adult: "I re-create it—brighter, better, more suitable to my purpose. . . . 'Since we cannot change reality, let us change the eyes which see reality,' says one of my favorite Byzantine mystics. I did this when a child, I do it now as well in the most creative moments of my life."[15]

To see with the eyes of faith is to trust that, beyond and even within the harshness of what seems to be reality, there is a partially hidden kingdom or rule of God, which is even more real. It will be perfectly fulfilled in the future; it is already breaking into the world in Jesus Christ. In it God is truly Lord of life, and the deepest yearnings of our hearts are met in him. Through parables and other sayings, Jesus pointed to examples of that kingdom or rule in even the most common experiences of everyday life, where most of us miss them most of the time.

If your life isn't the bowl of cherries you wish it were, try looking at it through other eyes. After all, who is to say which is the most accurate way of viewing cherries, through our naked eyes, which may be all too weak to see them as they really are, or through Kazantzakis' marvelous bucket of water?

O God, give us eyes to see! Amen.

Searching for Life

□

Strangers and Exiles

Speaking of Abel, Enoch, Noah, Abraham, Sarah, Isaac, and Jacob, the book of Hebrews says,

These all died in faith, not having received what was promised, but having seen it and greeted it from afar, and having acknowledged that they were strangers and exiles on the earth. For people who speak thus make it clear that they are seeking a homeland (*Hebrews 11:13-14*).

Do we not all feel, at times, like strangers and exiles who are seeking a homeland?

When young people are confused about where they are headed, we usually feel sorry for them, for we know that pain ourselves. But there is rarely very much growth without growing pains.

Sometimes seekers are closer to the homeland than those who take everything for granted. Jesus promised, "Seek and you will find" (*Matthew 7:7*). The seekers of this world often wind up finding more than those who think they have found everything without even bothering to look. In fact, if we hadn't found more than we realize, we probably wouldn't be seeking in the first place.

O God, as strangers and exiles, keep us seeking, that we may find our homeland in you! Amen.

Itchiness

In the movie *Streamers*, there is a scene in which two drunken sergeants sing a comic song to the tune of "Beautiful Dreamer," substituting the words, "beautiful streamers." It is written as if sung by a parachutist whose chute would not open. Then they tell about a soldier who, to show off, cast off his parachute on the way down to the earth, intending to grab the cords with his hands and to ride it down that way. But by the time he reached up to grab the cords, they were already twenty feet above him. The description is so vivid, it is hard to erase the image of a soldier reaching up desperately to grab a parachute that is beyond his reach. And all the characters in the movie, torn by conflicts within them, seem to be reaching up for something to save them that they can't quite grab hold of either.

To some extent, most of us are reaching up for something we can't quite grasp, usually without knowing exactly what it is. There is a restlessness about us, like having an itch and not knowing where to scratch. I notice it in myself, especially in the eagerness with which I look forward to the morning mail. It is usually only advertisements and bills, but I rush home each noon to see it anyway without really knowing what I expect to find— something new, perhaps, an unexpected fulfillment, something to scratch that itch. But even though whatever we are reaching for may always partially elude our grasp in this life, I, for one, intend to keep on reaching, for the reaching is one of the things which make life worth living.

We can live with not being able to quite grasp whatever it is we reach for, because the good news is that God reaches us where we are. In Jesus Christ, he reaches down to the earth, down to Bethlehem, down to Golgotha, down to wherever we live, and he catches us even when we least deserve it.

O God, keep us reaching even as you reach us! Amen.

□

Christ Is the Question

Those who watch the Johnny Carson Show will recall the parody of a mindreading act he does occasionally. He gives an answer, then opens a sealed envelope to read the question. We laugh when Johnny does that, but often we do the same thing in our churches. We like to begin with the answers, because we feel threatened by too many questions. But what good are answers unless there are questions?

Jesus asked a number of questions such as: "Who do you say that I am?" (*Mark 8:29*); "Is it lawful on the sabbath to do good or to do harm, to save life or to kill?" (*Mark 3:4*); "What does it profit a man, to gain the whole world and forfeit his life?" (*Mark 8:36*). It was such questions that provoked the authorities and led to his crucifixion. They and other people felt threatened by such questions.

Even more important than all of the questions he asked in his preaching, however, was the question he asked with his life and death. Both his manner of life and the manner of his death called into question most of the values people lived by then and live by now. Is Jesus only the answer, as the billboards say, or is he not more often the question?

O God, call our lives into question that we may find ourselves in you! Amen.

What's It All About?

According to his widow, T. S. Eliot liked to tell a story about himself, a taxi driver, and the British mathematician and philosopher, Bertrand Russell. Eliot stopped a taxi one evening. When he got in, the driver said, "You're T. S. Eliot." Asked how he knew, the driver replied, "Ah, I've got an eye for a celebrity. Only the other evening I picked up Bertrand Russell, and I said to him, 'Well, Lord Russell, what's it all about?' and, do you know, he couldn't tell me."[16]

I, for one, would be disappointed if life were about no more than what Bertrand Russell could tell a taxi driver during a short ride. Some seem to find comfort in their belief that there is no answer to the taxi driver's question. Others seem satisfied to end the search quickly with a few pat answers. Some search frantically, as if they will fall into complete despair if they don't find answers soon. For me the search is one of the most satisfying rewards of life.

"Seek, and you will find. . . ." Jesus said (*Luke 11:9*), and in my search I have found two things. The first is that the search is fun. The second is that even more rewarding than the search are those moments along the way when, usually more by chance than by intention, I manage to make some small difference in the lives of other people.

I remember, for example, being called back from a convention to share in the grief of a college professor whose wife had been killed in a tragic automobile accident at exactly the wrong moment in their lives. They had both just been awarded their Ph.D.s. The following week, they were to move to a new location where both could teach. The child they had waited to have until they completed their education had been born only a few months earlier.

I remember serving as pastor to a retired minister, the nearest person to being a saint I have ever known, and having the honor of conducting the funeral of one who had meant so much in the lives of so many. On my visits to him in the hospital, he always managed to minister more to me than I to him, but he was enough of a pastor to allow me to feel, at least, that my visits meant something. Then there was the year I shared some thoughts and tears in visits with one of my parishioners, a young faculty wife dying of leukemia. I remember the final day when she took my hands, thanked me for ministering to her, then told me the physicians had decided to "wind things up" that day. There have also been those rewarding moments when I have chanced to share in a special way the joyous experiences of others.

As I look back, I find such moments as these even more fulfilling than the search. In fact, perhaps they are a large part of the answer to the taxi driver's question. If so, don't tell me; I enjoy the search too much to want it to be ended by a complete answer.

O God, we thank you for life, whatever it's all about! Amen.

Staying Alive by Caring

Give a Damn!

In a poem called "Profile," which must be at least partially autobiographical, W. H. Auden wrote:

> He has often stamped his feet,
> wept on occasion,
> but never been bored.

Auden was a poet who cared. Anyone who cares experiences plenty of anger and pain at the world's injustice and suffering. Jesus shared fully in those emotions. The only way to escape them is to steel ourselves against compassion and caring. But while indifference can save us considerable pain, its side effect is boredom.

Later in the same poem, Auden wrote:

> Scanning his fellow
> Subway passengers, he asks:
> 'Can I really be
> the only one in this car
> who is glad to be alive?'[17]

Seeing the bored, indifferent, and empty faces of his fellow passengers led the narrator to realize that the pain of his caring was worth it. The only way to be fully alive is to care. Machines don't care. People who really live do. To force ourselves to be indifferent machines in order to escape a little pain is the best way I know to enter the living death of boredom.

One day, when we were living in New York, new signs and billboards appeared along all the expressways and subway routes. I have never learned their precise purpose or who put them up. I have never forgotten their message. They read simply, "Give a damn!"

O God, help us to care! Amen.

The Fire of Life

The minister of my home church during my teenage years was one of the strongest influences on my decision to enter the ministry. God frequently reaches us most decisively through other people. There were many things I admired about him—his brilliant mind, his love for culture, and his great capacity for friendship with many different types of people from all sorts of backgrounds. I remember most the intensity with which he lived. No issue was so insignificant that he would pass it by. Many times, after theological discussions had waxed hot, I saw his wife walk him around the block to cool him off. A mutual friend said he had enough fire for a hundred people. He cared.

There are many ways, of course, to be fully alive, but all of them involve caring. Indifference is the surest symptom of deadliness that we know in this world. The first letter of John says, "We know that we have passed out of death into life, because we love the brethren" (*3:14*). It is in caring, especially for other people, that we live.

We do not know much about what awaits us beyond death; "it does not yet appear what we shall be" (*1 John 3:2*). But when I see people who are full of life because they care, it is far more difficult for me to believe that physical death can quench the fire of that life than to believe that God, once again, will raise it up.

O God, fill us with your fire! Amen.

☐

Heart Trouble

Heart disease remains one of the leading causes of death in our nation. Fortunately, physicians are making great strides forward in its treatment. Techniques for heart transplants are still in their infancy, but other advanced forms of treatment have become routine. These days, I visit far more patients who have undergone angioplasties and coronary artery bypass grafts (already shortened to "cabbages" in the jargon of our local hospitals) than appendectomies.

Ezekiel was concerned about a disease of the heart that is even more deadly than the physical kind—hardness of heart. He wrote "get yourselves a new heart and a new spirit! Why will you die, O house of Israel? For I have no pleasure in the death of anyone, says the Lord God; so turn, and live" (*Ezekiel 18:31-32*).

The people had heart trouble. Without hearts that loved and cared, Ezekiel knew, his people were more dead than alive. When our hearts become hardened, it may *hurt* others, but it *destroys* us, so far as meaningful life is concerned.

Unfortunately, we cannot use any of the new medical techniques to bypass hard hearts, but there is an old cure. A large dose of God's love can soften our hearts and give us life.

O God, love softness into our hearts that we may live! Amen.

To Care and Not to Care

Near the end of T. S. Eliot's poem "Ash Wednesday" come the words:

> Teach us to care and not to care
> Teach us to sit still
> Even among these rocks,
> Our peace in His will. . . .[18]

That is the tension central to the Bible and within which we all must live out our lives as Christians in this imperfect world.

"Teach us to care," writes Eliot. The call to be caring and loving and to do what we can to make this world a better home for all moves across most of the pages of the Bible. Without it our lives would be ones of resignation, without responsibility.

But Eliot also writes, "Teach us . . . not to care / Teach us to sit still / Even among these rocks, / Our peace in His will. . . ." Across the pages of that same Bible moves the call to submit to God's providence, to trust in his will, to await his fulfillment in his good time. The Bible recognizes that finally our world can be healed only through God's grace. Without that call to trust God, our lives would be filled with despair when our human efforts failed, as they so often do.

To live without either resignation or despair, between working and waiting, caring enough to try as hard as we can, yet finally submitting ourselves to God's will and awaiting his fulfillment, is the tension within which alone there is true life.

Paul points to the same tension when he writes in Philippians, "work out your own salvation with fear and trembling; for God is at work in you, both to will and to work for his good pleasure" (*Philippians 2:12-13*). There is the plea for us to work and to do what we can, but at the same time to recognize it is God who works in and through us for his will and his good pleaaure, and that in the end, we can only trust in him.

Only in living with that tension can we find our true peace.

O God, teach us to care and not to care! Amen.

Joyous Living

The Party Has Begun

What would any of us be without a sense of humor? Without laughter, we take both life and ourselves too seriously. We turn molehills into mountains and put ourselves on the highest peak. That is always a precarious perch! How else can we lose ourselves in order to find ourselves, except by having enough good humor to laugh at ourselves?

H. A. Williams writes:

> God, we believe, accepts us, accepts all men, unconditionally, warts and all. Laughter is the purest form of our response to God's acceptance of us. For when I laugh at myself I accept myself and when I laugh at other people in genuine mirth I accept them.[19]

If God accepts us "warts and all," as Williams puts it, should we not also accept the lives he has given us, rough spots and all?

Early one morning, I received a call from two elderly sisters, both retired school teachers. The elder of the two had become seriously ill during the evening before, and the younger sister had fallen and broken a hip in trying to carry her to a bed. Neither could manage to reach the phone until daylight. When I arrived, both were still on the floor where they had been all night, *and they were laughing*. The one with the broken hip winked at me and asked, "Have you ever before seen two old maids in such a predicament?" I'm convinced it was their laughter that brought them through. Our problems never seem as serious when, in good humor, we don't take ourselves too seriously.

"Although we are still on our journey," says Williams, "when we laugh we know that really we have already arrived. The party has begun and we are there."

O God, fill our lives with your laughter! Amen.

□

Funerals and Wedding Feasts

Thinking of the miracle at the wedding feast at Cana mentioned in John's Gospel, Dostoevski noted in *The Brothers Karamazov* that it was to make people joyous that Jesus performed his first miracle.[20]

It is often at crisis points in our lives when we feel nearest to God—times of stress, heartache, and sorrow. We need him then, and he is with us in those times. But if Jesus is any indication, God is with us in the happy times as well.

In the Gospel stories, Jesus probably spends as much time eating with people as in doing any other activity. He was accused of being a glutton and a drunkard, and he refused to have his disciples fast. When he sought to picture the kingdom of God, he often used the image of a great banquet or meal.

When black preachers of an earlier day pictured heaven as a fried chicken dinner, they probably were in closer touch with Jesus' own imagery than were their white counterparts who borrowed visions of streets of gold and pearly gates from the book of Revelation. The First Letter of John says it was written so that "our joy may be complete."

Sometimes we act as though we thought there were something more Christian about sorrow than about joy. But if we are going to invite God to our funerals, I think we ought to invite him to our wedding feasts as well.

O God, we thank you that you are with us in all our times. Amen.

A Tricky Customer

Joy is "a tricky customer," wrote H. A. Williams. "It is unseen when most fully possessed. It is most often recognized when it has gone or when mixed with anxiety about its departure."[21]

The church in which I grew up enjoyed during my high school years what many of its members now think of as its golden age. Under a dynamic minister, it prospered and flourished in every way. It grew in membership. It had a healthy program. It reached out to the community and to the world. And it remodelled its sanctuary.

At the time, however, I didn't hear much about its being a golden age. There was more talk about the people who weren't in attendance than about those who were. From what I heard people say, I supposed the church was almost on its last legs. We rarely recognize our most fulfilling moments until they have gone and we miss them!

At a time when most religious people were preoccupied either with remembering what God had done in the past or hoping for what he would do in the future, Jesus, without playing down the importance of either, announced to his followers, "The kingdom of God is in the midst of you" (*Luke 17:21*). In at least a partial way, the joy of life in that kingdom is here already for those who have the eyes to see it.

O God, help us to love life as we live it! Amen.

The Laughter of God

One of the most likable and dedicated members of a church I once served was also the most inclined to look at the gloomy side of life. The economy, the political scene, and the environment were always on the brink of disaster. He would usually preface his dire predictions with the words, "I am no pessimist, but . . ."

One summer a drought hit the state. He told a group of us that such droughts usually lasted about six years in that part of the country, and that would finish out his lifespan. He fully expected to spend his last days in dust. It turned out that he had always believed he would not live beyond a certain age. When that birthday came and went without consequence and the drought lifted, he laughingly told me he guessed that now he would have to pick another date.

The thing that saved him was his very keen sense of humor. He delighted in telling the story about a wasp that lit on his forehead just as he was supposed to give a prayer as an elder during a church service. He simply swatted his forehead, crushing the wasp, and went on with the prayer. As nearly as I could tell, he always dealt with the troubles that actually did come his way in about the same way he handled that wasp, and he kept right on going.

Much of the tragedy in life is beyond our power to eliminate or even to explain. Why it must be, no one can say. But we can drown out the cynicism, which is usually its most devastating consequence and sometimes its source, with the joy and laughter of God.

O God, turn our cynicism into your laughter! Amen.

Living Sorrow

□

Abundant Life

Jesus said, "The thief comes only to steal and kill and destroy; I came that they may have life, and have it abundantly" (*John 10:10*). He does not offer constant pleasure, but abundant life.

Nikos Kazantzakis, author of *Zorba the Greek*, wrote a brief devotional book entitled *The Saviors of God*. In it, he said, "What is meant by happiness? To live every unhappiness. What is meant by light? To gaze with undimmed eyes on all darkness."[22]

Abundant life, I suspect, is not the absence of sadness, but the absence of death. Jesus' promise is not to protect us from all pain, but to save us from allowing either pleasure or pain to deaden us to the fullness of life.

The good news of the gospel is that God accepts us as we are, in our weaknesses no less than in our strengths. If he accepts us that way, should we not accept the life he has given us the same way—its sorrows as well as its joys, living the tears of it no less than its laughter?

The enemy, as Jesus puts it, is that "thief who comes only to steal and kill and destroy. . . ." The enemy is all that tempts us to deaden ourselves to life. Jesus came that we, "may have life, and have it abundantly."

O God, fill us with life! Amen.

Why Should I Fast?

When the first child born to David and Bathsheba became ill, David was stricken with grief, undoubtedly intensified by the guilt he felt over the whole affair with Bathsheba and Uriah. He fasted and slept upon the ground, and no one could rouse him. On the seventh day, the child died. The servants were afraid to tell David, fearing what the news might do to him since he had been already so distressed over the illness. But when David heard them whispering and concluded that the child had died, he, "arose from the earth, and washed, and anointed himself, and changed his clothes; and he went into the house of the Lord, and worshiped; he then went to his own house; and when he asked, they set food before him, and he ate" (*2 Samuel 12:20*). The servants asked David what accounted for the sudden change in his behavior. He replied, "While the child was still alive, I fasted and wept; for I said, 'Who knows whether the Lord will be gracious to me, that the child may live?' But now he is dead; why should I fast? Can I bring him back again?" (*2 Samuel 12:22-23*).

Lay theologian Mary McDermott Schideler tells of the death of her father during her college days when she was already in the midst of something of an emotional crisis. She asked a trusted professor whether it would be best to give in to her emotions by letting herself go to pieces, or to continue the exhausting effort to keep them under control. He wisely pointed out that there was a third choice, "Accept it, and thank life for it."[23]

I do not agree with the often repeated statement that "everything is for the best." Really to live on the basis that everything automatically works out for the best, which even those who make the statement rarely do, would lead to a completely passive life in which there would be no reason to try to change anything or to take any responsibility for one's own future. I do believe that, through God's grace, everything can be used for the best, if we accept what cannot be changed and lay hold of the possibilities it opens for us.

O God, help us to use all things for your glory! Amen.

Saving Tears

The eighth verse of Psalm 56 curiously reads:

> Thou hast kept count of my tossings;
> put thou my tears in thy bottle!
> Are they not in thy book?

Often, we try to bottle up tears ourselves. Most of us want to avoid them if we possibly can, and to shut them off as quickly as possible if we cannot. The trouble is, if we steel ourselves against tears, we steel ourselves against life. There is no more devastating form of deadliness than that of not caring.

The psalmist prays that God will put his tears in God's bottle. They are, after all, something we can offer up to God. As the giver of life, God undoubtedly is especially disappointed to see the deadliness of indifference in any of us. Our tears show that we care. In them we come alive. Perhaps our tears of caring are about all there is in any of us worth saving.

O God, put our tears in your bottle! Amen.

□

The Unanswered Question

"Why did God create germs?" Although I have no memory of the incident, the minister who baptized me said that I asked that question when I was eight years old in the pastor's class he was teaching to prepare us for baptism. At the conclusion of one of the sessions, he offered to answer any of our questions, expecting us to ask about the lesson. Evidently, I took his offer as an invitation to ask about anything. He said later that my question came so unexpectedly he was at a loss to know how to answer.

Through the years, whenever our paths would chance to cross, he would remind me of my question and laugh about how it had taken him completely by surprise.

The last time I chanced to see him was on a ship off the coast of Scotland. He was then suffering from an incurable disease, and he knew his days were numbered. One last time he reminded me of my question and said he had still not found a very satisfactory answer. Nevertheless, he faced his impending death with courage and acceptance.

On a theoretical level, there are a number of excellent answers to the question of why God allows suffering, but all of them lose their force when we are faced with concrete instances of suffering involving ourselves or those we love. While in some instances the Bible touches on that question, it does not offer speculative answers. Instead, it points to a way of coping with the suffering. It does not satisfy our curiosity, but it offers a way to deal with pain. It affirms that God is with us at all times, both good and bad:

> Whither shall I go from thy Spirit?
> Or whither shall I flee from thy presence?
> If I ascend to heaven, thou art there!
> If I make my bed in Sheol, thou art there!
> If I take the wings of the morning
> and dwell in the uttermost parts of the sea,
> even there shall thy hand lead me,
> and thy right hand shall hold me. (Psalm 139:7-10)

It is God's presence that makes our good times great and our bad times bearable.

O God, we thank you for being with us and for us! Amen.

□

Unloading

"Our obedience to God requires us to fight Him." So writes H. A. Williams, one of the most deeply spiritual of all contemporary theologians. If we take God seriously, there are times when we will not understand his ways or why he allows certain things to happen to us, and we will be angry even at him. God has created us to be aggressive, independent people. If we don't feel some of that aggression at times spewing out even at God himself, then it is likely either that we are not taking him very seriously, or that we are keeping the irritation bottled up, in which case it is apt to become so intense that it might warp our whole lives.

The ancient Hebrews had a way of unloading some of their anger at God in worship. In psalms of lament, they laid their frustrations before the Lord, even arguing with him at times. I suspect their honesty would appear blasphemous to many people today, but, as Williams writes, "What is really absurd and really blasphemous (since it defies the order of creation) is to imagine that we can love God without at times feeling highly aggressive towards Him. There is often more love in a 'Christ Almighty' than there is in a spiritually castrated 'Alleluia.'"[24]

The same is true in our relationships with other people. There are times when even those we love most deeply get under our skin. Unless we unload it at them on occasion, that irritation is apt to fester until it destroys the love. Our deepest relationships are not those in which our aggression is hidden behind a glaze of saccharine sweetness, but those in which there is enough love and trust that occasionally we can flare up. Genuine love is based on mutual trust, not on artificial sweetener.

O God, help us to trust you and each other enough to be ourselves! Amen.

The Sky on the Other Side

In a record album called *The Storyteller*, British actor Charles Laughton tells of a conversation with Henry Moore. Moore was a highly acclaimed sculptor and Laughton's friend. One of the striking features of his sculptures is that they often have holes chiseled through them. Laughton asked Moore what gave him the idea to put all those holes in his sculptures. Moore replied, "One day I cut so deep into the heart of the stone that I discovered the sky on the other side."[25]

It is often that way with our heartaches and griefs. If we face them squarely and look deeply enough into the heart of them, we can eventually find the sky on the other side.

Since none of us likes to hurt, we sometimes try to turn off our feelings when we are faced with emotional pain. Some of us become so good at deadening ourselves that we end up with scarcely any feelings at all. But when we numb ourselves to escape the hurt, we can't feel joy or love, or the warmth of God's grace either. Without feelings, we are more dead then alive.

Psalm 30 says, "Weeping may tarry for the night, but joy comes in the morning" (*Psalm 30:5*). If we close our eyes to the darkness, we may miss the sunrise. But if we have the courage to look into the heart of the darkness and to keep our eyes open, we will eventually see the light of day and find the bright sky on the other side.

O God, Give us the courage to feel! Amen.

Wise or Mean?

Several years ago I read an author who implied that suffering could give us wise hearts. The same day I read another author who said that he had never seen suffering make people kind; it only turned them mean. Probably the situation can go either way. The crises in our lives inevitably change us. Whether they change us for good or for ill depends on how we face them.

We sometimes try to "comfort" each other by saying "Oh well, it's all for the best." Perhaps in the long range scheme of things, God uses all things for his purposes. But in the short range scheme of a lifetime, not necessarily, not inevitably, not automatically do all things work out for the best, not by a long shot. But God stands with us in all of the crises of our lives, helping us to bring the best out of them, if we let him. Paul wrote, "We know that in everything God works for good with those who love him . . ." (*Romans 8:28*).

We can face hardships with trust and hope, allowing them to deepen our experience and make our hearts wise, or we can meet them with bitterness, so that they turn us mean. God is there to help if we let him, but the choice is ours.

O God, with you may we make the best out of the worst! Amen.

☐

Root-Room

Gerard Manley Hopkins climaxes his forty-seventh sonnet, in which he lets us see some of the pain within him, with the prayer, "Leave comfort root-room."[26] Comfort grows in us like the roots of a tree, and that takes time. So Hopkins, who saw about as deeply into the heart of things as any person could, does not pray for instant relief, but only that there be room within him for comfort to take root and grow.

None of us likes to hurt. We are impatient for healing to come. And, of course, if we are only feeling a bit down, even a little excitement can sometimes do wonders. But for our deeper griefs, when we have lost something really worth grieving for, quick remedies are usually short-lived. If we try to suppress those griefs, the pain may leave awhile, only to stab us again when we least expect it. In the psalms of lament in our Book of Psalms, we often read the phrase, "How long, O Lord, how long?"

It is these deeper, longer-term griefs that are usually of greatest value to us insofar as growth is concerned. The people, things, careers, or whatever else we cherish become a part of who we are. When we lose one and say, "It is as if a part of us has died," it is not only "as if." Part of us *has* died. But that makes room for a new part to be born that hasn't been there before, if we allow the old part to really die by permitting ourselves to grieve. That rarely happens overnight. Comfort needs time for its roots to take hold and grow.

O God, when we hurt, leave comfort root-room! Amen.

The Blues

In August Wilson's play, *Ma Rainey's Black Bottom*, Ma Rainey is a blues singer of the 1920s who finds her music being overtaken in popularity by a brighter but more superficial style to which people can dance and have a good time. She says, "You don't sing to feel better. You sing 'cause that's a way of understanding life. . . . This be an empty world without the blues. I take that emptiness and try to fill it up with something." Then one of the members of the band adds, "In the church sometimes you find that way of singing. They got blues in the church."[27]

Of course, we all prefer to be happy rather than sad, but rough times are a part of all of our lives. When our pursuit of happiness is no more than a shallow effort to paper over the rough spots, it doesn't hide them for very long, and we miss the enrichment that can come from working through the pain. Only a fool would go out looking for trouble, but when we look back on our lives, we can usually see that the tough times were occasions for our greatest growth as persons. Reflecting back on the most painful time in his life, a friend said, "I wouldn't go through that experience again for a million dollars, but I wouldn't take a million dollars for that experience." He felt it had given him a better understanding of other people and made him more of a person himself.

We may think that all we *want* out of life is a little happiness, but I suspect what we all really *need* is fulfillmemt—lives that are whole, full, and complete. Jesus did not say he came into the world to make us happy. He said, "I came that they may have life, and have it abundantly" (*John 10:10*).

Oh God, make our lives full! Amen.

Fearless Living

No Darkness

Many thought the old mystery programs on radio were far more frightening than any of the horror shows on television today. Visual images were left to our imagination. We usually could do more with them than even the most inventive director can put on the "tube."

Late one night, in my childhood, I listened to a radio show about the ghost of a woman which came back from the grave saying, "Comb my hair. Comb my hair. It hasn't been combed in twenty long years." The street light on the corner, filtering through the trees, made shadows on the wall of my bedroom. All night long I lay awake imagining I could see that woman's face in the shadows, with long tangled hair partially covering it. When daylight finally came, I never appreciated it more.

The first letter of John says, "God is light and in him is no darkness at all" (*1 John 1:5*). Even when we grow up, all of us have our dark shadows—our own private fears and worries—filtering up through the dark corners of our imaginations. But we do not need to fear even the darkest night of our souls, for, "God is light and in him is no darkness at all."

O God, thank you for the light of your presence. Amen.

□

□

Rough Seas

A storm arose and the waves almost swamped the boat. Jesus was asleep. The disciples woke him asking, "Teacher, do you not care if we perish?" Jesus calmed the wind and the waves saying, "Peace! Be still!" Then he asked the disciples, "Why are you afraid? Have you no faith?" (*Mark 4:37-40*).

To have faith is to trust in the kingdom or rule of a merciful God. The story should not be taken to imply, I suspect, that if we trust in such a kingdom, no difficulties will ever come our way. We all have our stormy times in life. On other occasions, Jesus said that God, "sends rain on the just and on the unjust" (*Matthew 5:45*) and implied that his followers could expect tougher times than most people (*Matthew 8:19-20*). Sometimes, when the seas of life are rough for us, it may appear that God is asleep and doesn't care, just as Jesus was asleep and seemed to his disciples not to care when their boat was caught in the storm.

To have faith in God's kingdom or rule, however, means to trust that, despite all appearances to the contrary, the storms and heartaches, which are a part of all our lives, are not the last word. It means to trust that, in the end, God's kingdom of grace and mercy will triumph, and that sharing in that victory is the final word in all our lives.

O God, we do not ask for constant smooth sailing, but only that we reach our destination in you. Amen.

Long-Leggety Beasties

A Cornish prayer reads:

> From ghoulies and ghosties and
> long-leggety beasties
> And things that go bump in the night,
> Good Lord, deliver us!

Perhaps none of us is too frightened any longer of "ghoulies and ghosties and long-leggety beasties and things that go bump in the night." We all have our "little green men," our own private fears and worries about things that never come about.

Paul speaks to all our fears when he writes:

> For I am sure that neither death, nor life, nor angels, nor principalities, nor things present, nor things to come, nor powers, nor height, nor depth, nor anything else in all creation, will be able to separate us from the love of God in Christ Jesus our Lord. (*Romans 8:38-39*)

> Nothing can separate us from God's love in Jesus Christ, and as the First Letter of John says, "There is no fear in love, but perfect love casts out fear" (*4:18*)

O God, save us from our fears! Amen.

Living Our Own Lives

A Little Salt

"You are like salt for all mankind," Jesus said, "but if salt loses its saltiness, there is no way to make it salty again. It has become worthless, so it is thrown out and people trample on it" (*Matthew 5:13, Today's English Version*).

We people need some flavor about us—some uniqueness, some distinctiveness, some strong convictions, to be worth very much to anyone, above all to ourselves.

One of the things my family and I enjoy on our visits to France is the good French bread, which we carry home fresh from the bakery each morning, and which actually has a taste. American white bread really is designed to hold sandwiches together. For that purpose, it is the best bread in the world. If you try to make a sandwich out of French bread, you're in serious trouble. Even if you have sharp teeth, it is virtually impossible to get them through two slices of it at the same time, and if you do, you can't taste the filling. American bread, intended for sandwiches, is made to have as little flavor as possible so as not to detract from whatever you put between the slices. With peanut butter and jelly it is great, but by itself, it is completely bland. It is really just an edible wrapper.

Years ago, I read a newspaper article about a convention of American bakers who said their goal was to produce a bread which would offend no one. They succeeded. American bread is so neutral in taste, I can't imagine how it could possibly offend anyone, but eaten alone, I don't see how it could please anyone either.

We people are the same. If we try to be too neutral in order not to offend anyone, we become worthless to everyone, especially to ourselves. We end up only as wrappers for what other people think. In order to be worth our salt, we people need to be at least a little salty.

O God, put the salt of your truth in our lives! Amen.

What I Do Is Me

Gerard Manley Hopkins wrote a poem about how we are what we do:

As Kingfishers Catch Fire

As kingfishers catch fire, dragonflies draw flame;
    As tumbled over rim in roundy wells
    Stones ring; like each tucked string tells,
        each hung bell's
Bow swung finds tongue to fling out broad its name;
Each mortal thing does one thing and the same:
    Deals out that being indoors each one dwells;
    Selves—goes itself; *myself* it speaks and spells,
Crying *What I do is me: for that I came.*

"What I do is me: for that I came," Hopkins wrote, and Jesus said, "Each tree is known by its own fruit. For figs are not gathered from thorns, nor are grapes picked from a bramble bush. The good man out of the good treasure of his heart produces good, and the evil man out of his evil treasure produces evil; for out of the abundance of the heart his mouth speaks" (*Luke 6:44-45*).

When, in a moment of uncertainty, John the Baptist sent his disciples to Jesus asking, "Are you he who is to come, or shall we look for another?" (*Luke 7:19*), Jesus did not enter into any discussion about who he was. Instead, he pointed to what he was doing. "In that hour he cured many of disease and plagues and evil spirits, and on many that were blind he bestowed sight. And he answered them, 'Go and tell John what you have seen and heard: the blind receive their sight, the lame walk, lepers are cleansed, and the deaf hear, the dead are raised up, the poor have good news preached to them'" (*Luke 7:21-22*). "What I do is me: for that I came."

69

Hopkins continues his poem:

I say more: the just man justices;
   Keeps grace: that keeps all his goings graces;
Acts in God's eye what in God's eye he is—
   Christ. For Christ plays in ten thousand places,
Lovely in limbs and lovely in eyes not his
   To the Father through the features of men's faces.[28]

The just man does justice; in what we do, we speak not only who we are but who Christ is as he lives in us.

O God, may we so live that we may be who we truly are, and allow Christ to be who he really is in us! Amen.

Headaches

Of all our presidents, Thomas Jefferson was probably the best prepared to assume that office. When President Kennedy gathered his staff of the "best and brightest" at the White House for a first dinner together, he quipped that so much brain power hadn't been assembled in those quarters since the days Thomas Jefferson dined there alone! Yet, from the day Jefferson took office until he left, he was plagued by excruciating headaches.

Although Jefferson was a slave owner, he was morally opposed to slavery. He introduced a proposal in the Continental Congress that would have forbidden slavery in any new territories. Had that resolution carried, there may have been no Civil War. It lost by a single vote. Perhaps because his political base was in the South, Jefferson did nothing about slavery during his presidency. Probably President Truman was right when he pointed to that inaction as the source of Jefferson's headaches.

We all have to make compromises in order to live together with people who hold convictions different from our own. But there is a rock bottom point beyond which we dare not go in compromising our integrity, lest we destroy ourselves as persons!

O God, help us to be true to you and to ourselves! Amen.

☐

I Gotta Be Me

> Praise the Lord from the earth,
>> you sea monsters and all deeps,
> fire and hail, snow and frost,
>> stormy wind fulfilling his command!
> Mountains and all hills,
>> fruit trees and all cedars!
> Beasts and all cattle,
>> creeping things and flying birds!
>> (*Psalm 148:7-10*)

Brian Foley begins a hymn reflecting on Psalm 148 with the words, "All things that are praise God by what they are." That includes us. We serve God best by becoming more fully ourselves, not by trying to be something we aren't.[29]

God does not expect any of us to be gods. Indeed, we get ourselves into some of our most serious problems when we act as if we were. We serve his purposes best by being genuine human beings.

The trouble is that we so rarely live up to what we were created to be. We are often confused about what we are, and so our notions of what it is to be ourselves are frequently distorted. Sometimes we even act as though we thought being ourselves meant being rather inhuman. Thus, in many cases, being ourselves may mean being different than we have ever actually been before. That is why we say that Christ makes us new. But the new life he brings us is the fulfillment of what God intended in the first place. We serve God best by living up to a motto on a plaque on my office wall that reads, "I gotta be me."

O God, help us to be us! Amen.

Humans or Sea Creatures?

Edward Albee's play *Seascape* is an unusual drama involving a conversation between a couple of creatures from the bottom of the sea, Leslie and Sarah, who are considering coming out on land to be more like people, and a human couple, Charlie and Nancy, who think they might like to go to the bottom of the ocean to be sea creatures rather than human beings. It turns out that the reason Charlie and Nancy are not certain they want to keep on being human is that they are nearing the end of their lives, and only human beings are aware they are going to die.

The problem, of course, isn't only that we are aware we are going to die in the end, but that we are uniquely aware of all the tragic things that might happen to us along the way. Being created in the image of God means that we have more of most things than the animals—more capacity for hope and fulfillment, but also more capacity for fear and anxiety.

The more we live up to that image and realize our unique potential, the more we seem to have of both fulfillment and anxiety. Rollo May wrote, "Creative people, as I see them, are distinguished by the fact that they can live with anxiety, even though a high price may be paid in terms of insecurity, sensitivity, and defenselessness for the gift."[30]

Small wonder we people are always tempted to escape to the comfort of being less than human, less than creative, less than loving, and less than caring. But when we are unwilling to accept the pain of being fully human, we forfeit our unique opportunities for fulfillment as well.

In the end, Charlie and Nancy decide that, despite the extra pain it entails, they want to keep on being human after all, and they urge Leslie and Sarah to do so as well.[31] Maybe together we can all find the courage to be more fully the creative and caring human beings that God created us to be.

O God, give us the courage to be what we are! Amen.

Truly Human

"Jesus Christ," said the early church, "is fully God and fully human." He came into the world in order to show us what it is to be truly human. We are not automatically human beings simply because we happen to have been born *homo sapiens*. None of us can claim much more than to be on the way toward becoming truly human.

The cross of Jesus Christ exposes the darkness in us all, which threatens at every moment to block out our humanity and turn us into beasts. But that same cross points to the way our darkness can be overcome. The only way I know to drive away darkness is with light. The one who hung on the cross for all our sakes said, "I have come as light into the world, that whoever believes in me may not remain in darkness" (*John 12:46*). The light of God's love, which shines from the cross in his willingness to give his own son for us, can drive away our darkness and love us out of our fears so that we can shoulder the pain and the joy of being truly human. As Gerard Manley Hopkins prays in a poem, "Let him easter in us, be a dayspring to the dimness of us, be a crimson-cresseted east."[32]

O God, make us more than we appear to be! Amen.

□

□

What to Say

"By your words you will be justified, and by your words you will be condemned," Jesus says (*Matthew 12:37*). And whether or not we believe in God's judgment, the truth of that observation, even on a purely human level, weighs heavily on us all.

Probably more than on any other matter, I am asked for advice on what to say. Getting through to each other with words seems especially difficult in our day, and, of course, there are many times when there are no "right" words. Yet silence can be even more unsatisfactory than speaking. Whether they are going to visit a friend in a crisis, deal with a conflict, conduct a meeting, or give a devotion for P. T. A., people come and ask, "What can I say?"

> The weight of this sad time we must obey,
> Speak what we feel, not what we ought to say.[33]

That is the advice of the best wordsmith of them all, Shakespeare, at the end of *King Lear*.

It is because Shakespeare was able to speak what he felt so well that his plays have endured for so long. What we feel is usually the hardest thing to say. But if you can manage to say it, you can rarely go wrong.

O God, give us the courage to speak what we feel! Amen.

75

The Search for Us

What is man that thou art mindful of him,
and the son of man that thou dost care for him?

(*Psalm 8:4*)

The psalmist is not alone in asking that question. Through the ages, we have wondered. What are we? Who am I?

One of the most important searches in all our lives is for ourselves. We struggle to become what we most truly are. We seek our humanity. Often without being fully aware of it, we yearn to be what we were created to be in the first place.

In the end, all of us must discover for ourselves the persons that we really are. But in Jesus Christ, the *True Person*, we can find some clues, which mostly point to the fact that the answers are ones we may least expect. We sometimes seek to be pillars of iron that cannot be touched by the world outside, but in his life we see that our true humanity consists in having the courage to be vulnerable—to open ourselves and to be moved and touched by the lives of others. In Jesus, we see that we are most able to find ourselves in those rare moments when we are willing to lose ourselves as he did. And most important of all, in him we see that we become most fully ourselves when we join hands together, so that the search for "me" becomes a search for "us."

O God, help us find ourselves in your Son! Amen.

Living Together

An Extra Flight of Stairs

During the great power outage that darkened the Northeast, our subway train had just pulled into a station when the current went off. We had to climb twelve long flights of stairs to reach the surface. At our apartment building the first-floor residents were using candles to escort those on the upper floors to their apartments. I was in too much of a rush to wait my turn. My wife was pregnant, and I was anxious to see whether she was all right. Thinking I could negotiate the nineteen flights of stairs on my own even in the darkness, I miscounted and walked up twenty. On the way down to our floor, I ran smack into another man on the way up. It would have been much better if I had waited for help.

None of us have many of the answers. We all grope in the darkness at times, but we can at least grope togetner. "Two is not twice one," wrote G. K. Chesterton, "Two is a thousand times one."[34] Even when none of us has the strength to lift up the others, we can usually find ways of leaning together so that we all are propped up. It sure beats falling on our faces separately.

O God, help us stand together! Amen.

☐

Part of Who We Are

"When Mark Twain's second child, Susy, died, he said that her death was like a man's house burning down—it would take years and years to discover all that he had lost in the fire."[35] Such is the impact upon us of those we love. I suppose we never know how much they mean to us until we lose them. They, and in varying degrees, all the people who are part of our lives, become part of us. People often say when they have lost someone close to them, "it is as if part of me has died." It is not only "as if." Part of them has died, for the others in our lives are part of who we are.

Thus, the second great commandment, which Jesus borrowed from the sages of Judaism, that we should love our neighbors as ourselves, is not only for the sake of our neighbors. It is for our own sakes as well. They are part of us. In loving them, we are loving ourselves.

Just as Mark Twain said it would take years and years for him to realize fully how much he had lost in the death of his daughter, when we destroy our neighbors, it may take years for us to realize how much of ourselves we have destroyed in the process.

O God, for our sakes, help us to love others as ourselves! Amen.

☐

In It Together

In the midst of a drought, the prophet Elijah went to the home of a widow asking for something to eat. All she had was a handful of flour in a jar and a little oil in a bottle, which she planned to bake as a last meal for herself and her son. Elijah told her first to bake a little cake of it to share with him. When she did, neither the jar of flour nor the bottle of oil ever ran out (*1 Kings 17:8-16*).

That story came to mind as I watched the best movie made in several years, *Places in the Heart*. Set in the South during the depression, it tells the story of a widow with three young children who is about to lose her home through foreclosure. At that dark hour, she opens her small farm to a unemployed black man named Moses, and to a former soldier, an emotional wreck blinded during the war, about to be sent to a state home.

Sharing together, they are able to coax enough of a cotton crop from her land to make the payment on the mortgage.

Of course nothing is ever perfect in this life, and Moses is run out of town by the Klan because the local cotton gin operator doesn't appreciate the shrewd business advice Moses has given the widow. But the imperfection of this life isn't the last word either.

There is a final scene involving the people of the town gathered in a church. The preacher reads 1 Corinthians 13, and they share in communion. As they do, the camera zooms in on the congregation, and you see that Moses, who had been run out of town, is there too. The widow's dead husband is there, and the black boy who had shot him during a drunken spree and was lynched for it is there. Even the banker who was about to foreclose on the mortgage and the cotton gin operator are there. They are all there, because that is what the Christian faith is about and that is what communion is about. When we share in that meal, we share it not only with God, but also with each other. And we share it not only with those who are present, but also with all God's children at all places and in all times, the living and the dead, the saints and the sinners, because in the end, we are all in it together.

O God, help us to share all our meals! Amen.

□

Time Out for People

The first chapter of Mark tells of a day Jesus spent preaching and healing at Capernaum. The following morning, Jesus went out to a lonely place to pray. Simon and the others followed him and said, "Every one is searching for you" (*1:37*). You can picture them, all those people with broken bodies, hoping for a cure from this new healer. But Jesus had even more than that to give. He said, "Let us go on to the next towns, that I may preach there also; for that is why I came out" (*1:38*). There were others who could heal, but his own unique mission was to proclaim the dawning of the kingdom or rule of God. To do that, he had to keep on the move.

On the way to another place, a leper came to Jesus saying, "If you will, you can make me clean" (*1:40*). To come into close contact with a leper excluded one for a time from participation in the synagogues, and it was in the synagogues that Jesus preached. To heal the leper would mean a serious interruption in what Jesus saw as his first priority—the preaching of God's kingdom. Without hesitation, Jesus not only healed the leper, but touched him— a touch which must have meant everything to the leper, who had been excluded from human contact—a touch that was also a serious infraction of the law. It would further hamper Jesus' efforts to carry on what he saw as his first mission, the proclamation of God's kingdom.

When Jesus was forced to choose between a person and what he saw as his chief task, he took time out for the person. Can we do otherwise?

O God, help us always to take time out for people! Amen.

Our Saints

A document found in an old New England Church concludes, "Be it resolved: That we are all saints." I do not know whether the resolution carried, but even if we are not all saints, at least we all have our saints—the special people in our lives who have somehow helped us along the way. Laurence Housman said, "A saint is one who makes goodness attractive."[36]

One of my saints was my sixth-grade teacher, Florence Orr. I saw an old photograph of her the other day. In connection with the closing of the grade school I attended, my hometown newspaper ran a picture of its teaching staff taken the year before I entered the first grade.

She doesn't look much like a saint in the photograph. In fact, I can now understand why we had more respect for our teachers' authority than many school children seem to have for theirs today. Judging from the photograph, it was a rather terrifying crew of teachers we faced when we entered Jefferson Grade School in Bartlesville, Oklahoma.

That sixth-grade teacher, however, had a way of inspiring us to want to make something of ourselves—never at the expense of others, always for others. Through the years my memory has softened some of the harsh lines in her face, taken some of the sternness out of it, and transformed it into the face of a saint. I wouldn't be surprised if her face as it appears in my memory were a more accurate description of who she really was than is the face in the photograph.

One of our greatest illusions is that we are self-made people. There are no self-made people—only, I am afraid, ungrateful ones. All of us have special people in our lives—some we remember, some we have forgotten, many we have never even met, but apart from them we would not be who we are, for good or for ill. Those who have made us better are our saints!

O God, for all our saints we give you thanks. Amen.

Good Health to Your Belly Button

There is a Yiddish phrase that goes, *A gezunt dir in pupik*! Literally, it means "Good health to your belly button!"[37] It is used as an expression of thanks for small favors. That is about all the gratitude most of us are due.

We all should be more grateful than we are for the help we receive, but when we are doing the giving, we are apt to overestimate how much gratitude we are owed.

There are a good many Americans, for example, who still believe the United States can take all of the credit for the amazing economic advances made by tne Japanese since World War II. We helped them off to a good start. We treated them as well as any conquered nation has been treated by its conquerors. Of that we can be proud. There are things we could have done to prevent an economic recovery, and to our credit, we didn't. That recovery itself, however, was due in large measure to the ingenuity of the Japanese, and it ill behooves us to suppose our help entitles us to take credit for everything the Japanese may achieve from the end of World War II until doomsday. I think I detect in such talk the distinct odor of sour grapes.

The same is true of the help we give our individual friends and neighbors. To demand eternal gratitude humiliates them and deprives them of the satisfaction of feeling they have achieved something tnemselves. A wish of good health to our belly buttons is probably all of the gratitude most of us deserve most of the time.

O God, may we help each other because we want to, not for what we want out of it! Amen.

Real Gold

One New Year's Eve, a few friends gathered at the parsonage for a party. We asked them to write poems in honor of the New Year, and we voted for the best one.

Among our guests was the owner of a local grain elevator. That year there was a shortage of boxcars to take the processed corn to market. None had arrived in our little Missouri community. The elevator and all of the cribs were full. The streets near the railroad tracks were blocked by huge golden piles of shelled corn awaiting the boxcars, which seemed never to come.

That evening our guest was only able to compose two lines of a poem, which didn't even rhyme:

> The gold is in the streets.
> Hope to hell it doesn't rot!

We voted his poem the winner. Considering his state of mind that evening, even managing two lines was a victory of sorts. Of course, we were voting more for the person than for the poem.

Finally, the boxcars came and went, carrying away the corn. Our lives too have carried us away in different directions. But we were all together one New Year's Eve. That was the real gold. I am still casting my ballots for people!

O God, help us to find the true gold! Amen.

□

□

Holding Hands

Whenever I have failed people—failed to give them a helping hand when they needed it most—found excuses not to go where I should have gone—it has usually been from fear. I suspect that is true of others who went to help as well. Laziness, selfishness, indifference, and lack of understanding may all play roles in our neglect of each other, but the greatest hindrance of all is fear— fear of the awkwardness, fear of rejection, fear of being unable to handle the pain we see in some, fear especially of the silence when we don't know quite what to say.

I was moved, therefore, when I read a piece written by a nurse with a terminal illness to help her fellow nurses better understand how to care for persons in her situation. She said that all she really wanted was for someone to hold her hand.

As I read her words, I thought of a sentence in the prologue to John's Gospel: in Christ, "the Word became flesh and dwelt among us, full of grace and truth" (*John 1:14*). It wasn't the words he said that were the most important, but that in his flesh and bones God's Word was there living for us. And maybe it would help us overcome the fear that separates us from others if we would realize that it is not the words we are able or unable to say that are the most important, but rather our physical presence there in flesh and bones with them to hold their hands when they too are afraid.

O God, deliver us from fear! Amen.

A Pat on the Back

My junior high school band director used to say, "a pat on the back never hurts anyone, as long as it is low enough and hard enough." There are times when we all need that kind of pat on the back. There are moments, however, when we need the ordinary kind as well.

When I finished the field examinations for an M.A. degree at the University of Chicago, I was convinced I had failed. Because of confusion brought about by a change of the secretaries who administered the exams, I was given only an hour to write each one in the series, whereas those who had taken the exams before me had been allowed all day to write each essay. Looking back, I suspect the shorter time limit helped me pass. Undoubtedly, the professors who read my essays appreciated their brevity. It took them almost four months to read them as it was! At the time, however, I did not see how my one-hour essays could possibly compare favorably to all-day ones.

Returning home that day in a daze, I was convinced that my whole life had just gone down the drain. When I opened the door, my little dog jumped up and gave me a few good licks on the face. That did it. It suddenly occurred to me that the dog didn't care whether I had passed or failed, and maybe I shouldn't either. All it took was a couple of licks from my dog to bring me back to the land of the living.

If a dog's lick can mean as much as that one did to me, just think how much a person's pat can mean when we are down. Sometimes it's all we need to get us through another day.

O God, thank you for all the dog licks and person pats in our lives. Amen.

The Direction of Love

God's love was directed toward people. Our love for God should move in the same direction. The author of the First Letter of John says,"If anyone says, 'I love God,' and hates his brother, he is a liar; for he who does not love his brother whom he has seen, cannot love God whom he has not seen" (*1 John 4:20*).

Lofty talk about love of God can be no more than an empty slogan unless it is brought down to earth by loving him in the flesh and bones of the people for whom his Son died. God came to earth so that he would be more than an abstract idea or slogan for us. When he did, he incarnated his love for us in a person, his Son and our Lord. Our love for him ought to move in the same direction—toward people:

> For Christ plays in ten thousand places,
> Lovely in limbs and lovely in eyes not his
> To the Father through the features of men's faces.[38]

O God, help us to love you in your people! Amen.

☐

A Coffee Break

Several years ago, I underwent surgery. My condition was not serious, so it was probably a good experience for me. It is usually people I visit who are in that predicament. Although the surgery had been scheduled for days, the surgeons still had not arrived when I was wheeled into the operating room. After what seemed an eternity, the anesthesiologist evidently concluded they would show up eventually and went ahead and put me under. The last thing I remembered was a voice paging the physicians over the public address system.

The surgeons were both my friends, or at least I thought so until then! So, the next day I felt free to ask them, "Where on earth were you guys yesterday? Here I was, laid out on the butcher's block waiting for you to cure or kill, and it looked as if you were never going to show up!" "Oh," they responded, "we were down in the cafeteria having coffee when they paged us, and we didn't want to waste any." To me that operation was a big deal. To them it was all in a day's work and of somewhat less importance than the morning coffee break.

Of course, I wouldn't have wanted a surgeon whose hands were shaking as much as mine were that day, but the incident goes to show how our perspective is changed by how close something is to us. It is only a sign of human nature that we are apt to think first of ourselves and those nearest us. However, we need to try to compensate for that biased perspective, since the needs of people aren't reduced any by their remoteness from us. When Jesus answered the question, "Who is my neighbor?" by telling a story in which the unlikely Samaritan proved to be the most neighborly, he declared all people everywhere our neighbors.

O God, may we offer help on the basis of need rather than geography! Amen.

The Seeds Cry Out

The Apostle Paul wrote:

> The creation waits with eager longing for the revealing of
> the sons of God; for the creation was subjected to futility,
> not of its own will but by the will of him who subjected it
> in hope; because the creation itself will be set free from its
> bondage to decay and obtain the glorious liberty of the
> children of God. (*Romans 8:19-21*)

Not so long ago, it was difficult for us to understand verses of
this kind. What sense did it make to talk about the liberation of
the physical universe? What could it mean for plants and animals
and the earth itself to be set free? Western theologians were
inclined either to ignore such passages or else to chalk them up to
a type of primitive thinking that no longer made sense in a scien-
tific age. But now we have been alerted to how easily the misuse of
our environment can destroy and poison it, along with ourselves.
Talk about the liberation of the physical universe does not seem
so strange.

Nikos Kazantzakis wrote:

> Even in the most meaningless particle of the earth and sky
> I hear God crying out: "Help me!" . . . A stone is saved if
> we lift it from the mire and build it into a house, or if we
> chisel the spirit upon it. . . . If you are a laborer then till
> the earth, help it to bear fruit. The seeds in the earth cry
> out, and God cries out within the seeds. Set him free! A
> field awaits its deliverance at your hands, a machine
> awaits its soul. You may never be saved unless you save
> them.[39]

Our future well-being is bound up with the well-being of the
whole universe more than we can imagine, just as our own interests are bound up with the interests of people everywhere much
more than we usually can see.

O God, heal our nearsightedness! Amen.

Living with Differences

Singing in Different Keys

Charles Edward Ives was an insurance broker, whose firm, Ives and Myrick, became the largest volume life insurance brokerage house in the United States. His new ideas for the insurance industry, aimed at improving the retirement income of common people and estate planning, are part of the trade today.

He was also a gifted composer and organist at Central Presbyterian Church in New York. With its use of dissonance and unusual harmonies, his compositions are now heralded is anticipating many of the trends of contemporary serious music.

In his later years, he published many tracts at his own expense, always championing the right of the dissenters and lone voices who dared to be different to be heard.

James W. McClendon, Jr. has shown that Ives' music, with its dissonance and use of quotations from widely different sources, and his view of life, with its appreciation for those who dared to be different, were of one piece. It was a vision in which uniqueness, individuality, and differences were accepted as part of a larger whole. One of its sources, says McClendon, was the influence of Ives's father, a high school band and church choir director. He taught Ives to accept and even to appreciate the occasional sour notes and off-key singing and playing of church congregations and high school bands, as part of a larger musical and spiritual whole.[40]

Whether or not we like Ives' music, we can learn much from his vision. The church ought especially to be a place where our differences can be accepted and appreciated as a part of the whole body of Christ. As Paul wrote, ". . . we, though many, are one body in Christ, and individually members one of another" (*Romans 12:5*). Even though we don't always sing in the same key or think in the same way, we are all one in Jesus Christ, and we ought to act like it.

O God, help us to accept and to rejoice in our differences as parts of one body of your Son! Amen.

Colliding People

Physicists believe that for each type of subatomic particle there is a corresponding anti-particle with properties and behavior just the opposite of that particle. When a particle chances to collide with one of its anti-particle counterparts, they annihilate each other. Their mass is transformed into energy, which is released in the form of gamma rays.

We people sometimes behave much like subatomic particles. On almost every issue, some of us are pro-people and others of us are anti-people. When a pro-person and an anti-person collide in a discussion, common sense, at least, is apt to he annihilated. In the case of these people collisions, however, the energy released is usually hot air or steam rather than gamma rays.

We have made much progress toward harnessing the energy released by the collision of subatomic particles, but we are still a long way from harnessing the energy released by colliding people. If we ever learn to do that, I suspect we will see wonders far more spectacular than those wrought by nuclear physics.

O God, when we are too hot under our collars, cool us off! Amen.

□

We Need Faces

"How can we meet [the gods] face to face till we have faces?" C. S. Lewis asked.[41] We have to have some sense of our own unique identity before we can relate to God, just as we do before we can relate to other people. Faceless people wouldn't make very interesting friends.

Since our relationships with God require that we "have faces," that we be the unique individuals we were created to be, each of us will have his or her own unique relationship with God. There has never been another person exactly like any of us, and there never will be. No one ever has nor ever will have a relationship with God exactly like ours.

As Mary McDermott Schideler put it, "To each of us God gives a different name and speaks a different word. With each of us he has a separate covenant, and from each of us he calls for an individual response."[42]

The most certain way to destroy other persons is to force them to be like us. Heaven forbid! However good any of us may be, one of each of us is quite enough! The quickest way to destroy the faith of others is to try to force them to relate to God in the same way we do.

When we have had a joyous experience of God, it is only natural that we want to share it. But to suppose that others aren't Christians simply because they haven't had the same experience, or don't believe exactly the same things about God that we do, is nonsense. God is not that small! Who do we think we are to try to cut God down to our size? God is much more than any of us can ever exhaust in our beliefs about him or in our ways of relating to him. There is room in his infinitely large heart for us all.

O God, help us to love our faces and those of others! Amen.

☐

Only One Leg Nearer

The story is told of a little boy who came home to his parents with the news that he had won first prize in a quiz. The question had been, "How many legs has a horse?" He had answered, "Three." When his mother asked in astonishment how he had won first prize with such an answer, he explained that all the other children had answered, "Two."

It is like that in our search for truth. In our efforts to understand what life means and how we should live, etc., some may be closer to truth than others, but none is much closer than the little boy who, with his answer that a horse had three legs, was just one leg nearer to being correct than the others who had answered, "Two." Paul wrote, "Now we see in a mirror dimly" (*1 Corinthians 13:12*). He wrote that statement to the Corinthians who were famous for making mirrors of polished metal in which images were always blurred, unlike the sharp images in the silvered glass mirrors of today. Those words are in Paul's response to a very haughty group of people in the church at Corinth who thought they were superior Christians, possessing gifts even Paul lacked and certain they were right in all matters.

We need strong convictions, but we also need enough humility to remember we are only people, not gods.

O God, free us from arrogance! Amen.

There But for the Grace of God Go I

Late one night, I headed for the church to pick up a book I needed and stepped into an open manhole. It was unmarked, and in the darkness I couldn't see it. Fortunately, only one leg went in. Although it went clear down, it was still attached to the rest of me, and I was able to pull it out and keep going. I have heard of people winding up in the gutter, but I nearly wound up in the sewer. I thought of that old phrase. "There but for the grace of God go I."

Those are good words to remember. Once Jesus asked why we look at the speck in our brother's eye and pay no attention to the log in our own (*Matthew 7:3*). Part of the answer, I suspect, is that we know more about the reasons from our own pasts that lead us to some of the irritating and otherwise incomprehensible things we do than we know about such reasons in the pasts of other people.

We should probably never use the reasons from our past as excuses for our own behavior. I remember hearing a psychiatrist say that we should take charge of our own lives; if there are reasons in our pasts that cause us to do what we don't want, then we should invent new pasts. But that is sometimes easier said than done, and realizing that there are such reasons in all our pasts can help us be more understanding of others. There but for the grace of God go all of us.

O God, help us to understand! Amen.

Life's Temptations

Lousy Gods

In *The Wizard of Oz*, the little dog Toto tips over a screen, and Dorothy and her three companions see that the wizard is really only a little old man. They had just risked their lives to obtain the wicked witch's broom for the Wizard in exchange for promised rewards. Realizing that since he isn't a wizard at all he probably can't keep his promises, Dorothy blurts out, "I think you are a very bad man." The Wizard replies, "Oh, no, my dear! I'm really a very good man, but I'm a very bad wizard. . . ."[43]

All of us have the potential to become very good people, but none of us make very good wizards or, for that matter, very good gods. From the point of view of the first part of the book of Genesis, the very worst sin any of us can commit is to try to set ourselves up as gods. We act like Adam and Eve eating the forbidden fruit in order to "be like God, knowing good and evil" (*Genesis 3:5*), like Cain killing Abel, a prerogative that belongs only to God (*Genesis 4:8*), or like people building a tower with "its top in the heavens" to "make a name" for themselves (*Genesis 11:4*). People get themselves into their most serious trouble when they try to act like they are gods.

Whenever we pretend to be gods, as, for example, when we lord it over others and treat them only as things made to serve our purposes, we have committed what, in the eyes of the book of Genesis, is the very worst sin of all.

Within all of us, there is a lust for power that tempts us to try to run the lives of others as if we were their gods. We aren't! We are people, as are they. Our most serious conflicts arise when we forget that. We all can become very good people, but only when we remember that we make lousy wizards and lousy gods.

O God, help us always to remember who we are! Amen.

When the Rooster Crows

At the Mount of Olives, Jesus told his followers that they would all fall away. Peter protested, "Even though they all fall away, I will not." Jesus answered, "Truly, I say to you, this very night, before the cock crows twice, you will deny me three times" (*Mark 14:27-31*). When the hour came and Jesus was arrested, Peter was asked three times if he were a follower of the Nazarene. He meant well, but courage failed him as sometimes it fails us all. Three times he denied that he knew Jesus. After the third denial, he heard the crow of a rooster for the second time that morning.

We all have known the rooster crow of conscience many times. It is good that we have. Just as, if our reflexes are intact, physical pain can warn us to take our hands off a hot stove before they are seriously burned, our conscience, if it is well formed, can warn us when we are about to do what we should not. The trouble is, just as our burnt fingers can keep hurting even after we have jerked them back from a hot stove, so our conscience can keep crowing even after it has served its purpose of warning us of moral wrong. It can even paralyze us instead of turning us toward new life. What can we do when the rooster crows and keeps crowing?

When the risen Christ appeared to Peter and several other followers, the Gospel of John says that Jesus asked Peter three times if he loved Jesus, giving Peter three opportunities of affirmation corresponding to the three denials. Jesus' responses to the three affirmations Peter made that day were: "Feed my lambs," "Tend my sheep," and "Feed my sheep" (*John 21:15-17*). He did not want from Peter the kind of continuing remorse that can paralyze life. Rather, he asked Peter to involve himself in the needs of other people. If the rooster keeps on crowing even after it has served its purpose, our best course is to involve ourselves in caring for the problems of others so that we can forget our own. To be preoccupied with a guilty conscience, even after we have stopped doing whatever made it hurt, is a form of self-centeredness that benefits neither God nor us. The way out of remorse is to reach out to others with a helping hand.

O God, let our conscience crow only when that helps. Amen.

Things Worthwhile

In a technological age, it is easy to be lured into thinking that technique and style are everything. Corporations conclude that producing worthwhile products is less important than their appearance and developing the right techniques to sell them. So, more money is spent on style and advertising than on material and workmanship; we wind up with scores of highly seductive commercials for attractive gadgets that fall apart almost as soon as we take them home from the stores. Worst of all, we become convinced that developing the right style and technique for getting ahead is more important to us than what we are inside; we see multitudes of outwardly successful people with empty lives. Depression has become one of the most common conditions associated with success.

A recent local television editorial criticized our mayor's budget for allocating too much to "luxuries"—such as a new garden and a center for the arts—and not enough for "necessities," like streets and sewers. It bothered me that streets and sewers were assumed to be self-evident necessities when not so long ago both indoor plumbing and automobiles were seen as luxuries. It bothered me more that things which might make our lives full, like gardens and an art center, were viewed only as luxuries.

The apostle Paul wrote, "Finally, brethren, whatever is true, whatever is honorable, whatever is just, whatever is pure, whatever is lovely, whatever is gracious, if there is any excellence, if there is anything worthy of praise, think about these things" (*Philippians 4:8*). I don't think he had in mind only indoor plumbing. A society that can't see beyond its streets and sewers may be headed straight for the gutter!

O God, help us always to think of things worthwhile! Amen.

A Use for Demons

Storyteller Hans Christian Andersen wrote to a friend:

I feel a desire to be rude to somebody. I must have air!
Would you do me the truly friendly favour of insulting me
this evening, so that I may have cause to give vent to my
rage, there's a kind soul! After all, I'm not asking something very difficult, am I?[44]

All of us have a dark side, or at least a side of us we evidently
think is dark, since we waste so much energy trying to hide it even
from ourselves. I am thinking of our anger, fears, aggression, and
those things that differ from our image of what we think we ought
to be. Usually the best way to deal with those supposed demons
within us is neither to fight them nor pretend they don't exist, but
to put them to use for some good purpose.

Jesus, for example, vented a good deal of anger at the hypoc-
risy of the Pharisees and the injustice of the money changers in
the temple. He put the anger to work for what was right. He said,
"You have heard that it was said to the men of old, 'You shall not
kill; and whoever kills shall be liable to judgment.' But I say to
you that every one who is angry with his brother shall be liable to
judgment. . . ." (*Matthew 5:21-22*). He was evidently thinking,
however, of the bitter, destructive anger that can lead to murder,
rather than of the constructive anger he made use of in his dis-
putes with the Pharisees and during the cleansing of the temple.

Our anger is most apt to turn into the dark, destructive kind
when we try to pretend it is not there, or when we try to keep it
bottled up. The best thing to do is to use it for a good purpose.
We are the human beings God made us to be. Our most serious
trouble usually begins when we try to pretend we aren't human,
instead of using what we are in the service of what is right.

O God, help us to put all that we are at your service! Amen.

Vending-Machine Christians

I do not get along with vending machines. They seem eager to take my money but often refuse to give me any merchandise in return. One of the world's worst vending machines was in an apartment building where we once lived in New York City. In exchange for our coins, it was supposed to dispense small grocery items, but it almost never did. One night we returned after an evening out to discover that someone had taken an ax to it. Judging from the location of the blows, it did not appear that the ax wielder was after the machine's money. He or she was simply fed up with the blasted thing. I did not wield the ax, but I confess I sympathized with the person who did.

We Christians are sometimes like vending machines—prepared to take in God's grace, but unwilling to dispense much of it in return in our dealings with other people. That is what Dietrich Bonhoeffer called "cheap grace"—treating grace as if it placed no obligation on us. "Are we to continue to sin that grace may abound?" asked Paul. Then he responded to his own question, "By no means! How can we who died to sin still live in it?" (*Romans 6:1-2*). God's grace means little unless it softens our hearts so that we treat other people the same way God treats us.

Vending machine Christians, who take in grace but refuse to dispense any, are as irritating as vending machines that take money but won't give out merchandise.

O God, soften our hearts with your grace! Amen.

☐

Only the Kingdom

Fred Allen once quipped that a celebrity is one who works to be known, then wears dark glasses so as not to be recognized. It is an almost universal human experience to discover that the achievement of many of our goals is not as fulfilling as we had expected. That is why we usually want more and more of whatever it is we go after. There never seems to be quite enough achievement to make our lives full. Some fail to achieve their goals and are frustrated. Others achieve them and are disappointed. There is much truth in the old saying, "Beware of what you want in your youth, because in your old age you will probably get it."

Most of the goals we set for ourselves are good ones, but few are worthy of being the center of our whole lives. It is the Christian claim that only God, his kingdom, and the fulfillment of our lives in him are good enough to be objects of our ultimate commitment. Of course, we all want other things as well. It is proper that we should. Many are worth a great deal of effort, but nothing less than God's kingdom is worth our whole selves. It is the "pearl of great price" Jesus talked about, and part of its value is that it frees us from centering our lives on anything less. There *is* something sad in not liking what you wanted when you get it, and part of what is sad is that either you wanted the wrong thing or some right ones more than they were worth.

O God, free us from centering our lives around anything less than you. Amen.

Living Our Commitments

□

Not an Easy Thing

In his play, *Gideon*, Paddy Chayefsky has Gideon say to the Israelites, "It is not easy to be loved by God."[45] The great prophets of the Bible discovered the same thing. That is why they tried as hard as they could to decline the honor of being prophets when God gave them the nod. All of them would rather have stayed home dressing sycamore trees.

"It is not an easy thing to be loved by God." God's grace does not make life easier. Legalistic religion is always the easiest way, which is why it is always the most popular. When religion is reduced to a few petty do's and don'ts, as is usually the case with legalism, or even when it is made a matter of lofty requirements, all that is necessary is to meet those requirements. Then the price is paid; all obligation ends. Adherents of legalism always know, or think they know, where they are going before they even start on their religious journey. That always makes for an easier and safer trip.

In contrast, God's grace calls us to a grateful response that knows no end. One who has been moved by that grace never knows where it may take him. God's grace calls for a response of following. When Jesus called his disciples, he said, "Follow me" (*Mark 1:17*). Who knows where that adventure may lead?

God's grace is free, but not cheap. It is, however, the only way to true life. God's grace does not make life easier; it makes life, in any sense that really matters, possible.

O God, give us the courage to be loved by you! Amen.

Going to Church

Amos Wilder, a New Testament professor and brother of playwright Thornton Wilder, wrote in a poem:

Going to Church is like approaching an open volcano
where the world is molten
and hearts are sifted.
The altar is like a third rail that spatters sparks,
the sanctuary is like the chamber next to the atomic oven:
there are invisible rays and you leave your watch
outside.[46]

That is how it ought to be, but, I am afraid, seldom the way it is.

We preachers must shoulder much of the blame. Because we think it is expected of us, we often console rather than challenge, entertain rather than provoke, and tranquilize rather than excite. We could all learn from Father Mapple's sermon in Herman Melville's *Moby Dick*:

Woe to him whom this world charms from Gospel duty! Woe to him who seeks to pour oil upon the waters when God has brewed them into a gale! Woe to him who seeks to please rather than to appal! Woe to him whose good name is more to him than goodness! Woe to him who, in this world, courts not dishonor! Woe to him who would not be true, even though to be false were salvation! Yea, woe to him who, as the great Pilot Paul has it, while preaching to others is himself a castaway![47]

Part of the problem also lies with the listeners. So few things excite us any more. We confuse sophistication with indifference. We like to play it cool. We think being immovable is a sign of strength, when, in reality, it is allowing ourselves to be moved that takes the courage. We want to feel good rather than to be challenged to goodness.

If the sparks don't fly and ignite something in us when we go to church, it may be because there is no flint in the preacher. It may be because there is no kindling in our hearts.

O God, let your sparks fly! Amen.

Goodness from Badness

In Robert Penn Warren's *All the King's Men*, Boss Willie Stark says that if you want goodness, ". . . you got to make it out of badness. . . . And you know why? Because there isn't anything else to make it out of."[48]

That is what orthodox Christianity means by original sin. It means that, fallen as they are, creation in general and people in particular, don't have much natural goodness in them to build on. On our own, we are all pretty much wrapped up in ourselves— our own fears, our own heartaches, our own aspirations. That doesn't leave much in us with which to reach out to others. Yet the fact is never seen as an excuse to relieve us of responsibility. That is our predicament. We feel helpless sometimes to do the good we want and know we should do, yet at the same time responsible for not doing it.

And since badness is about all there is around, out of which goodness can be made, Christian orthodoxy has spoken of God's grace as the only power that can make it. "Since all have sinned and fall short of the glory of God," says Paul, "they are justified by his grace as a gift, through the redemption which is in Christ Jesus, whom God put forward as an expiation by his blood, to be received by faith" (*Romans 3:23-25*). Only God's love in Christ can love us out of ourselves enough to enable us to love others.

Yet just as original sin is not seen as an excuse that relieves us of responsibility, so God's grace is not seen as a magic potion that works the way a snake oil cure is supposed to work, without involving us. It is the power that makes it possible for us to make goodness out of all that badness. "Work out your own salvation with fear and trembling," says Paul, "for God is at work in you. . . ." (*Philippians 2:12-13*). The fact that God is at work in us does not relieve us from working but makes it possible for us to work. Grace doesn't let us off the hook; it is the power that hooks us.

O God, we thank you for your grace, which enables us to make goodness even from badness. Amen.

Hit the Target Without Aiming

Whenever I have a Tuesday evening free, and one of our church's bowling teams is hard-up for a substitute, I lend a hand. Nothing I do improves my score much, but I always do better if I don't try too hard. Fortunately, that is easy on the team for which I substitute. Most of us are so bad that it doesn't matter much whether we try or not, and the better bowlers are charitable enough not to keep after the rest of us. But if I try very hard, my score drops from bad to worse.

It is said that some Zen Buddhists teach archery by helping students learn to hit the target without aiming. The art is intended to be applied to the whole of life. Sometimes we can better hit the target if we aren't too anxious about the aiming.

That is why Martin Luther once wrote, "We are soon defeated if we try too hard not to sin."[49] Indifference isn't good, but trying too hard can easily lead to the kind of self-righteousness that drops our score from bad to worse.

God's grace empowers us to do what we sometimes cannot do by trying too hard. That grace usually appears in the most unlikely ways, at the most unexpected times, often when we least deserve it.

As Charles Péguy puts it, "Grace doesn't travel along the paths known to us. Grace takes the road it fancies and it never takes the same road twice over. Grace is free. It is the source of all freedom. When grace fails to rise like a spring of water, it may well be percolating surreptitiously."[50]

If we trust in God's grace and remain open to its surprises, it may help us to hit the target in life without too much anxious aiming.

O God, help us to do what we cannot do ourselves! Amen.

The Good We Dream

"I do not do the good I want, but the evil I do not want is what I do." These are not the words of a sociopath or a hardened criminal, but the confession of the greatest Christian of all—the apostle Paul (*Romans 7:19*). I wonder if there is anyone who has not had a similar experience. We dream of goodness we would do, but usually we are too wrapped up in our own problems and frustrations to live those dreams. Even when we manage to translate our dreams into action, we sometimes end up doing more harm than good.

It may be only a dream, this good which we hope to do, but even dreams are important! If we dream enough, we may do at least a little. And in a world where not too much good gets done, even a little can sometimes mean a lot.

O God, help us both to dream and to do! Amen.

Finding Life by Losing It

An Interesting Lock of Hair

At first glance, there may appear to be a contradiction between Paul's advice that we should not think of ourselves more highly than we ought (*Romans 12:3*), and Jesus' assurance that, for God, even the hairs on our heads are numbered (*Luke 12:7*).

One of the most famous theologians of this century, Karl Barth, once said to a group of his students while grasping a strand of his gray hair, "There is not a lock of the hair on my head that is not infinitely interesting to God!"[51] When we realize that, we don't need to prove ourselves or go around thinking we are the center of the universe. God loves us. That is enough. And that's what it means to live by grace.

I heard Karl Barth deliver a lecture series near the end of his life when his fame was at its peak. Rockefeller Chapel at the University of Chicago, a gigantic, cathedral like structure, was packed during every lecture, with people coming from all over the United States to hear Barth. I confess, I don't remember a single thing Barth said at those lectures. His words have long since been blended in my mind with all the other words I have heard from or about him. I do remember his waving goodbye after the final lecture.

All of the dignitaries of the University were on hand that day to award Barth an honorary doctorate. It was a solemn occasion. It was so solemn, in fact, that even when the university president, a biologist who knew little of theological terms, started to misread the citation and refer to Barth as the world's leading dogmatist instead of dogmatician, we were afraid to laugh. But at the end of the lecture, there was jovial old Karl Barth, with an impish grin on his face and a twinkle in his eye, waving goodbye as a child might. It was as if he were letting us know he was not overly impressed by all of the fuss being made over him, and that we in the audience shared with him a joke on all the dignitaries who were taking him and the occasion so seriously.

When we realize we are important to God and loved by him as we are, we don't need to take ourselves so seriously. The weight of the world and of our own self-esteem drops from our tired shoulders, and we can join in the laughter of God. That is grace!

O God, give us your grace! Amen.

□

Giving Ourselves

When we recall Jesus' call to find our lives by losing them, the first thing we are apt to think of is martyrdom. There are still, of course, those times when Christians feel called to give their very lives. One thinks of the confessing church movement in Germany during World War II, or more recently of similar situations in some third world countries.

The odds, however, are so much against finding ourselves in such situations that too much emphasis on giving our physical lives can divert our eyes from the little risks we are called to take every day. The willingness to stick out our necks for others, to reach out to them when we know we may be rejected, to crawl out of our protective shells, to touch other lives and be touched by them, to love when we may not be loved in return, are some of the most common forms of risk-taking.

In fact, as theologian H. A. Williams writes, "People continually give themselves without their (or anybody else) often realizing what they are doing. Self-giving is not (thank God) confined to what are technically acts of piety or compassion."[52] Through the help we give others in our jobs, clubs, personal relationships, or other places, we are fulfilling Christ's call, sometimes without even realizing it. Whenever we give of ourselves, even just a little for even "the least of these," we are saving our lives by losing them. To let go of ourselves, our fears, our false pride, etc., is the only way to be alive in any sense that much matters.

O God, help us to remember that little risks are as necessary as big ones! Amen.

The Last Digit

Playing Cupid is not a good idea. I have always believed every person is entitled to make his or her own mistakes! On only one occasion have I broken my rule against it.

The woman was an attractive school teacher in her early thirties. A statement she made following her father's death so touched me that I made up my mind on the spot that I was going to find her a husband one way or another. A high school principal, who had been a member of another church I had served, moved to town. I knew he was the man. With the help of her brother, a Sunday school class, and many other members of the congregation, I carefully orchestrated a series of encounters leading up to a party designed to bring them together. It worked! They are now the parents of two children, one of whom they named after me. Since I had planned their wedding before they met, this seemed the least they could do.

There was only one period of uncertainty. It was weeks after the party when the principal finally phoned the school teacher for a date. At the wedding, I asked him why on earth he took so long to call. He replied that he had started to dial her number many times during those weeks, but he had lost his nerve when he came to the last digit. As nearly as I can tell, he has never regretted, for long at least, that he finally took the risk.

Unless we are willing to risk the wounds they may sometimes inflicted on us, we cannot know the joy of relating to other people. To live in any way that really matters always involves taking risks. In our relationships to other people, as in other areas of our lives, Jesus' words remain true: "Whoever seeks to gain his life will lose it, but whoever loses his life will preserve it" (*Luke 17:33*).

O God, help us not to fear the last digit! Amen.

Bearing New Fruit

Jesus said, "Truly, truly, I say to you, unless a grain of wheat falls into the earth and dies, it remains alone; but if it dies, it bears much fruit" (*John 12:24*). Growth is never easy, but in order for the new to come, the old must die. It is always painful to let go of that to which we have become accustomed. No wonder it is always tempting to stay where we are. It takes courage to sacrifice the security of what we know for a future we don't know.

Despite the pain of new growth, God calls us to live lives that are ever new. Those who value comfort more than adventure will find little comfort in the Bible. God called Abraham to leave the security of his home for the adventure of a new land. God called Moses to a new task of leading his people out of Egypt, a job for which Moses did not feel qualified any more than the great prophets felt qualified for theirs. When a man wanted to follow him, Jesus pointed to the insecurity that decision would involve: "Foxes have holes, and birds of the air have nests, but the Son of man has nowhere to lay his head" (*Luke 9:58*).

There is the promise, however, that when we allow the old to die, new life will come. As Paul says, "if anyone is in Christ, he is a new creation; the old has passed away, behold, the new has come" (*2 Corinthians 5:17*).

O God, teach us to risk bearing fruit! Amen.

☐

The Source of Life

The Destroyer of the Destroyers

When the seventh trumpet sounds during the vision of the battle between good and evil in the book of Revelation, there is as much fire and brimstone flying around as at any point in the Bible. Suddenly a heavenly chorus of twenty-four elders breaks forth in a song, announcing God's purpose of "destroying the destroyers of the earth" (*Revelation 11:18*). In other words, God's purpose is to prevent the destruction of the earth by destroying those who would ruin it.

Even in judgment, God's purpose is constructive. There is no hint of retaliation or revenge. God's judgment is not a matter of getting even. God judges the world in order to save it. As Jeremiah implied centuries earlier, God plucks up and breaks down and destroys only in order that he may then build and plant (*Jeremiah 18:7-9*). Would that our human judgment were always that constructive!

O God, help us to pluck up and break down only when we intend to plant and build! Amen.

☐

God Never Gives Up

Most of us have moments when we are ready to give up on ourselves. We make mistakes. We have failures. We do things of which we are not proud. Sad as it is, the temptation to give up on ourselves at such times is often quite seductive. It relieves us of any need to keep on trying. Sometimes it is hard to escape its appeal.

God, however, never gives up on any of us. He knows what he created us to be and what we can become. In three great parables, the lost sheep (*Luke 15:1-7*), the lost coin (*Luke 15:8-10*), and the lost or prodigal son (*Luke 15:11-32*), Jesus spoke of a God who is even more concerned with the lost than with the found! The last of the three passages ends with the father still pleading with that stuffy elder brother, whose self-righteousness and jealousy prevented him from attending the banquet celebrating the prodigal's return. If God didn't give up on the elder brother, he is not apt to give up on any of us.

Jesus reached out to the lost so often that he was accused of keeping the wrong sort of company. Most of his followers were people who, for one reason or another, had given up on themselves. By believing in them, Jesus lured them into believing in themselves.

We may lose faith in ourselves, but God never loses faith in us. That is both good news and bad. It is bad news in that it demolishes our excuses for giving up. It is good news in that it opens possibilities for us to become more than we ever dreamed. God never gives up on any of us. Who are we to question God?

O God, don't let us go! Amen.

Have You Not Heard?

Jerusalem was in shambles. The Hebrew leaders and many of the people had been taken away from the promised land, and had lived long years of exile in Babylon. They had lost three of the pillars which had given stability to their lives—the temple in Jerusalem, their king, and their land. Babylon was a powerful nation with magnificant cities. Undoubtedly, many of the exiles were tempted to think that all of that power and splendor and the victory of the Babylonians over them was proof enough that the Babylonian God Marduk was the true one. It must have appeared to many that Yahweh had been defeated along with them. The majority of people in every age have been unduly impressed by power and success.

At that lowest moment in ancient Hebrew history, a prophet wrote:

Have you not known? Have you not heard?
The Lord is the everlasting God,
 the Creator of the ends of the earth.
He does not faint or grow weary,
 his understanding is unsearchable.
He gives power to the faint,
 and to him who had no might he increases strength.
Even youths shall faint and be weary,
 and young men shall fall exhausted:
but they who wait for the Lord shall renew their strength,
 they shall mount up with wings like eagles,
they shall run and not be weary,
 they shall walk and not faint. (*Isaiah 40:28-31*)

Outward appearances notwithstanding, in the end the God of patient, steadfast love will prevail over all of the power and might of the Babylonians or anyone else.

Centuries later, God sent his Son into the world to save it. He did not look much like a winner either. Born in a stable, of all places, he gathered about him followers who, to the eyes of most religious people of the time, must have looked like riff-raff. Deserted by most of them, and, in the end, even by his closest disciples, he died a humiliating criminal's death in the most degrading manner possible. Yet, out of that death came new life and hope that, despite all appearances to the contrary, the patient, steadfast love of God will win over all other forms of power.

O God, when we are discouraged, renew our strength! Amen.

Reward or Source?

St. Catherine of Siena was asked one time what we can possibly give to God—which is ours to give—in return for his love. She replied that the only thing we can offer God of value to him is the gift of our love to people as unworthy of it as we are of his.

God's Son came into the world showing that God loves and accepts us whether or not we deserve it. "God shows his love for us in that while we were yet sinners Christ died for us" (*Romans 5:8*). We are called to deal with other people in the same way. "You have heard that it was said, 'You shall love your neighbor and hate your enemy.' But I say to you, Love your enemies and pray for those who persecute you" (*Matthew 5:43-44*). Our lives are miserable when we feel we must merit God's love and treat others as though they must merit ours.

It matters little how virtuous our lives may he in other respects if we lack hearts large enough to receive the love and acceptance God freely gives and to share that love and acceptance with other human beings.

We will never be perfect. We will never find perfect people with whom to deal. However, genuine love does not wait for perfection. It reaches out regardless of merit, and in so doing, it makes more perfect all of the lives it touches. Love is not a reward for virtue, but its source.

O God, give us hearts that are large! Amen.

To Be One of Us

In Mark Medoff's moving play, *Children of a Lesser God*, Sarah, a deaf person who has learned to speak only in sign language, raises the question of whether the world of speech, toward which people are pushing her, really is better than the world of silence. That is an interesting issue, considering a lot of the things we use our powers of speech to say. It is absolutely certain, however, that the last thing she and the pupils at the State School for the Deaf want is sympathy.[53]

Of course, there are times in all our lives when we don't mind being spoiled temporarily by a bit of sympathy. To have people feeling sorry for us on a more permanent basis, however, is humiliating and degrading. The long-term response from others for which we all hunger, whatever our situation, is not sympathy, but empathy—the capacity of others to share in our feelings. All of us yearn to be understood and accepted for what we are.

That is what God offers to all of us. I know of no hint in the whole New Testament indicating God sent his Son into the world to show that he felt sorry for us, miserable creatures though we all may be. Rather, He sent his Son into the world to be one of us that he might share in our experiences and feelings, joy and pain, life and death. He came to love and accept us as we are and for what he knows we have it in us to become. It is in sharing in the feelings of each other and in accepting each other despite our differences that we become most fully like him.

O God, help us to accept each other as you accept us! Amen.

A Day Late and a Dollar Short

According to the Gospel of Matthew, Jesus told a parable about a householder who went out early in the morning to hire workers for his vineyard to whom he agreed to pay a denarius for a day's work. Needing still more workers, he hired others at the third hour, still others at the sixth, the ninth, and finally even some at the eleventh hour. When the day's end came, he paid them all the same, a denarius apiece. Adding to the apparent injustice of that action, he paid those who worked the shortest time first. When those who had worked all day complained about receiving no more than those who had worked only briefly, the householder replied, "Friend, I am doing you no wrong; did you not agree with me for a denarius? Take what belongs to you, and go; I choose to give to this last as I give to you. Am I not allowed to do what I choose with what belongs to me? Or do you begrudge my generosity?" (*Matthew 20:13-15*). Jesus introduced the parable by saying that such is the kingdom of heaven.

The initial reaction of most people to the parable is one of sympathy with the complaints of the all-day workers. Most of us identify with them and are puzzled by the apparent unfairness of equal pay for those who did so much less than they. But, as the householder said, if we receive what we bargained for, why should we begrudge the generosity toward those who did less? Is it not because we are all at least selfish enough that we don't like others getting off with less work than we? And if we all are that selfish, does it not mean that by the standards of the kingdom we are all more like the eleventh hour workers than those who started early? And if so, should we not all rejoice in the news that, even so, we shall receive the full measure of the joy of God's kingdom?

When it comes to that kingdom, we are all "a day late and a dollar short," so thanks be to God that its joy is ours anyway.

O God, thank You for your grace! Amen.

□

Blessing and Cursing

Suppose a boy steals an apple
From the tray at the grocery store,
And they all begin to call him a thief,
The editor, minister, judge, and all the people—
"A thief," "a thief," "a thief," wherever he goes.
And he can't get work, and he can't get bread
Without stealing it, why the boy will steal.
It's the way the people regard the theft of the apple
That makes the boy what he is.[54]

So wrote Edgar Lee Masters in "Aner Clute" from *Spoon River Anthology*. When we carelessly name the boy a thief, we encourage him to be one. "How great a forest is set ablaze by a small fire! And the tongue is a fire" (*James 3:5-6*). "With it we bless the Lord and Father and with it we curse men, who are made in the likeness of God" (*James 3:9*). Our words to others can either bless or curse, for we encourage persons to become whatever we call them.

How fortunate we are that the word God spoke to us in Jesus Christ as *the Word* is the word of grace. The twelve, Mary Magdalene, Zacchaeus, and all that motley crew that followed Jesus were made new people because he treated them not as the sinners they were, but as the saints he knew they could become.

"God shows his love for us in that while we were yet sinners Christ died for us" (*Romans 5:8*). He does not wait for us to become saints but loves us already as though we were; thereby he empowers ue to become far more than we could ever dream.

O God, help us to bless rather than to curse! Amen.

Better News

Our deepest feelings come from very secret places. Sometimes we scarcely understand them ourselves. But part of the good news of the gospel is that God understands.

We talk a good deal about how God revealed himself to us in Jesus Christ and opened up for us some of the secret places within himself. That is important. But perhaps even more important to us is the good news that he knows and understands us and all of our secret places. I suspect that one thing we all want even more than to understand is to be understood.

Paul wrote, ". . . if one loves God, one is known by him" (*1 Corinthians 8:3*). It is good news that, in Jesus Christ, God opens our eyes to some of the mystery within him. It is perhaps even better news that, in Jesus Christ, God shows us that we are fully known and accepted, even in the secret places of our hearts where tears come from.

O God, We thank you that you understand. Amen.

□

Holding It Together

Have you ever felt torn apart by the decisions you must make? I notice that feeling most in deciding how to use my time. How much of it do I owe to my church? How much to my family? How much to the community? How much to myself? Should I use my work time to recruit new members or to visit the existing ones who need a pastor? In most decisions we make, we are torn between conflicting loyalties. That is why we all need a center for our lives—a supreme commitment under which all of our lesser commitments can fall into their proper places.

The world also needs a center which can pull it together. Yeats' wrote about what happens to the world when it tries to live without a unifying center:

> Things fall apart; the centre cannot hold;
> Mere anarchy is loosed upon the world,
> The blood-dimmed tide is loosed, and everywhere
> The ceremony of innocence is drowned;
> The best lack all conviction, while the worst
> Are full of passionate intensity.[55]

The letter to the Colossians says that both we and the whole universe can find such a center in Jesus Christ. "All things were created through him and for him. He is before all things, and *in him all things hold together"* (*1:16-17*).

Of course, even with Christ as our center, there are still hard decisions we must make between the lesser commitments toward which we feel drawn. Much of the anxiety, however, vanishes from those decisions when we know our only ultimate commitment is to Christ.

O God, hold our lives together in your Son! Amen.

To Have Needs And Know It

Jesus told a parable comparing the kingdom of God with a banquet. The host invited many of his friends, but all of them sent regrets. The first said, "I have bought a field, and I must go out and see it." Another said, "I have bought five yoke of oxen, and I go to examine them." A third said, "I have married a wife, and therefore I cannot come" (*Luke 14:15-20*).

Their excuses show that they were all good, substantial people—the kind of people who marry, own land, and carry out the work of the world. They received the first invitations to the kingdom banquet, but all of them thought themselves too busy to come.

Then the host said to his servants, "Go out quickly to the streets and lanes of the city, and bring in the poor and maimed and blind and lame" (*Luke 14:21*). It was these, who had no other hope, who came to the kingdom banquet. Only those who knew they had needs showed up for that banquet.

We all have needs, of course. But if life has gone too well for us, it is easy to fool ourselves into thinking we are self-sufficient. That does not exclude us from the kingdom banquet. It may cause us to exclude ourselves.

In Luke's version of the beatitudes, Jesus says:

Blessed are you poor, for yours is the kingdom of God.
Blessed are you that hunger now, for you shall be satisfied.
Blessed are you that weep now, for you shall laugh. (*Luke 6:20-21*)

Blessed, in other words, are those who have needs and know it; only they are likely to be willing to receive God's gifts. Blessed are those who see that, in our relationship to God, we are all beggars—poor, maimed, blind, lame beggars—bleeding from what we have done or have failed to do—for only they are apt to want to come to the kingdom feast.

O God, help us not to miss your feast by supposing we do not need it!

Peeking Beyond Life's End

All Things New

If we thought about it long enough, I suspect most of us would be depressed at the thought of any fulfillment of our lives being only an endless repetition of the present—the same old problems, the same old routine, the same old experiences repeated over and over again, *ad infinitum*.

That is the importance of all the talk of newness in the book of Revelation as it moves to its conclusion with a vision of the final victory of God:

> Then I saw a new heaven and a new earth; for the first heaven and the first earth had passed away, and the sea was no more. And I saw the holy city, new Jerusalem, coming down out of heaven from God, prepared as a bride adorned for her husband; and I heard a great voice from the throne saying, "Behold, the dwelling of God is with men. He will dwell with them, and they shall be his people, and God himself will be with them; he will wipe away every tear from their eyes, and death shall be no more, neither shall there be mourning nor crying nor pain any more, for the former things have passed away."
>
> And he who sat upon the throne said, "Behold, I make all things new." Also he said, "Write this, for these words are trustworthy and true." And he said to me, "It is done! I am the Alpha and the Omega, the beginning and the end. To the thirsty I will give water without price from the fountain of the water of life. He who conquers shall have this heritage, and I will be his God and he shall be my son." (*Revelation 21:1-7*)

Here the hope is not for an endless repetition of the same old life, but for a new life, in which "the former things have passed away," and there is "a new heaven and a new earth" created by a

130

God who says, "Behold, I make all things new." It is a vision of a future so different from the present that it cannot be precisely described in our present language, but only pointed to with these images of newness. Yet the vision looks forward to a newness that need not be feared, as we often fear the unknown, since it is still life with God. The voice from the throne says, "Behold, the dwelling of God is with men. He will dwell with them, and they shall be his people, and God himself will be with them." It is also a hope for "a new earth," as well as "a new heaven." The passage speaks of "the holy city, new Jerusalem, *coming down* out of heaven from God" to this earth. Sometimes interpreters have puzzled over this verse, since a few verses later the author sees it coming down again (*21:10*) But throughout the whole vision of God's final victory in the concluding chapters of Revelation, things keep coming down to this earth, offering in a partial way new life already, here and now in this world, from the God who "makes all things new."

O God, make us new! Amen.

☐

The End Is Not Yet

"And when you hear of wars and rumors of wars, do not be alarmed," says Jesus, "this must take place, but the end is not yet" (*Mark 13:7*). The resurrection hope is faith in an end beyond the apparent end. It is faith that the wars, heartaches, failures, frustrations, and suffering, which we all face from time to time in life, are not the last word. As Fred Craddock says, "Only God deals in final conclusions."[56] Despite apparent defeats, new beginnings are always possible both now and in the life to come.

Of course, if it is to be life that is really new, we cannot know precisely what awaits us beyond physical death, anymore than we can foresee what unexpected opportunities will come our way to make possible new beginnings when the future seems closed to us in this life. We know that, above all, it will be life with God. "Beloved, we are God's children now; it does not yet appear what we shall be, but we know that when he appears we shall be like him, for we shall see him as he is" (*1 John 3:2*). Because God in Jesus Christ is present with us in both, we need not fear either life or death.

O God, we thank you for your presence in both this life and the life to come! Amen.

□

Notes

1. Joe Williams, *Bartlesville: Remembrances of Time Past, Reflections of Today*. TRW Reda Pump Division, 1978, pp. 89, 97.

2. Hugh Leonard, *Da*. Atheneum, 1978, p. 82.

3. Clyde Reid, *The Return of Faith: Finding God in the Unconscious*. Harper & Row, 1974, p. 86.

4. Sholom Aleichem, "The Town of the Little People," in *Favorite Tales of Sholom Aleichem*. Avenel Books, 1983, pp. 1, 2.

5. Gyles Brandeth, *871 Famous Last Words*. Bell, 1979, p. 130.

6. Rosalind Fergusson, *The Penguin Dictionary of Proverbs*. Penguin, 1983, p. 53.

7. Lillian Hellman, *My Mother, My Father, and Me*. Random House, 1963, p. 24.

8. Eduard Schweizer, *The Good News According to Mark*. John Knox Press, 1970, p. 46.

9. Gilbert A. Harrison, *The Enthusiast: A Life of Thornton Wilder*. Tiknor and Fields, 1983, p. 113.

10. C. S. Lewis, *Poems*. Harcourt Brace Jovanovich, 1977, p. 65.

11. Dag Hammarskjold, *Markings*. Alfred A. Knopf, 1964, p. 56.

12. John Donne, "Meditation XVII," in *The Complete Poetry and Selected Prose of John Donne*. Modern Library, 1952, p. 441.

13. Ed Graczyk, *Come Back to the 5 and Dime, Jimmy Dean, Jimmy Dean*, as performed at Carpenter Square Theater in Oklahoma City, Oklahoma, April 19, 1985.

14. Mary Chase, *Harvey*, in Burns Mantle, ed., *Best Plays of 1944-45*. Dodd, Mead and Co., 1946, p. 184.

15. Nikos Kazantzakis, *Report to Greco*. Simon and Schuster, 1965, p. 45.

16. Valerie Eliot in a letter to the *London Times*, cited by Annie Dillard in *Pilgrim at Tinker Creek*, pp. 168, 169.

17. W. H. Auden, *W. H. Auden: Collected Poems*, Random House, 1976, pp. 581, 583.

18. T. S. Eliot, "Ash Wednesday," in *T. S. Eliot: The Complete Poems and Plays (1909-1950)*. Harcourt, Brace and Co., 1952, p. 67.

133

19. H. A. Williams, *Tensions: Necessary Conflicts in Life and Love*. Templegate, 1976, pp. 111, 120.

20. Fedor Dostoevski, *The Brothers Karamazov* Dell, 1956, p. 250.

21. H. A. Williams, *The Joy of God*. Templegate, 1979, p. 12.

22. Nikos Kazantzakis, *The Saviors of God: Spiritual Exercises*. Simon and Schuster, 1960, p. 79.

23. Mary McDermott Schideler, *Consciousness of Battle*. Eerdmans, 1970, pp. 151, 152.

24. H. A. Williams, *Tensions*. Templegate, 1976, pp. 30, 34.

25. From *The Story-teller . . . A Session with Charles Laughton*. Capitol Records TBO 1650.

26. Cited in Amos Wilder, *Modern Poetry and the Christian Tradition*. Charles Scribner's Sons, 1952, p. 165.

27. August Wilson, *Ma Rainey's Black Bottom*. New American Library, 1985, pp. 76-77.

28. Donald Davie, ed., *The New Oxford Book of Christian Verse*. Oxford University Press, 1981, pp. 249-250.

29. Brian Foley, "Psalm 148," *Cantate Domino*. Barenreiter, 1974, p. 28.

30. Rollo May, *The Courage to Create*. W. W. Norton and Co., 1975, p. 93.

31. Edward Albee, *The Plays, Vol. III*. Atheneum, 1982, p. 135.

32. Gerard Manley Hopkins, "The Wreck of the Deutschland," in *Poems of Gerard Manley Hopkins*. Oxford Univerity Press, 1948, p. 67.

33. *King Lear*. Act V, Scene iii, lines 324-325.

34. Cited in Frederick Buechner, *The Alphabet of Grace*. Walker and Co., 1970, p. 65.

35. Frederick Buechner, *Ibid.*, p. 78.

36. Frank S. Mead, ed., *Encyclopedia of Religious Quotations*. Fleming H. Revell Co., 1976, p. 586.

37. Fred Kogos, *A Dictionary of Yiddish Slang and Idioms*. Citadel, 1967, p. 19.

38. Gerard Manley Hopkins, "As Kingfishers Catch Fire," in *The New Oxford Book of Christian Verse*. Oxford University Press, 1981, p. 250.

39. Nikos Kazantzakis, *The Saviors of God*. Simon and Schuster, 1960, pp. 120-122.

40. James William McClendon, Jr., *Biography as Theology*. Abingdon, 1974, p. 173.

41. Cited in Mary McDermott Schideler, *Consciousness of Battle*. Eerdmans, 1970, p. 146.

42. Mary McDermott Schideler, *Ibid.*, p. 181.

43. Frank Baum, *The Wizard of Oz*. Award Books, Inc., n. d., p. 145.

44. Cited in H. A. Williams, *The Joy of God*. Templegate, 1979, p. 73.

45. Paddy Chayefsky, *Gideon*. Random House, 1961, p. 105.

46. Amos Wilder, "Electric Chimes or Ram's Horns," in *Grace Confounding*. Fortress Press, 1972, p. 13.

47. Herman Melville, *Moby Dick*, Pocket Books, Inc., 1956, p. 54.

48. Robert Penn Warren, *All the King's Men*. Harcourt, Brace and Company, 1946, p. 272.

49. John M. Todd, *Luther: A Life*. Crossroad, 1982, p. 307.

50. Cited in H. A. Williams, *The Joy of God*. Templegate, 1979, p. 127.

51. Quoted by Elizabeth Achtemeier, *Preaching as Theology and Art*. Abingdon, 1984, p. 90.

52. H. A. Williams, *The Joy of God*. Templegate, 1979, p. 32.

53. Mark Medoff, *Children of a Lesser God*. James T. White and Co., 1980.

54. Edgar Lee Masters, "Aner Clute" in *Spoon River Anthology*. Collier Macmillan, 1962, p. 77.

55. William Butler Yeats, "The Second Coming," in *The Collected Poems of W. B. Yeats*. Macmillan, 1937, p. 215.

56. Fred Craddock, *Philippians*. John Knox Press, 1985, p. 34.

"A concert of souls. A collective journey of spirit. Life lived hard and the lessons of uncovering one's truths. Five phenomenal women across generations, race, and personal geographies lend an ear to one another. *The Dream Catcher's Song* is their testimony.

"These pages are one telling of the creative space women can shape for one another through communal listening, deep witness, and the intention of entering the mystery raw. As you read one voice, you can hear the other women in the circle listening, and feel how listening shapes work. '…A journey to reclaim my authentic self…' writes Princene Hyatt, 'So, don't ask me if you're not ready for my truth.' The ante is upped. You in?"

– Annie Rachele Lanzillotto
Author and Performance Artist

"This quintet of Brooklyn writers writes memoir, poetry, and fiction with a quiet power, a wild tenderness, and a faithfulness to their own experience I've seldom seen before.

"Funny, sometimes angry, richly sensual, vivid as the families, acquaintances, and living, contradictory feelings they explore. Five glowing, intense voices full of insight and power."

– Donna Minkowitz
Author of *Ferocious Romance*

"A wise and patient cook knows that complexity of flavor can only be achieved by simmering slowly, and it's obvious that the authors of *The Dream Catcher's Song* have mastered the art of literary depth-by-simmer.

"This collection of compellingly rich writing defies definition and genre. Funny, sad, defiant, sexy – and incredibly readable – *The Dream Catcher's Song* is an accomplished and surprisingly satisfying treasury crafted by writers who offer up a rare marriage of imagination and insight. Readers will, by turns, be delighted, touched, disturbed, and humbled."

– Sunshine O'Donnell
Author of *Open Me*

Legend of the Dream Catcher

Native Americans of different Nations believe the air is filled with both good and bad dreams. Historically, dream catchers were hung in the tepee or lodge and on a baby's cradleboard. According to popular legend, good dreams reach the sleeping person through the center, while bad dreams get caught in the web, only to disappear at the break of day.

THE
DREAM CATCHER'S
SONG

An Anthology
Presenting Five Emerging
Brooklyn Writers

Gabriella M. Belfiglio
Kim D. Brandon
Princene Hyatt
Olivia S. Taylor
Rita REB Wilson

Edited by Margarita M. Suarez

BELLA PRESS
BROOKLYN, NY

We dedicate this book to everyone who has shined a light against the dark, who has led a march for peace, justice, or equality.

9/10/17
Brooklyn

To Joy + Darryl,
with gratitude to
know you both.
Happy Reading —
And also to wishes
of catching your
dreams —
love,
Gabrielle

We thank our fellow members, friends, and family at Brooklyn Society for Ethical Culture for bringing us together and providing us with the space and platform for our work.

We also express our appreciation to Joel Shatzky for giving us the idea to make this book and starting us off on the process.

Thanks to Annie Rachele Lanzillotto, Donna Minkowitz, and Sunshine O'Donnell for taking the time to read our manuscript and for their heartfelt responses.

Much appreciation goes to Elvira Morán for her generosity and design advice.

And finally, our gratitude to Margarita M. Suarez for her vision and many hours of hard work to make this, our first group publishing effort, a reality.

Table of Contents

Introduction

Our writers' group came together about three years ago. Kim Brandon initiated the concept of a writers' workshop. She approached Lisel Burns, the leader at that time of Brooklyn Society for Ethical Culture, and together they introduced members and friends of the Society who shared the common thread of writing. Kim Brandon became the facilitator of our group, helping to organize and center our creative forces.

As a group, we decided to meet twice a month and to welcome everyone with a desire to write. There have been poets, novelists, short story writers, memoirists, and people who move between the genres. There have been brand-new writers, published writers, and folks in between. We have welcomed writers of all ages, genders, and backgrounds. Writers come and go as their schedules allow. However, a core group of us has emerged: Gabriella M. Belfiglio, Kim D. Brandon, Princene Hyatt, Olivia S. Taylor, and Rita REB Wilson. Our work is included in this first anthology.

Most meetings are held at Brooklyn Society for Ethical Culture. Some of us are members of the Society and some are not. Our group does not represent the Society, but we enjoy the friendship and gathering space they offer us. We also meet at cafes, libraries, restaurants, and each other's homes.

The meetings are warm and encouraging. Each meeting begins with an icebreaker exercise offered by one of the members. For example, one Sunday Gabriella brought in a box of old photographs that she had collected from flea markets and such. She gave one to each of us, and we had to write a back-story for our photo. Another icebreaker was the topic, "What if you won the lottery?" We are often amazed with one another as we explore the spontaneous creativity that happens at these moments. Many of our icebreakers have turned into longer pieces. Above all, they help us immediately become present and focus on the transformative power of language. We have included sample icebreakers in this anthology to reveal part of our process, so that the reader can follow the evolution of our work.

The lion's share of the meetings is dedicated to sharing and discussing prepared works. As you will soon find out, our core group is a mix of writers expressing themselves across different genres. Writers bring in a story or poem or other works-in-progress for the group's feedback. We have heard some remarkable work and have nurtured, inspired, and strengthened the writing process in each other. The following pages showcase examples of each writer's work.

Prefacing our icebreakers and more polished work, we have each included a short piece regarding our influences and inspirations as a writer. We hope this will give you a context of what has shaped and grounded our voices and help you connect more deeply. The five of us have found many places where we overlap as individuals and many places where we are different. We feel strength lies in keeping open minds and hearts and celebrating both our similarities and our differences.

We invite readers, writers, and thinkers to hear our voice, our song: *The Dream Catcher's Song.*

Inspirations

How I Got Here

Gabriella M. Belfiglio

It's hard to figure out how we end up like we do. Is it fate, genetics, will? Humans will forever try to figure out the mysteries of the universe, try to unlock the chaos. The way I see it, there will always be some unknown, despite the mind's relentless pursuit of clarity. On good days, I call it magic.

Many times over, I might have chosen *not* to be a writer. Listening to one's heart and following the path that leads you on is not easy – especially in the midst of family, friends, and society's constant nagging of more practical choices that should be made. Often it feels like swimming upstream, the crack and roar of the creek akin to a battle.

Even before I could write, I was making up stories, fascinated with words and the worlds they created. I was born last in a line of siblings, which gave me a certain freedom. I have clear memories of meandering home from Oakmont Elementary School, lost in an enchanted world. As I walked, I would collect stones and acorns and beautiful weeds, all of which would factor into my tales. Muriel Rukeyser, one of my countless influences, wrote: "The world is made up of stories, not of atoms." By the time I made it to the pink house on the corner of my block, I had been transported to places far outside the suburban streets that took me home.

Stories, in the form of prose or poetry, helped shape and form me from the very beginning. My magnanimous mother, who used to read to me, supported my dreaminess. One of our favorite books was Robert Louis Stevenson's *A Children's Garden of Verses*. I remember her pushing me on the rusty-chained swing, in the playground next to St. Dennis School, singing his words:

> How do you like to go up in a swing,
>   Up in the air so blue?
> Oh, I do think it the pleasantest thing
>   Ever a child can do!

The first poem I ever memorized was a Christina Rossetti poem:

> Who has seen the wind?
> Neither you nor I.
> But when the trees bow down their heads,
> The wind is passing by.

I love the rhythm of it, the cadence, but even more, I love the attempt to express mystery. To illuminate invisibility.

As long as I can remember, I've had a book by my side. The thrill and horror of Washington Irving's "The Legend of Sleepy Hollow" provoked me. The more domestic tales of Judy Blume's *Tales of a Fourth Grade Nothing* and *Are You There God? It's Me, Margaret* spoke to my own experiences. I found companionship in books more than I did in my peers. I was not loyal to any one genre, the fantasy of C.S. Lewis' *The Chronicles of Narnia* and J.R.R. Tolkien's *The Hobbit* as real to me as the trials and heartbreak of Louisa May Alcott's *Little Women* or Betty Smith's *A Tree Grows in Brooklyn*. Whether it was Lucy, Bilbo, Jo, or Francie, I started to see options of identity, mostly examples of courage and strength that inspired me.

As I grew older, my voracious desire to get lost inside a book only intensified. I remember finding Emily Dickinson: I would yell her verses to the trees, the summer I turned fourteen and left home to help make a new trail in the Colorado mountains:

> I'm nobody! Who are you?
> Are you nobody too?
> Then there's a pair of us — don't tell!
> They'd banish us, you know.

I was blessed with a house full of my parents' books. In high school, I'd stay in on a weekend night, camped out on my bed or on our screened-in porch reading, rather than hang out at someone's house drinking while their parents were away. I found Dostoevsky and Tolstoy, Emerson and Thoreau, Dante, Baldwin, and more. I picked up any book I could and fell into it. In history class, I repeatedly got in trouble for hiding novels inside my big boring textbooks.

After finishing each new book, I was high on the discoveries they allowed me. I remember that energy: I became buoyant after reading a great book, declaring to anyone who would listen: "This is my favorite book!" Till the next one, when it happened again. I remember thinking: *If I can make even one person feel the way I do now, from my own writing, my life's purpose will be complete.*

In 10th grade, I was assigned *The Bluest Eye*. It changed my life. Toni Morrison showed me a power and perception in language that awed me. She revealed a depth of the responsibility of my identity that I had before taken for granted. Her form also had a huge effect on me. She showed me just how little difference there is between poetry and prose. I continue to read her books, copies hot off the press, and they never stop taking my breath away.

At the end of high school, my humanities teacher told me to read Sylvia Plath – another life-changing experience. He recognized a sorrow beneath my sunny appearance that few could imagine. The cathartic value of writing became clear to me as I read Plath. I blurred the lines of reality as I created my final project, interchanging my own journals as Plath's and vice versa.

In college, I discovered Audre Lorde and Adrienne Rich. Lorde's wisdom enlivened a fierce hope inside me. Rich's intricate web of language and thought examined on the pages once again gave me the freedom of identities I had not known before. I found yet other parts of myself reading each of them.

During this time, I first read Pablo Neruda as well. Like a waterfall, his words reminded me of the play of expression, the astounding beauty of it. I went full center into his poetry, got drenched.

There is no way I could tell you of all my influences – there have been so many, and continue to be so. It is like asking a piano player to name her/his favorite five keys on the piano – the real song comes from chords, from the endless combinations of notes and silence.

For everyone I could name: Anne Sexton, Rita Dove, Gloria Naylor, Sharon Olds, June Jordan, Barbara Kingsolver, Richard Wright, Gwendolyn Brooks, Wislawa Szymborska, e. e. cummings, Nikki Giovanni, Joy Harjo, Marilyn Hacker, Alice Walker, Rainer Maria Rilke, Gertrude Stein, Grace Paley, Lucille Clifton, Ntozake Shange, Ai, Jorie Graham, Naomi Shihab Nye, Italo Calvino – and I have to force myself to stop – there are countless more writers who I feel guilty for neglecting to mention. It feels like I am cheating on them, my saviors.

I have had many loves.

It is no exaggeration to say that writing and reading have saved my life. Some might say that being a writer is a choice; some even say it is a selfish and naïve one. For me, I know it's the only one.

My Inspiration

Kim D. Brandon

I was two years old when my family moved from Baltimore to New York City. I grew up with six siblings: Derek, Gale, Sylvia, Andre, Harlan, and Linder. My father's name was Charles Lindberg Brandon, but everyone called him Bird. He was a barber and a great storyteller. I spent most of my time at his knee. He entertained his customers by telling wonderful stories and tall tales about growing up down South and the hard work involved with country living. The funny thing was that my dad watched his older siblings work hard. He was his mother's baby, and she didn't want him to work. To hear him tell it, he worked from sunup to sundown all on his own, and in his spare time he taught their cow to count. "Laugh and the world laughs with you" was his motto. My mother, O'Nell, was another story all together. She was a fighter, an activist, and she still is a powerful force.

I grew up in Brooklyn and went to public school. I remember in the 1970's, my teacher telling us, her students, that she got paid whether we learned or not. She implied that we could act a fool, or melt into the wall, or study the substandard text that was provided. She didn't care one way or another. It was our choice. She only said that directly to me once, my mother saw to that. What this teacher didn't do was share the power of words with us. I was starved for them while in home economics classes that tried to turn me into someone who had just enough of a trade to possibly land a minimum wage position or become one of the underemployed. It was a setup. They needed us to contribute to society by holding it up, like the back legs on a desk that are load-bearing but not adorned – that aren't carved by the master but by his new, inexperienced apprentice – or worse still, by the older craftsmen without any real skills. A whole host of these rejected, ineffective, and lifeless teachers paraded through my public school education. But every once in a while, I came across a real jewel, a diamond of a teacher that made it all worthwhile.

So when I discovered James Baldwin in seventh grade, I discovered myself. I was there on the page, between his words and at the end of each of his sentences. I was right there, and James Baldwin knew it. He knew that we too needed a voice, and he was generous enough to make room for anyone who wanted, needed a safe haven from the pain of being missing on the page.

And even worse than being missing on the page was being exploited by images in books and movies that created damaging portraits of us and did not reflect who I was and – more importantly – who I could become.

I was someone who wanted to read. Everything else – playing outside and socializing with friends – came second to "If Beale Street Could Talk." It wasn't cool to be held up in my room, which I shared with my sisters Sylvia and Gale, reading. As my ability to read grew in the 1970's, I discovered everyone. Richard Wright, Zora Neale Hurston, Toni Morrison, Maya Angelou, Langston Hughes. Later I got into Alice Walker, J. California Cooper, Walter Mosley, Nikki Giovanni, and Ntozake Shange. I read everyone. It is writers from the African Diaspora that resonate with me most. I love opening a book and finding myself somewhere on the page.

I enjoy reading the classics, and I draw inspiration from anything related to self-discovery, motivation and spiritual growth.

The late Eric Butterworth led me on my path to the discovery of human potential.

I am also motivated by a young writer, a poet: my nephew, Prince Larry Smith. Larry writes of hope, happiness and beauty. Here is one of his poems:

Dream

I was sitting in a room
Playing a piano
When I heard a beautiful voice
With my musical heart
I allowed someone to bloom
I followed its scent
And we played beautiful music together
So I could bloom too.

I am inspired, supported and motivated by other writers. We encourage each other. I really can't see when I have selected the wrong word. I see what I wanted to say. Editing my work is really difficult, so the workshop process is invaluable for me. Being in our writers' group has been unlike anything I have ever experienced. Each writer brings their voice, their power, and their grace. So, I welcome the support and friendship that I have found here. Never in my wildest dreams did I think that I would have the pleasure of publishing a book with such beautiful, spirited people.

Today, I am still in Brooklyn, with my daughter, writing. At the end of the day, I guess that teacher was right. I don't remember her name, but over 30 years later, I still remember her statement. The truth is that it is my choice, and it will always be my choice. Her mean-spirited, racially motivated statement changed me. I realized back then that I could be classified, marginalized, adorned, or I could be Kim – it was my choice.

Books: Inspire, Encourage, Engage, Enlighten

Princene Hyatt

My love of books began when I was a toddler. My aunt, an elementary school teacher, gave me several books. I toted them around all the time – waiting for my mother or someone to sit and read Little Orphan Annie, Little Red Riding Hood, Goldilocks or whatever. Once I started school I always read – ahead of assignment. As I was an only child, homework became my companion.

Literature was my favorite subject in college until I became involved in necktie collages.

Miss Gwendolyn Brooks would probably head the long list of writers I admire and love.

I share a certain southern identity with Dr. Maya Angelou. I bought her greeting cards for myself and kept them in view because I needed to internalize the message they brought me.

The book *Creative Visualization* fell apart in my purse. I continue to carry it around. Thank you, Shakti Gawain!

Tennessee Williams' work speaks openly and honestly about his life experience. One director said, "Everything in his life is in his plays, and everything in his plays is in his life." Recently, I saw *Cat On A Hot Tin Roof* again – on Broadway. Williams' masterful work is a powerful reminder of life in the South. I identify with his personal life on many levels: his struggle with depression, family history of insanity, alcohol addiction, superficial Southern lifestyle, controlling mother, and family secrets.

Unlike Tennessee's my life took a radical, right turn. I was able to find the professional help and support I needed to begin the healing process.

I am deeply grateful to writers who motivated me to manifest my own destiny: Dr. Arthur Janov, Dr. Deepak Chopra, Dr. Wayne Dyer, Caroline Myss, Marianne Williamson, Louise Hay, Jacquelyn Small, Gary Zukav, Ishmael Beah, Eckhart Tolle, and many others.

Sharing my story of recovery is not inspired by an overpowering need to write; I do not see myself as a writer beyond my memoirs. My hope is that my words will inspire someone to gather the necessary courage to take charge of their own suppressed, confused, unhappy, addicted life. And I hope that they decide to take back their power – find their own voice with which to speak for themselves – as I am doing.

If one does not take charge of life, there is a very good chance that life will take charge and run away – out of control, out of reach.

14

My Inspirations as a Writer

Olivia S. Taylor (Pen Name: Sally Bill)

I come from a family of storytellers. My desire to write stems from a childhood spent listening to their stories. I was enraptured. I loved to listen to the elders relate many life experiences in stories.

I grew up along the Gulf Coast, which today we refer to as Katrina/hurricane country. Most of the men in the area (and, during World War II, some women) had worked in the many shipyards along the coast of the Gulf of Mexico, and they brought their stories home to their families. They had worked out of Pensacola, Florida; Mobile, Alabama; Gulf Port and Biloxi, Mississippi; New Orleans, Louisiana; and Galveston, Texas.

I was fortunate enough to have had a father who was a gifted storyteller. He, along with a neighbor, Mr. Bill Smith, had worked or docked in most of these ports at one time or another.

It was my delight to sit on the front porch bench swing with Mr. Bill, in the early evenings, and listen to the many stories he told. I would go home and tell of the places I visited during storytelling time with Mr. Bill. Then, I would be ready for more stories from my father!

After learning that we both had the same last name of Smith, my three or four-year-old mind could not accept that we did not have the same first name. So I adopted Billy as a middle name, which I always wanted to have. I became their new daughter.

To capture the joy and rapture of my youth listening to stories, I now write many of my stories to recreate a moment in time when times were hard, yet simple. I learned early to enjoy reading Mark Twain: *The Prince and the Pauper, The Adventures of Tom Sawyer, Huckleberry Finn*, and others. By fifth grade, I had read pieces on his life and admired his love of the rivers, the Missouri and the Mississippi, and the adventures of the waters.

I read that Mark Twain's real name was Samuel Clemens. He would watch the men working on the docks as they anchored the ships. They would call "Mark!" then "Twain!" to measure the depth of the water. This affirmed my decision to take on a pen name, and I wrote my first story as Sally Bill.

My given name is Olivia, but nobody pronounced it correctly. I was called Ophelia, Olive, Oliver, Ollie Mae, and one day someone called me Olive Oyl. Then I decided to have my own renaming ceremony for myself at the age of four. My new first name became Sally, since I had learned to spell it from my brother's primer, and my new last name became Bill. The first did not stick, but the latter became my pet name especially with my father and brothers until this day.

My mom, too, was an avid storyteller and often used her stories to teach important lessons to her children. When my mom was annoyed, I became Olivia Billy Smith, and given the extent of her annoyance I became Olivia Sally Bill Smith.

We, seven sisters and brothers, had no television until we older ones were in our teens. We told stories, read and recited poems, imitated the characters we heard on the radio, and read comic books. We created our own forms of entertainment. My father called one of us daily to read the evening paper; he listened to how well we read. On Sundays the main attraction was the funnies. We were expected to read them and take on the voices of the cartoon characters.

Both of our parents were full of good stories. They taught us to love reading. My mom introduced us to the writings and poems of Langston Hughes and Paul Lawrence Dunbar. We learned the importance of these two poets, and the role they played in the world of literature. They remain my favorites.

Writing enables the storyteller to share the nature of an experience through a story or poem that must be told. Paul L. Dunbar captured the plantation life of Black folks in the Deep South. Langston Hughes captured life in the urban cities when Blacks fled from the segregation of the South, but found another kind of oppression in the northern cities.

Some of my other favorite writers are Zora Neale Hurston, George Bernard Shaw, Nathaniel Hawthorne, Pao-Lu Hsu, and James Baldwin. One of my favorite novels is *God's Bits of Wood* (1960) by Senegalese author Sembène Ousmane. He uses a strike of train workers, telling the history, the culture, and the uprising of the people in Senegal. It was not just a strike against the Dakar-Senegal train empire but it was a blow against colonialism in French-occupied Africa. The women are heroines in the struggle. It no longer was just the workers' fight but became the entire community's struggle.

Some of my favorite poems are "The Wreck of the Hesperus" by Henry Wadsworth Longfellow; "Invictus" by William Ernest Henley; "Freedom's Plow" by Langston Hughes; "Annabel Lee" by Edgar Allan Poe; "Still I Rise" by Maya Angelou; and "In the Morning" by Paul L. Dunbar.

In writing, I strive to put down in words various experiences of life in simple words and in story form. I hope to convey stories that are of importance to family rituals. I am one who was consciously shaped by people, places, and the patterns of human interaction. And I continue to be inspired.

Inspiration

Rita REB Wilson

I become inspired at different times, by different writers under different circumstances. For example: one Sunday afternoon, TJ Wilson read a part of her story about a female character that had two lovers: each one served a purpose for the character's life though turmoil was inevitable. The reading stimulated me to take another look at my character in a story with a different theme that was in progress. Also, MJ Nelson sent a piece of poetry; it awakened thoughts that flowed through my brain and on to paper that appears in this anthology.

I get inspiration from Mrs. Taylor when she reads about her siblings, be it cutting down a Christmas tree, or the boots of a fisherman. I go with her to the woods where the tree is waiting, or to the bank where the fish are jumping almost in the boat.

Gabriella inspires me to hang on to words and meanings. Also, she stimulates me with details that can make me smell bread that isn't actually being baked, or imagine sitting inconspicuously on a stool, viewing for a fleeting moment … a love interest.

Miz' Kim asks inspiring questions and gives stimulating examples, which is shown in her work. Whether her character has been bathed and well scrubbed with bubble bath or regular soap, the process is there, and it inspires me to include details without vacuous writing.

Princene Hyatt is hy-at writing from her mind and creating through her mind and fingers artwork that inspires me and speaks for itself. Her memoirs exhibit artistic honesty: "I don't know nothing about nothing, you understand?"

I'm inspired by other writers too, yet these folks are nearby and I can immediately say, "tell me more; I like that sentence, paragraph, story, poem." "It was inspirational," or "I need more so that it will stimulate my interest."

Icebreakers

19

Topic: What gets in the way of your writing?

How to begin [writing] /
How (not) to begin.

Gabriella M. Belfiglio

First, you must make the coffee – grind the oily beans, boil the water, let the coffee steep into a delicious dark brown, then transform into a shade of caramel as you add the cream. Carry your smoky cup of coffee to your desk, pick out a CD that will hold you, yet not distract you – no words – or if so, in another language – something like Cecilia Bartoli's Vivaldi album. OK, now light a stick of incense, maybe cinnamon to foster your intuition. You're close now. Sit at your desk; get grounded. Do a quick puzzle like Sudoku or play a game of solitaire on your computer to help clear your mind. Now, pick up your favorite pen and open to the first blank page of your notebook. Wait – check to see if you turned off the burner on the stove, you swear you smell gas. While in the kitchen pour yourself a glass of water, add a slice of lemon to help it go down. Return to your desk. Firmly write today's date at the top of the page. By now you have to pee. After washing your hands, you realize they are dry – search for the hand cream. Remember you used it last night while you were watching some stupid crap on television. From the coffee table beckons the Con Edison bill you meant to pay last night. Decide you better pay it now. Write a check, find a stamp, and slip the envelope in the crack between front door and wall, so you won't forget it. Return to your desk. The phone in the bedroom rings. Promise yourself *not* to answer it. Your curiosity gets the better of you. What if it's Astraea calling you to say you won first place in the poetry contest, expect your $10,000 grant any day now, or your mom, who has fallen down while climbing the step stool in the kitchen to reach the mixing bowls up high, she needs your help? You peek at the caller I.D. It's your stupid job (the one that pays you). Return to your desk. Light a second stick of incense: cedar to help you focus. Pick up your pen. Look at the blank page. Look out the window – notice the neighbor's yard: their trashcan lids have blown off and are chiming into the fence. A pudgy blue bag pokes out the top of a can. In the other, an empty Corona bottle rattles delicately on the bottles beneath. Return to the white page. Write something down. Anything, the first thought you have. Read it. Scribble it out. Remember to breathe. Start again. Write. Don't stop yourself. So what if you have no idea where the image of an elephant-shaped cloud came from, or what it's supposed to mean. Keep writing. Don't judge. Let your hand take orders from your brain. Do not stop to fix your mistakes. Fill the page with glorious words. Don't look back.

Topic: Write about remembering happy times.

Happy Times

Princene Hyatt

1. Anticipating morning coffee while water boils – which flavors should I mix today? One part Jamaica Blue, sprinkle with Irish Crème, add one part Zimbabwe. Pour boiling water slowly around filter – add one ounce half and half, one ounce almond milk. Uh! Uh! Uh! Perfect!!!

2. Soaking in a hot bath – scented with lavender – giving thought to how grateful I am for the life I live.

3. Really comfortable shoes for serious 6 A.M. walks across Brooklyn Bridge with friends.

4. Brooklyn Botanic Garden – oasis in the heart of the city. When I come face to face with those who make it so, I tell them how much I love their work. Every square yard of the Garden is more delightful than the last, if that's possible. Magnificent trees embody the earth's wisdom.

    I must touch! Fragrance from roses nourish my senses, exquisite water lilies floating on fishponds take my breath away. What a sight!!!

5. Springtime in New York when thousands of orchids from around the world flaunt their exotic beauty – amidst O-ohs and Awes! Branches overloaded with cherry blossoms sway ever so softly with gentle breezes.

6. Xian Zheng conducting the New York Philharmonic in Prospect Park while a surrealistic full moon kept watch over her shoulder. Her entire body played every instrument. She was enchanting!

7. Hugh Masekela in concert at the Bandshell on a perfect summer night. What a wild, rhythmic, screaming good time!

8. Sharing an exceptional meal with friends anywhere – even on a bench in Union Square Farmers Market. Live music was perfect with smoked fish and fresh baked bread.

9. Finally reaching the door of Ice Cream Factory – barely squeezing my body inside to see which flavors are on the menu – salivating every step as the line moves along – ever so slowly.

10. Romance under the stars – ferryboat ride in the arms of a very special young man.

11. Meeting fellow tourists every morning to witness a spectacular sunrise from the deck of a cruise ship.

12. Completing a collage that I see as being quite good.

13. Huge cotton dresses that touch only my shoulders to wear in 90-degree temperatures with matching humidity.

14. Hilarious dolphin encounter in Bahamas.

Topic: Start each thought with "I remember."

I Remember

Rita REB Wilson

I remember my first train ride: it was with my maternal grandmother. She lived about 35 miles away, and we were returning to her house to prepare for her youngest son's wedding reception. Her son, my uncle, had gotten married in the city and had a reception. My grandmother hosted a reception for him with family members and friends who did not attend the city reception. I was privileged to attend both, because I could ride the train free, and I was favorite to my grandpa, who did not care to ride the train and was not particular about riding the bus either.

I remember running to my grandpa after Grandma and I dismounted the train. He picked me up, and I hugged his neck. I can still smell the tobacco and hear the roar of the train as it sped away. Grandpa had a wagon and a mule to transport us to the house: it was an adventure to ride on such a mode of transportation. My dad had a car, and I had just gotten off a train that seemed to have flown from one point to the other. I did like the realness of a wagon helping to get you where you needed to go. My brother and I had a wagon. Sometimes we were pulled to the store by a cousin, to buy an ice cream cone or a johnnycake cookie.

I remember the reception: my new aunt having flowers in her hair – they smelled of Jergen's lotion. That was the sweetest smell that I had known; I don't remember any comparison. I was less than four years old, yet I remember.

Also, I remember the delicious chocolate cake that was sweet enough to keep me watching guard over it. Also, I remember the fried chicken, cornbread with meat in it that was called cracklin' bread. I remember Grandpa saying, "Give it to Pete," whatever it was, "Give it to Pete." That was me.

Topic: Describe a memory that is always with you.

Knocking

Kim D. Brandon

I sometimes recall "The Raven," by Edgar Allan Poe. My mother would read "The Raven" to us kids. I don't recall her reading anything else. I will have to ask my sister Gale if there were other stories. Gale remembers everything.

It was kind of creepy that she didn't know how wonderful it could have been for me to hear wonderful little sweet stories. Yes, I was a really fearful child. But no, it was "The Raven." "Who's that knocking..."

On lonely nights I pretended that my mother's presence overshadowed the beckoning of doom. I was conflicted.

But thirty years later, I still recall her voice; it was huge, dark and magical. She could have been on stage somewhere. She had the pipes.

After re-reading "The Raven" as an adult, I realized like most people, my mother read us her favorite parts of the poem. She read the parts that she enjoyed most. She was giving us a piece of herself. Not the mother piece, but another piece.

I walk away from "The Raven" a better storyteller – my voice looms high and towers over my own stories just like Poe's and my mother's. We thrill, haunt, and entertain. I guess I will share "The Raven" with my daughter, too. Luckily, she is really into scary stories.

Topic: Write about remembering happy times.

Our Funny Lovely Christmas Tree

Olivia S. Taylor

My parents were great pastry makers and cooks. It was Christmas Eve and Momma and Daddy had been working all week long late into the evening. Their work was plentiful this holiday season. It seemed as if every family that could afford to have a catered holiday party did. Schools were already closed for Christmas break. Almost every house in the neighborhood had sparkling lights. Some yards were even decorated. Our house was bare.

That morning before our parents left, they had given clear instructions to all of us children. Everyone had chores that had to be completed. The oldest one would supervise the cleaning of the house and all would do their fair share. We would clean the kitchen and have all of the pots and pans ready for Momma and Daddy to do the holiday cooking.

They had gone to an afternoon party. Momma and Daddy were expected to be home before dark. They had promised to bring the Christmas tree. The day at home went smoothly. All of us did our chores and waited patiently for our parents to return that afternoon or early evening.

My older sister Doretha prepared the lunch of spaghetti that my mother had directed. We ate, quickly cleaned the dishes, and took vigil on the front porch taking turns anxiously watching for our parents. The afternoon began to slip away; usually if there was an important message for us, a neighbor around the corner would appear. But no one brought a message.

Frost had come early this year forcing many of the small creatures that were their prey to burrow in to early hibernation. Now the wild cats were lurking near the edge of the woods where they were scavenging for food. All of the children in the neighborhood had been warned not to go into the woods because a bobcat had been seen lurking in the forest.

Every year, a week and a half before Christmas, my brothers Jason and Jeffrey would go with their friends into the woods and chop down our tree. But this year some families had bought trees, or fathers had gone and gotten trees to keep the boys out of the woods.

We children said it was decision time. What were we to do? No tree, no money, no message from our parents. We knew our parents would surely come home too tired to go in the woods for a tree. With a flashlight and a rifle or shotgun, all of us children gathered in the front room to figure out our next step.

Jason and Jeffrey agreed that they could go and see if they could meet Momma and Daddy and maybe help them carry any packages. And if they got off too late to buy a tree, they could help them home quickly. Then they could go with Daddy and chop down a tree.

I said, "But if you walk to the highway to wait it will soon be getting dark."

My older sister Doretha said, "Now you can't go back into the woods until the stray cat is caught."

"Well," said Jeffrey, "We might be able to find a small tree on the edge of the woods, but all the fir trees and evergreen trees are going to be gone. Do you think we can bring the rifle?"

"Don't be silly," said Doretha. "Every neighbor from streets around will be waiting to tell Momma and Daddy they saw you going into the woods, or stop you before you get to the corner."

"No, you know everybody has gotten the trees on the edge of the woods," replied Jason. "Even if we saw a tree, how would we get it? We cannot take an ax. We can't hide it. Well maybe we can take the hacksaw and a hatchet. Hopefully we can find a little pine on the side of the ditch."

As they approached the last road at the edge of the woods it was clear that there was no fir, spruce or evergreen, not even a small pine tree. Everything was taken. Starting back home like ones without hope, Jeffrey spotted a breathtaking holly bush. He stopped to stare at it. It was so filled with clumps of red berries, it looked to him as if an elf had decorated it. The holly sat just over the other side of a thorny rose bush that was smothered with the dead vines of winter, but her cluster of thorns was visible.

Jason said, "I think we should take the holly tree."

"I don't know, it is pretty, but it is a poor excuse for a Christmas tree," uttered Jeffrey.

Jason smiled and replied, "Well, one thing's for sure: we will be able to say we never had anything quite like it before."

The boys decided to chop down the holly tree. The more they looked at it they saw a magical beauty. They agreed that the little holly bush would be as enchanting as any tree. They felt that if Daddy brought the big tree there would already be a little tree for the three younger children.

When the boys got the tree home, everyone was excited just to see a tree come through the front door. The boys quickly hammered a stand for the holly tree as if it were a spruce. Doretha pulled over a small round wicker table from the corner of the room and dressed it with old Christmas paper. We placed it by the side window.

We got down the box of Christmas ornaments that Momma used every year. Each one of us picked out our most favorite ornament and placed it on the holly tree. Then something

magical started to happen. We took turns again choosing another ornament and placing it on the holly tree. We shared the
feeling of excitement, fun and peace with this holly tree, deco-
rating it, and had more fun than ever before. The night when
the tree was decorated we would always have hot cocoa and
popcorn. Doretha, Jeffrey, and Jason got all of the goodies
ready, and we sang Christmas carols late into the night.

It was very late when Momma and Daddy came home. We
had turned off the lights of the Christmas tree and were still
singing our favorite carols. We heard them on the front porch
and went out to meet them. Almost simultaneously, they
started to speak about the tree: "Maybe we will have to get up
at the crack of dawn to go get a tree. Every place was closed or
all sold out. The only thing we could find was a wreath."

When we got them and their packages inside, Doretha
turned on the lights of the little holly tree. We all hoped they
would be pleased and know we had not disobeyed their request.

The compassionate look on their faces showed us how
proud of us they were for trying to keep Christmas alive with
the lovely little holly tree.

Not a year goes by in our home now that the little round
wicker table is not pulled out to hold our Christmas tree. That
little holly tree made the round wicker table our annual Christmas tree table.

Topic: Write about something somebody taught
you that you internalized.

Christmas In a Women's Shelter

Kim D. Brandon

Maybe ten years ago I volunteered to spend the night at the
Father Dempsey Center on Christmas Eve. See, all the Sisters
who usually stayed with the women at night all wanted to go to
Midnight Mass. Going to Midnight Mass was huge. So they
advertised for a volunteer, and my spiritually evolved behind
decided to do it.

I arrived at the Center early, and one Sister and I set up ten
to twelve beds. She also set up a little fake Christmas tree in
the corner. We restocked the refrigerator and made sure that
everything was ready, so that the women could come, eat,
shower, sleep and leave first thing in the morning. A bus
would bring women who were classified "not too crazed or
dangerous or violent" to spend a night at the Father Dempsey
make-shift shelter.

Apparently, the Sisters rolled up the beds and there was a
daycare center in the space during the day and a host of recov-

ery meetings in the early evenings. So the space was always in use around the clock – thanks to the Sisters.

At the foot of each bed, the Sister placed a small wrapped gift, then turned off the overhead lights. The glow from the tiny tree's lights made the place feel warm and cozy. I started to feel like I was throwing a holiday party. *This was wonderful,* I thought. I couldn't wait for my guests to arrive. My excitement ended when the good Sister told me to get the ladies situated, and then lock myself into a small storage room with a bed. Fear took over and I wanted to run. I pictured this bunch ripping the gold fillings from my mouth. *What in the hell was I thinking? Who were these people?*

I started to pray for protection and that God would let me know the moment to retreat and to lock myself in and hide. What had the Sister said except sleep behind a locked door? But I was off to the races.

She thanked me again for taking her shift and was off to Midnight Mass.

I was alone in an empty center and started walking around turning on lights. It was time to wait at the window for the bus to arrive. Well, the bus arrived and I placed a small gift on each bed too, and then opened the door. I welcomed each woman into the toasty warm space, with a smile and a gentle touch of the hand. The bus had pulled off before all of the women reached the door. Most of the women knew each other and had been to Father Dempsey's before.

"Hello, Chickie," one woman said to me. They all looked surprised to see my black face there, and then proceeded to tell me the deal. They sized me up immediately. This was the pink Cadillac of shelters, and they felt like they had won a lottery just getting picked to come to Dempsey's for the night. They had to make the most of their hours here, and I was to keep things moving. They wanted a shower, a meal, and a good safe night's sleep.

To my surprise the women were just like me! One woman went to work every day – she had unfortunately lost her apartment and was trying to keep the news from her co-workers.

They took turns showering, changing in to PJ's, and eating the food that the Sister had put out. Some of the women cooked food from the refrigerator and cleaned up their dishes. A few of us stayed up talking and watching Sammy Davis, Jr., in a holiday movie on TV. The ladies started turning off light after light until only the light from the TV and kitchen remained on. We were asked to speak in low whispers, and I was the last woman to go to bed. The Sister came back to relieve me and found me still awake.

I left while the ladies were still sleeping. I owed them, in the way that you can only share real stuff with strangers whom you may never see again. They were kind, determined, and some were even regal. They gave me something priceless that night. It was a present that I kept forgetting. But it was something like: don't let someone else's fear of who they think another person is, block this same someone from touching your heart.

The stories they told that Christmas Eve are stored in the back of my mind, now. But they were my sisters, my beautiful sisters, and there but for the grace went I.

Topic: Start each thought with "I remember."

I Remember

Gabriella M. Belfiglio

I remember flying last night.
I remember how the sky looked:
    full moon
    round   radiant
    lighting my way.
I remember the way the air felt:
    like a soft push on my skin
    a nudge, leading me
    into the blueblack.
I remember how free my heavy bones became:
    gravity a mere idea.
I remember flying last night.

I remember waking up this morning:
    a crowd of thoughts ringing like an alarm
    crashing me back to earth.

Topic: Write about something somebody taught you that you internalized.

A Life-Long Teaching

Olivia S. Taylor

Do what you've got to do whether somebody is looking or not. The art of self-discipline was given to me by my parents. The importance of its application was taught to me by Mrs. Pace, a fifth grade teacher who got a bunch of us noisy children to be quiet whether she was in the classroom or not. It took only a few days to do the task.

Simply encoding, nobody knows you better than you know yourself. Be your own boss. She stopped leaving a monitor or a well-mannered or so-called well-behaved student in charge to take names. Her principle was not to tell on anyone unless you started with "I," telling on yourself, and this principle worked. If she walked away from the classroom for a few minutes, we read a book, did an assignment, wrote a story, or read ahead in one of the textbooks. The class remained silent.

When I began teaching, I applied similar techniques of academic discipline. I saw that the system worked 99% of the time. I, indeed, accept that children enjoy a challenge. I found that this method of self-discipline was indeed far more valuable than having a student just behave. It instilled a desire for learning.

One morning we awaited the teacher's arrival. At the time we were to start devotion, she still had not arrived, so we carried on. We did devotion and proceeded with class as usual. We began with our daily routine of oral reading. Every student in the class (of about 30) did their reading. When the teacher arrived at school we were all doing our math lesson. She had stopped by the principal's office to let her know that she was in and that she had car trouble earlier. The principal followed Mrs. Pace to the classroom to let her know how amazed she was by us. The principal had been totally unaware that our teacher was late, for the class had been so orderly she thought she was at her post.

This application of self-discipline that I learned in fifth grade has remained a life-long virtue.

Topic: Describe a job you've held.

Chock Full of Nuts, That Heavenly Coffee

Rita REB Wilson

The job orientation was held in the office of the site supervisor. The head counterperson was very clear and precise about how to quickly serve, collect money, and give change. I was one of the two workers in the first section, ready and eager to earn a paycheck with hopes to work there for a long time. Also, it was emphasized that there would not be any time to fraternize with friends. They could see you at work, through the glass, as they pass by 125th Street and 7th Avenue, where Chock Full of Nuts was located beneath the Theresa Hotel. (7th Ave. is now named Adam Clayton Powell Blvd.)

The first day at work was wonderful for me. At day's end, the head counterperson held a pep talk and suggested that my counter partner take note to how well I was handling the customers and keeping the counter clear. Of course, it was my pleasure to show that I could work with ease and confidence. Second day went well and so did the third day, until about 2 P.M.

Around that time, Congressman Adam Clayton Powell, Jr., walked in and sat on a stool in my section. He placed his order while talking to others that recognized him. I began to fill the coffee cup, which I allowed to run over, and on top of that I dropped the cream cheese and walnut sandwich on the floor. My counter was shaped like a helix; therefore he sat facing the door. When the door was opened, a few napkins flew in his face. When I finally had the coffee in place, he asked for the sugar, and I gave him the saltshaker.

Congressman Powell took it all in stride and continued to talk as people interrupted him from eating. I was so embarrassed I could have gone through the floor, yet he was encouraging and not bothered by the incident. I didn't return to work the next day. The anticipation of long-term employment ceased after three days. I wasn't terminated; I was clumsy and mortified.

Topic: What is in your suitcase?

Lady Baltimore

Kim D. Brandon

I woke up at 6:00 AM, and before brushing my teeth, I pulled down the tan matching Lady Baltimore luggage from the closet. I was going home. Just like that. It was time. I opened three suitcases of varying sizes and put them onto the bed.

My makeup and accessories went into the carry-on. Two pairs of dark glasses, a navy blue and gray scarf to hide in, if I didn't feel like being noticed, which was most of the time. On stage I was queen. But other than that I wanted no fan base and rarely signed autographs.

In the middle-sized bag I placed all my delicate items: slips, nightgowns, a silk robe and enough sexy underwear to make Omar, my ex-lover, proud.

My shoes, black and navy platform pull-ons, were placed in the bottom of the case, held by elastic bands. Then I pulled out two suits for the day and two full-length stage gowns to perform in. Then I thought: *Hell, Mrs. Clara, in East Baltimore, would have something hot and smoking waiting for me in her shop.* So I put the black strapless number back in the closet.

I took out a small navy blue hat and put it on the chair by the dresser. It was time to go home. I thought of my Momma, and just knew that it was the right thing to do. First, I needed to get clean and scrubbed. I had long ago outgrown her need for brown soap.

Topic: Write about the changing of the seasons.

The First Day of Fall

Princene Hyatt

In the fall of last year I invited an old friend from my C.O.R.E. (Congress of Racial Equality) days to vacation with me in New York. Rita was a New Yorker by birth, but had moved out of the country some thirty years ago. Since she now lives in suburban Philadelphia she was really excited to feel the pulse of this city again.

We met at City Hall on a beautiful, bright day – perfect for walking the Brooklyn Bridge into the Heights where we had a delicious organic breakfast. We then walked the promenade overlooking the East River and lower Manhattan where I first fell in love with the Heights area and decided to make it my home. After visiting other C.O.R.E. friends in Midwood we called it a day.

The next day we met at the pier. I always enjoy the water. After a lunch cruise around Manhattan Island we window-shopped, caught up on old times, enjoyed a live band on the campus of New York University while waiting for Ghenet, my favorite Ethiopian restaurant, to open for dinner.

Cruising up the Hudson River to Palisades Park and Bear Mountain is really spectacular on a fall day. The many shades of oranges, reds, golds, yellows, and greens are a visual feast. They give me such a sense of well-being and peacefulness with my world.

On our last day together we visited The Studio Museum in Harlem, then walked several miles for a serious eating experience at Raw Soul Restaurant.

Late fall has a kind of sadness and quietness for me – when leaves begin to fall. I love leaves!

Bare trees sadden me on some level. I always feel that summer has been too short and pretty soon we will have to put on our heavy coats.

It was really good getting together for an extended visit after so many years. We had a great time!

Rita and I totally enjoy talking, walking, and eating.

Topic: Narrate an old photo, chosen at random.

Look

Gabriella M. Belfiglio

It is the kind of day where you know you're in the middle of winter – the sky pressing down a white gray onto the empty benches of the parkway. The trees bare of leaves – empty like skeletons waving in the wind. There are only the two of us visible on the other side of the crisscrossed wire fence: My nanna and I. She is holding me up like a trophy. I was the latest one born in her growing tribe of grandchildren. I don't remember the day – but I remember the white hat she knitted for me: it was soft and warm, and the best part was it had two fluffy balls that I would twirl around, the strings itchy against my neck when she tied them together. My nanna liked to make everything tight against my body – as if she were dressing me in some kind of armor against the evils of the outside world.

We lived just around the corner – still my dark coat was fastened, no button missed, ankle to chin. On my feet: white leather shoes echoing my hat and the sky and the snow that was threatening to fall. When I look at the two of us, I barely notice how small I once was; instead I am amazed at my nanna's broad face, her brunette hair, her strong arms, lifting me higher than the metal fence, showing me off with a tired yet proud smile – "Look," she seems to be saying, "I *love* this child."

Topic: Start off with the line, "Four years ago I won the lottery – a huge sum of money – it changed my life...."

Four Years Ago I Won the Lottery for a Huge Sum of Money: It Changed My Life in Various Ways

Princene Hyatt

I was panic-stricken, shocked, terrified, elated, etc., etc., when winnings were confirmed. As soon as I was physically and mentally able, I made reservations aboard a cruise ship going anywhere – I needed to sort things out.

A classmate of mine is a retired estate planner – I needed him to tell me how much money I had in real terms and approximate just how far it would go if conscientiously invested. I had no need for huge sums personally; it made sense to use it to help others live a better life. It has always been my belief that ignorance – on all levels – is far more damaging than actual poverty; I would make a "dent" in both ignorance and poverty by educating students who are at risk, yet have potential.

After three months of living leisurely and overeating, I claimed my winnings through my legal advisors – trying to remain as anonymous as possible. My friend would invest and look after my good fortune, with me learning while looking over his shoulder. I would build a big beautiful home in a warm climate for my close friends and I to escape New York winters.

(Renting makes more sense – is less demanding.)*

I invited educators, community advocates, social workers and others who have experience promoting students' best interests. We put together a plan and support system to redirect focus and see students through public school and the college of their choice. Academic excellence was expected. Community service would be a part of their "give back" plan.

I am retired and had no intention of working full time again, but that's what I'm doing. As a matter of fact – I work many hours overtime. It is most rewarding work – life-changing to be exact – and worth all the effort I'm investing in the project. Actually, I've become a second mother to dozens of teenagers.

*(Afterthought.)

Topic: Start off with the line, "Four years ago I won the lottery – a huge sum of money – it changed my life...."

I Won the Lottery

Rita REB Wilson

Four years ago, I won the lottery... a huge sum of money; it changed my life drastically!!! My children, grandchildren, other immediate family members, and friends reaped the benefits of my selection of six numbers, plus the bonus number. I was the one and only winner of this money, and I wasn't featured in the newspaper. It was only announced that there was one winner for all of that money.

I became a philanderer, no, no excuse me, I mean a philanthropist. My aim was to help humanity in a way other than casual love, which I don't suggest. I sought the whereabouts of my long-lost relative that moved to Liberia.

I took the trip and found Thomas Jones who had migrated there in the early sixties as an experiment in the Back-to-Africa Movement. He and his wife Lela remained there after having five additional children. When they made the move from Boston, Mass., they had one son, Raoul. That son and the other children are raising families. Thomas and Lela had twenty-five grands, nine great grands, and they owned an export-import business that couldn't afford all family members to have work. The small village didn't have sufficient employment to sustain themselves and they were not able to take care of the ones that were ailing and needed medical help. Sometimes the smaller children were the caregivers, and when there was sickness, they would often miss school.

Thomas and Lela were happy to see me, though guarded when I asked questions. Lela was very candid: "Are you here to record information and report your findings on how we live, or did you come to help?" I managed to gain their trust and was very happy to share the good news of revitalization and expansion of their village.

The brightness of the future beamed through the windows of possibilities when the banks and attorneys agreed that money was available, the architecture plans were in place: ready and willing to design, erect, expand the schools, the hospital, the factories. Also, build a library with new books and computers; restore the church house and the juke joint. Both would be well attended by the same members and patrons.

Topic: Write a piece based on a randomly chosen newspaper caption.

"The Improbable Moralist"

Olivia S. Taylor

It was a solemn memorial service as I sat and cherished my memories of a dear friend. Everyone thought Tom was a monk upon first meeting him. The only thing that was missing was the dreariness of his monastery. I met Tom at a lecture at the Heritage House annual banquet for new members. He was bright-eyed, bouncy, full of energy and willing to please everyone. He never had a bad word to say about anyone or anything. He spoke as an idealist surrounded in a utopian villa. All the world would soon be one loving bundle; every creature would be at peace. There would be no need for capitalism or communism: just a loving social interaction of all human beings. When I asked Tom how this would be accomplished, he replied: "With unconditional love." He always insisted upon informing me that people in all corners of the world were just distant cousins.

One day I met Tom for lunch. I had some shopping to do, and he came along. While I was plowing through a selection of

outfits, Tom's pet words were "dazzling," "dashing," "for another customer," "possible," "that works well," or "now *that*
you can't leave." After I had made my selection of two outfits,
a woman walked over to us and asked if we could help her pick
out an outfit. She was carrying her selection of three outfits.
We both asked her whose funeral was she attending, and she
sheepishly said: "I am going to a difficult wedding."

Looking at the outfits which all were black, Tom asked the
woman: "Whose wedding is this?" She replied: "My husband
and I have been invited to the wedding of his ex-wife. I don't
know why I agreed to go, and now it is too late to bow out po-
litely. I decided to wear the most stunning black outfit I could
find." Tom and I looked at each other and smiled. Tom said:
"We are going to help you look ravishing, but we are going to
put all of that black back."

Tom proceeded to walk the woman over to a rack of dresses
that were for tall women. He began looking through, and
asked the woman to look at several outfits. He said: "Now we
can go glamorous." We spent a good while helping the woman
get ready to dress to make a statement. By the time we finished, Tom had gotten so many discounts on the purchases,
and the woman said, looking at the beautiful peach suit and
lilac dress on her arm: "I have two outfits for the price of any
one that I was going to buy."

"Now we can go and get some sassy shoes with your savings," Tom said.

The woman asked: "Will you help me do that?"

I said: "Why not?"

Tom chimed in: "You got to go high stepping."

It was a magical shopping spree. Tom had been a buyer for
Saks Fifth Avenue, but he always said he loved to shop at
Bloomingdale's. He would inspect every stitch and seam. In
addition to the bonus coupons I had in my purse there were
more deductions when Tom finished with the manager. As we
were leaving, I said to Tom: "Seems as if she was a long lost
friend." "Remember, we are all distant cousins," he retorted.

His memorial service was in a room filled with guests and all kinds of beautiful balloons. I sat silently and listened to the many accolades, but I was smiling thinking about so many pleasant experiences with Tom. He surely helped us all know the meaning of painting the town red.

– Sally Bill
Summer 2008

Kim D. Brandon

Excerpt from
Baltimore City Blues

Kim D. Brandon

The following excerpt is from the novel Baltimore City Blues, *which spans the lifetime of Miss Sista, a soulful blues singer. Some have called her gifted, some have called her evil, and there were others who knew the truth. Each choice made to further your dream can lead you into the light or plunge you deeper into darkness.*

This chapter takes place in Baltimore, Maryland, in the 1940's. Years before finding her place as a blues legend, Sista tries to hold on to her grandmother, who is the only family that she has ever known. Sista wants to remain in her grandmother's shadow where music reigns and interlopers are kept at bay.

Songs My Mother Used to Sing

In those quiet moments between the noises of my life, I always heard Mo. She doubled as my grandmother and my mama. She was in reality my only treasure. Her giant booming voice towered over the other working-class ladies in church. She sang like her ass was on fire and like the bass in her voice would put out the flames. It was all loud and hurried, like she needed to get to the punch line first. Her sheer volume dragged the other choir members along with her. Even "Amazing Grace" was lit up and set on fire when she sang it. This didn't fit well with the "saving a wretch like me" part. The sentiment was completely lost by Mo's speed and force. The whole atonement thing was trampled on and then set to the side.

In hushed whispers, the other choir members shared their disgust at what they called "a disgrace before God." They said more than that to each other in pitiful codes to fool us, which included the knocking of elbows, prolonged looks in each other's eyes, and low pitched clicks with their teeth. They didn't fool me and when Mo wasn't looking, I'd return their looks and clicks. None of them dared mention shit to my mama or ask her to slow down or leave the choir. They were stuck with us just like a blind mouse under a fat cat's paw.

You see, Mo blew in the church like a gusty wind before the storm. I could have told them heifers to wait it out, because just like rain, she would be gone before the rainbow started to appear.

It seems like everybody has a period where they discover God. This was Mo's. She discovered Jesus. I was ten. So for a year of Sunday's, she greased my hair down, polished my good shoes, and dragged my boney ass along, some eight blocks, with her to the left row, second pew, and second seat of Mount Holy Baptist Church. There I sat in school clothes all starched and creased everywhere, waiting for the all-day service to end. There were five offerings. Plates would come around three times, and two times everyone had to come up front to give. Mo told me to save my pennies for the stand-up offerings. More than all that begging, I hated the preaching most. Big pig-like men would get up on stage and yell at everyone, sweat and spit threatening to fly over the first row, over the makeshift altar and hit me. Every other sentence was peppered with "sin," "sinner," or "evil ways."

It wouldn't have been so bad if Mo, who was wearing her Sunday best with a little blue and white-beaded hat and white gloves with pearl clustered closures, had looked at me from time to time. She didn't see me as long as I didn't pull up my dress or commit any other public sin. I was just below her radar. And I hated it.

Instead her eyes were locked on Deacon Wilson. I bet he was a big-pig-foot-sucking fool. So when the deacon got up to pontificate on evil, the same speech that he gave every Sunday, she looked over at me and said, "He is a fine man." Before I could say "yes ma'am," she was back in her trance. The deacon looked more like an old horse, probably from years of pulling at his cheeks and chin to look like he was a thinking man, which he wasn't.

I hated him. It wasn't long before "Demon Wilson" was at our house for dinner. After church, we would rush home, in Sunday shoes, almost running the eight blocks and in minutes flat. I wanted to ask Mo if I could bring my tennis shoes in a sack next time. But somehow I knew that Mo would slap me or bark at me for some newfound affront to her newfound lord.

Before the big-headed "demon" arrived, Mo had a hot Sunday supper on the table – biscuits, hot fried chicken, greens with fatback, butter beans, okra and corn and to top it all off her favorite dessert – chocolate cake with lemon icing. Coconut flakes were added all throughout the cake and covered the top of it. She called it "old snow"; it was a joke that made the cake even less appealing. It was an acquired taste. Mo was an acquired taste her damn self. I always ate "old snow" because it was sweet, sugar was hard to come by, and because Mo made it. Still, I'd spit out the dry coconut flakes when she wasn't looking.

All that good old Blues music, that had sustained us, was now a sin. No more Memphis Minnie, Ethel Waters, or the Smith's; Bessie; Mamie and Clara or anybody. We didn't sing it or hum it together or play it on Mo's record player. But sometimes, whenever she was in the bathroom, I could hear that sin, in her whispering voice, singing – everybody, Ma Rainey, Skip James, Papa Charlie Jackson, Ida Cox and Mo's, all-time favorite song: Louie Lasky's "How You Want Your Rollin' Done?"

The good "demon" Wilson told Mo that I needed to be educated so that I could teach. "That gal has a gift, Sista Maureen. You keep an eye on har. She smarta than most. You had betta make sure da she gits da right start. We needs mo Negro teachas up at da school house. Praise da Lord."

Mo nodded, like she was simple or something.

After he butted in, my notebook was checked, and I had to read for two whole hours everyday. I had to write my lessons twice. Once was for practice and once was for show, "for the teacher to see you is smart child," Mo would say.

The "demon" didn't know Mo, and now he had set her loose on me. Mo and I had a good thing going. We were two peas in a pod. We went to the Reilly's house at 5:30 every morning. Mo made and served breakfast. I ate what the white folks ate for breakfast: fresh fruit, soft-boiled eggs, and buttered toast. After breakfast I colored in my fancy store-bought coloring book – only doing one page every couple of days to make it last, while Mo started cleaning and dinner, until it was time for her to take me to my bus for school.

Schooling came real easy to me, so I was moved up a grade. Mo' hadn't even noticed that I was skipped at all, until the "demon" had her speak with my teacher. That was the worst thing ever. The teacher, Mrs. Avery, told Mo that I was definitely the smartest girl in her class and the laziest girl she had ever taught. She told Mo that I had to sit in the front row "cause she caught me sleepin' on several occasions."

Mo had taken off from her second job at the Billings, the folks that gave her all our new furniture, their old furniture, to meet with my teacher and she was not happy with my report. I listened as Mo recounted Mrs. Avery's words.

"How could you shame us so badly? I ain't never axed nothin' of you, daughta, but ta do your studies. I never even axed you to wash one fuckin' fork or spoon. I irons your clothes and cooks ya food. And you fuckin' sleepin' at the schoolhouse. I oughta beat ya narrow ass. I tell you one thang, you gonna wish you had minded your teacher." Mo stomped along on the way to the bus yelling at me and dragging me along by the wrist. She didn't see the faces of people who thought to come to my rescue and then thought better of it and fled.

I knew not to say a word and just listen. But, I had done what was asked of me. "I did do all my studies," I whispered.

"You gone wish you had done all your studies."

It was a threat; her eyes were in a trance, not like at church, much meaner.

"You gone wish you had," she hissed again.

We got back to the Billings house just in time for Mo to make a hurried dinner. I sat in the corner of the kitchen pretending to look out the window. I studied Mo's moves. They were jerky and forced. I watched as she banged those people's things – banged their pots on the stove, their dishes in the sink, their food from the new icebox onto the counter. Somehow, unwisely, I forgot that all this banging noise was about me, and started to relax and hear music in her movements: I matched it up with "This Little Light of Mine" (bamm!) "I'm going to let it shine" (bang! bang!).

Later, the song ended in my head and I noticed that I didn't get my usual treat: some sweet tea or a cold piece of fruit waiting for me in the Billings' icebox – frozen orange slices were my favorite – mmm mmm.

"Mama, may I have something cold to...?" in mid sentence, I remembered and it, was way, way, way too late to pull it back in. If only I could suck the words back down my throat. I looked over and Mo was looking through me. She put down a large bowl of cornmeal she was mixing and headed towards me. My heart began to race; I wanted to disappear. The tears began to flow from my eyes. She hated me!

My world got smaller, then smaller still, with every step that she took towards me. She was all I had; somehow, I always felt that I had much more. Her slap hit my mouth and nose at the same time, and my nose began to bleed.

"You goin' wish you had done your studies... I work hard – three jobs, take six bus rides, to and from those jobs and your school. That's when I have the money, walk when I don't. So that you can be up at the school house and you there sleepin'. You know how many toilets I have to wash in a day, six days a week? And yo ass is up at the school house sleepin'," she screamed.

"Tiny, is everything okay in there?" A voice came from the outer room.

"Yessum," Mo snapped back still looking at me.

Then a really white woman with a powdered face and pretty red hair, that was long and wavy, like the women at the picture show, stuck her head in the kitchen. She was wearing dime store make up, red lipstick and a smart tan blouse. It was funny, but I had never seen this woman up close, in the same room before, after having been in her home for years.

"Okay then," she said looking at Mo and then looking at me. "You have a rag for that gal's nose?"

I sat there trying to look any way that wouldn't make "Tiny" madder. The fear was now replaced by a drumbeat in my head; my body heard the funeral march. I knew that things just got much worse; Mo didn't talk to the white people unless it was necessary, and somehow she managed to keep all of them out of any kitchen that she was in. I had spent much of my life in their kitchens, as long as I could remember; I never really saw the white people and Mo made sure that they didn't see me either. They knew we were in their homes, but if Mo heard a sound, a voice or a footstep heading toward the kitchen, she rebounded from whatever she was doing, made her way through the door, and stopped whomever in their tracks.

"May I help you?" or "yesum" or "yessa" would slip from her lips – never with the sweet gentle tone that she should have been aiming for. She would fill their request quickly (a cold glass of water, a sliced apple, run an errand); then she would return, and order would be restored to the kitchen. I never made any noise. Except sometimes when Mo knew the house was empty, we sang together and even played their piano.

Songs like "Good Biscuits," "Ice Man (Come on Up)," "Special Delivery Blues" and a whole host of the Blues. Our favorite cleaning song was "This Is the Maid's Day Off." Other than that I knew to keep my place. If Mo sang "My What-You-Ma-Call-It" it meant that the house was empty and I could play on the piano and sing while she worked.

I tried to be true. I tried loving you. I got lost last night
Baby, I made a left when I should have made a right
I was out all night looking for my what-you-ma-call-it.

Today was not a day for singing. I listened to the ticking of the clock and wondered if Mo would give me a dry rag or another slap. Looking out the window was my only option. The blood dried on my hands and face. Mo finished her work and we walked home, what seemed like 30 blocks, in silence, Mo always a good ten steps ahead of me, in an old print cotton dress, a well-worn sweater and run-over shoes. I noticed that I was better dressed than Mo. She wore one of three cotton dresses during the week and always the same sweater.

As the blood dried, I was able to rub some of it off. I made certain that none of it got on my school clothes. I had five outfits for school – two more than most of the kids in my class: a brown jumper with a matching blouse, two navy blue skirts, and a black skirt with short and long sleeved white blouses. Sometimes, I wore one of the white blouses under the brown jumper; that made five outfits.

By the time we got to our house, I noticed that I did manage to get three drops of blood on my white socks. My feet were sore and hurting. I still cowered real low like a mutt with its tail between its legs. Mo was the top dog.

I was torn between needing her, wanting things back the way they were, and needing to bark like a big dog about the long walk home. We had never walked the entire way back from the Billings. They had more money than a body had the right to have, so they lived as far away from everybody else as was possible. I wanted to bark, to howl. I had done everything that stupid old Mrs. Avery had asked. She never asked for more, and now Mo is acting like I slapped that woman or peed on my books.

She walked straight through the house and out the back door. She came back with a small tree. She was breathing hard, like she had run a race. As usual, I was too curious to be terrified. She pinched her fingers together around a branch and slid all the leaves off. That must be painful. I thought. It wasn't until all the leaves were off and littering the dinning room that I realized what was about to happen. Mo pulled each of the smaller branches off and was left with one giant branch; the top was the width of a dime. She twirled each branch around in the air and listened to the low whistles each one made.

I watched as if I was struck dumb. The whistling comforted me and I wanted to play with the branches too. I let my head rest on my left shoulder as I sat down in a chair to watch.

"They are whistling." I said, "Sounds like the blues, also like a harmonica. Right Mama?"

It was as if I had broken a spell and the ritual dance came to a screeching quick stop. This mistake had attracted Mo's attention to me and she looked over almost dumbfounded by my interest in the music. She looked at me for at least a minute before asking.

"Do you know why the switches whistle?" She was pulling off her sweater. She looked like a mad woman.

I thought about it for some time and wanted to ask if she could play two switches, one in each hand.

"To drown out your screams!" she continued. "Now git dem school clothes off."

I wanted to change into my everyday clothes, but didn't. I just started to pull the brown jumper over my head. I took off the matching blouse, my shoes and socks with the three little bloodstains.

"Maybe if I had taken a lickin' to your mother she wouldn't a been such a no-account."

This couldn't get any worse. Mo took great pains to never mention her daughter, my mother, Lottie Mae. My heart was beating so fast, I felt like I was about to faint. This wasn't a lickin'. This old lady was gonna kill me.

"Now take them drawers off and bend over that chair."

I wanted to whine or plead for my life. But my mouth didn't open. I pulled off the panties with the homemade elastic waistband, which was tied in a little knot to keep them from falling down. I threw my body over the back of the chair.

"No! Not like that, I want ya butt up in the air!" she yelled.

I pulled the chair completely out from under the table, laid across the seat and waited. I had never been beaten like this before, and my bare ass was unfamiliar to the dining room. Mama looked like a wild dog – she was really the top dog. I continued to wait there with my panties around my ankles.

She walked back out to the yard. I could just hear her voice. She was talking. So I got up and looked out the kitchen window and there she was ringing her hands together, walking around in small tight circles and crying. No, it was more like pleading for something. This was the first time that I had seen this; I didn't know that she had tears. She took the world as she found it, never begging for anything. She simply stomped along with the force of a mule – me tagging behind.

I pressed my face against the glass plane. The more she cried, the more I cried. After a few minutes, I ran to the back door, butt naked, panties at my feet and yelled – "please don't cry, Mama. I won't be a no-account. I promise" – only anybody in the alley could see all my business.

"I AM GOING TO WHIP YOU," she screamed.

In one giant step she was up the back stairs and in the house. She grabbed for the switches on the table and knocked them all on the floor. I ran in the living room and hid beside the sofa – which Mrs. Billings, the red-haired lady, had given Mo when she got a new one.

"I am going to whip you, gal."

I came out from behind the sofa, and the elastic band had come loose so I held my panties up. The giant looked so lost, so small. I lay back on the seat of the chair, my panties fell down below my butt, and I braced my bare ass for the storm that was coming.

Mo kind of slid down on the floor and sat among the leaves and smaller branches. She looked at the blood dripping from her thumb and continued crying and moaning. The moaning got louder as she held the notes and lower as she broke the notes into short, stabbing groans. It was like a mourning song. I'd give anything to hear her sing "Midnight Mama" or "I've Got It, This Time."

I thought about Mrs. Billings calling Mo "Tiny." That family had been calling her that for over twenty years. Mo wasn't a fat woman but she was big and solid. I looked over and I could see how hard her life had been and how she never ever stopped to complain or hide from anything. I wanted to do something to stop her sadness. I wanted to make sure that no one ever called her "Tiny" again. She was so beautiful. I must have fallen asleep, because when I woke up I was in Mo's bed, in my nightshirt and it was the next morning.

My clothes were laid out at the foot of her bed; I got dressed and came downstairs. The leaves were gone; the chair was back under the table. I grabbed my books and waited for Mo, my mama, at the door. There she was in the doorway, five times as big as I remembered her – with the grease and brush in her hands. She combed my hair down and put it into three plaits. Then we left for the Reilly's. I promised myself that I would never let Mo down again.

At school, I went to my classroom early to talk with Mrs. Avery. She was sitting at her desk looking peaceful. So I relaxed too. Once she saw me, her face soured like she was sucking on salt.

"Good morning, ma'am, Mrs. Avery, ma'am."

"You are early; go wait in the gymnasium with the other children."

"I was thinking. Mrs. Avery, my mother was hoping that you would give me extra work and suggest some books on music and history for me to read while she is cleaning. My mother would like it if I had some extra work to make up for my not paying attention."

"You were not paying attention. I see what your mother means – you have a much weaker command of the English language than I initially surmised," she said without looking directly at me.

It was done. I didn't have to like Mrs. Avery to get her to help me. I had asked for more homework and if she had any books that I could take home to read. She gave me plenty. Somehow I knew not to ask frog face to help me in class and I was right.

First I did all the homework, and then I would read the books from cover to cover. Then I'd start the books over again. I love books about animals, history, people's lives and anything that had to do with music. I read on the bus, in the white folk's kitchens, and everywhere else. Somehow, I thought that if I was a good student then my world would get bigger again, and I could find a way to stop the Billings from calling my mother Tiny.

My teacher loaned me ten books over the summer break. I read each one at least once. But it was a book about great ladies of music that I read at least twenty times.

Every night Mo would say: "Gal that is enough – ya goin' hurt ya eyes." She would smile and kiss my forehead.

I was skipped a grade, for the second time, to the seventh grade that August. "Demon" Wilson took credit for my "new interest in being educated."

One Saturday night he showed up with a gallon tub of butter pecan ice cream.

"Look a here, girly, you done gone and done da right thing. So git yourself a big dish and enjoy dis here cream."

I made three dishes of ice cream while Mo dressed for company.

"So, what you want me ta do for you now da you is a smart, girl?" he asked me, speaking to me directly.

"Deacon Wilson, sir, I want to sing in church on Sunday."

"Now you wait one minute. You gotta have something special to git up in the pulpit at Holy. We don't just open da
floodgates. Now say 'I wanta sing in church' again."

"I want to sing in church on Sunday, Deacon Wilson, sir."

"See that there right there is the problem. Did ya hear it?"
He sat down at the dining room table.

"Hear it sir?" I handed him a dish of ice cream.

"Yes, there it go again, gal ya sound like a cross 'tween a cow
and a frog. No wonder ya hid yourself aways from company."

And just like that I started to belt out "Oh Freedom."

"Well I'll be godam! Y'all sure is full of surprises, ain't you?"

By the time I got to "go on to my Lord and be free," Mo
was in the living room, looking sweet and clean.

"Deacon," Mo chimed in, in her best Sunday church lady
voice. "That is my child."

"Sista Maureen, this here gal got some pipes, she could sure
nuff teach singin' up at da college."

Mo and I looked at each other and decided not to respond
to the deacon's goals for college, unless and until we saw him
pull the tuition and board out of his wallet.

So after Sunday dinner the deacon would listen to me practice "Amazing Grace," which was his choice.

"A lil' more work on softing up parts and you be ready ta
sing in front of folks," he would say.

"Yessir," I would reply.

Other than singing the same slow ass song, I had barely said
two words to the deacon. Weeks were going by, and I still
didn't like the idea of him always coming around. We both
talked to each other through Mo for the most part. I mainly
asked Mo if the deacon knew when I was to perform my solo at
Mount Holy? Months went by. I dreamt about being in the
forest coming out of a cave and chasing down a ruined version
of the deacon. In the dream, I roasted him on a spit and
chopped off his head and ate the rest of him. I used his sharpened bones to make weapons. I woke up with chills and decided
not to share the nightmare with Mo. She was really taken with
the deacon.

Every couple of Saturday nights he would take Mo out. She would put on her Sunday best – minus the hat and gloves. They would go to the picture show or out "walkin" as Mo called it. I was left with my books and supper in the oven. Mo told me to sleep in the basement and she set up a mat on the floor for me. She did this every time he took her out.

One of those nights I came upstairs to pee. I looked into Mo's bedroom on my way to the toilet, and there was the deacon. He was sleeping in Mo's bed. He was lying out there with Mo – butt naked. I could see his wiener and then some. I clicked on the light in my room, made my way to the bathroom and closed the door and started to pee. I sat there and wondered what to do? *What were my choices?* Nothing came to mind. So, I turned off the bathroom light and headed back downstairs. I peeked into Mo's room. The "demon" and his wiener were gone. Mo was still there, sound asleep half under a white sheet. I wanted to wake her and ask her about the "demon" but knew not to. I was right; he really was a demon, no maybe a snake.

I went down to the basement and lay on my mat when the backdoor creaked shut.

The "demon" didn't come for any more Sunday dinners after the "big sleepover" at our house. He still took Mo out on Saturday nights, only they came home later, and he dropped her off at the door. As promised the deacon arranged for me to sing in Church on a cold Sunday morning – almost five months later. What a putz head! I sang "Amazing Grace" all slow and proud. I even touched my heart every time I sang "a wretch like me." I had learned what not to do in Church, by watching Mo singing. I got a round of hand clapping, about ten "amens" and three "hallelujahs." I must have stayed on stage too long wishing I knew another church song, darn it, because someone cleared their throat all loud and I got the message. I sat back down next to Mo. She kissed me on my forehead. I was wearing the black skirt with one of my white blouses. I wished I knew more church songs. Folks wanted more and I knew not to sing Bessie Smith at Mount Holy. I could study one of the books of hymns while folks were preaching; hey, maybe even join the choir. The next time, I could sing "This Little Light of Mine" or "Come Closer Yonder to Thee My Lord." I was so excited.

The very next Sunday, Mama and the deacon must have had a big falling out – because we sat in our usual seats in church. And then right before Deacon Wilson was to talk, Mo jumped up, put her purse under her arm, and I followed her to the back of the church. It seemed like all the good sisters were glaring at us. We listened to Deacon Wilson drone on about sin and how a saved woman is a treasure from God. He finally got to his real message.

"Brothers, a ha ha, men, a ha ha, keep yourself holy, a ha ha, keep yourself clean – don'tcha be lead by evil... Walk with the Lord, but keep your eyes open cause the devil. I said the devil will put on a pretty dress and put perfume behind the ears and whisper, a ha ha. I said whisper ya name."

He jumped straight up in the air and the church went wild – fans flying, "Amens" ricocheted off the walls, and men jumped to their feet. "...Keep one foot in front of the other one, and one foot on the floor. Stay the course..."

This meant war. Mo stomped out of the church before the good deacon was finished. Heads turned, necks popped as we left. I followed behind hoping that the church folks knew that I was a saved woman – even if I had seen the deacon's wiener and the side of his big old flat hind parts.

We never went back to Mount Holy. I never asked Mo about the deacon's wiener and why it was a sin for her and not for him. I never joined the choir and that next week Mo brought out her old blues music and played her records full blast and shimmied as she served our Sunday dinner. She seemed like she was in a good mood – happier than the church lady that she was pretending to be. So I asked.

"Mama, did you know that Deacon Wilson said that when I talk, I sound like an old cow and a frog at the same time?"

"That son of a bitch." She came closer and stroked my chin. "You will grow into that voice of yours and then him and his kind will line up, two across, to kiss your ass."

I wanted her to say that I didn't sound like an old cow or a frog when I talked. But I knew I did. So singing was my true language; it was how I translated my world, mostly for Mo and myself. But I would sing to a mangy cat with one eye, cause I needed to.

"Mama, did Deacon Wilson tell the church that you and I were sinners?"

"No baby, he said that I was a singer." And with that we laughed and danced around the living room.

"Sista, it ain't for him to decide who I is. It is for me to decide and I done decided. I am going to be a topsy twirly dancer at the Hat Check Room." Mo and I shook our tot tats to the beat, while singing "No Body In Town Can Bake A Sweet Jelly Roll Like Mine." We were accompanied by Bessie Smith on the record player. It was our first of many performances at the all-new imaginary Hat Check Room.

The reality of us was a whole different matter.

Olivia S. Taylor

The Old Fisherman

Olivia S. Taylor

The Old Fisherman has gone. He sits high upon a
hillside with his right eye watching the waves and
roars of the muddy waters of the Mighty Mississippi
River. And his left eye guarding, The Flatlands of
Plaquemines Parish, watching Buras, Venice and
Sunrise. He left Mobile Bay for the Port of New
Orleans and followed the River far south down to her
mouth, and there he would stay.

The Old Fisherman has polished and shined his boots
for the very last time. He has set them up to rest.
He saw the erosion of the land and the river gobble
the sand. He said the River has been dammed up,
jammed up, and can no longer deposit her fertile silt.
He walked the shores where the river now ran. He
navigated the old River and bayous, three score plus
ten. He talked of time on the river according to which
storm, against the might of Camille from 1940 to 2005.
He said none was meaner except Katrina.

The Old Fisherman speaks of yesteryear's history. He
recorded it in how fierce was the hurricane. He had just
come off the river when Flossie came ashore. Her
forceful winds sent her into the Gulf of Mexico. All
were warned to go to higher ground. He sent his family
away but he did stay. From that point on, he always
remained in the flatlands to ride out a storm. With
events he would call them by name.

The Old Fisherman had a story for every hurricane. After
the surge of Flossie in 1956; Audrey in '57 flooding the
land; Ethel in '60 damaged the orange crop; Clara in '61
caused most of the farmers to flee. Now a fifth season,
storm season was a new reality. The area was quiet for
a few years until old Betsy came roaring through.
She forced wind and water up and down Route 23 and
carried into the river the old Catholic School and Church
that refused to integrate. Hurricane Camille, grandma of
all seasons, soured in '69. She was the worst of the last
half of the century.

She tore up the Gulf Coast. Along with some other bold souls
we rode out her gales. Securing a fleet in Venice so they
could later set sail. Her winds were so strong and her surge
so steep many big men were knocked off their feet. They
moaned and groaned praying, "Lord please don't take me
home." The Old Fisherman said, "She did much damage at
Old Miss' mouth. The storm wreaked havoc over the land.

She veered east with her winds so strong; she came ashore bringing yachts, ships, trollers, and sailboats and parked them on the land. She washed out Highway 90. After each storm people counted their losses, mourned, and then went on and rebuilt with the might of their hands, as they always did."

His hands were the hands of a fisherman. Calluses and corns defined the years of his hard work. He added to his labor the skills of carpenter and welder, which he passed on to the hands of his sons; they mended many wrecked ships and boats to keep them afloat, with skills inherited from the Fisherman's hands.

His hands were as large as those of a seven-foot man. He was a hell of a guy, only five and a half feet high. At age 80, he could do the work of a man of 35. He went out on the river while all were sleeping. He was an early riser. When most were getting up to go on their way, he was returning with the catch of the day.

The Old Fisherman sat down to reflect, after he had shined his boots, with a twist of his mouth and a scratch of his brow. "A day of reckoning with the river will be the scientists, legislators and fishermen who will develop a lesson: Geography 101." If the Congress would have convened two days after Katrina on a barge floating in Louisiana's blazing hot sun, with no bug repellant, the job would have gotten done. No way. No, six months after Rita and Katrina, the people of New Orleans or anywhere else on the Gulf Coast should still roam and not be able to go home. Blind as could be, deaf in one ear, he said, "I know these waters I can smell the fog, thinking about putting me a boat back on the water, for the only true shrimps are in Louisiana's waters."

I bowed my head and thought about a wedding that had been postponed because of the storm. I was met as the great, great, great aunt, and I wondered how could it be. I remembered, I had a brother almost 93.

The Old Fisherman has gone. He is no longer the elder of the eldest. Now he has joined the ancestors: Lela Mae; Henry P.; Woote; Esther; Mary; Louise; Eugene J.; Marion; Lou Verda; Marvanel and others' names do call.............
I will not know I could not see if his newly polished boots were placed on his feet.

– Sally Bill
February 2008

Cleotis and Whimpey

Olivia S. Taylor

Cleotis was a nine-year-old boy who lived with his father and grandmother. His best friend was Herbert, but everybody called him Herbie. They were the same age. Herbie had an older cousin named Clarence who was eleven. The three boys often played, fished, hunted wild game, and roamed the nearby woods together.

It was a splendid July morning. The summer sun had risen early. Its bright rays struck the Mississippi Delta with full force. This was the first in several days that torrential rains had not fallen in the area. Cleotis, Herbert, and Clarence had all planned to go fishing. The banks of the nearby rivers and streams were full. Grandma always said, "The heavy rains fertilize the fish." An abundance of fish was always to be caught after every heavy rainfall.

Cleotis quietly crept out of bed. He did not see anybody else was up, but to his surprise Grandma had packed a lunch for him. It was sitting on the table. He knew that his father had gone to work, and Grandma had prepared breakfast. She had set his food in the warmer on the stove and gone back to bed. He hurried and ate. He was glad that he did not wake his grandmother. Soon he was finished eating. He heard the familiar whistle of Herbert.

Just as he was about to go out the back door Grandma yelled, "Don't take Whimpey with you. The river is too high today for the dog."

"I won't," replied Cleotis.

"Okay, Son. Catch plenty of fish."

Cleotis heard Herbie's whistle again. He did not bother answering but made a quick dash for the backyard instead. "What took you so long? We started to leave you," said Clarence. He was the oldest of the three boys and always liked to boss the other two around.

"Oh, I woke up a little later than I had planned," said Cleotis.

"Come on, hurry up! Let's take the shortcut through the woods," said Clarence.

"Do you think we ought to do that?" asked Herbie.

"Come on and stop whimpering," yelled Clarence.

"The footpath in the woods would be very muddy because of the rains," added Cleotis.

"Half the day will be gone if we go down the road the long way," said Clarence.

"Let's throw for it," Cleotis said. He knew that some times he could throw a rock much farther than either of the other two boys, and he wanted to support his friend Herbie. All three of the boys chose rocks and threw them in the clearing past the shed. They went out to find the rocks. Clarence's rock was a footprint ahead.

The trail was far soggier than they had expected. They had no problem digging for earthworms, which they used for bait, along the way. The fish loved the earthworms they hooked on the ends of their fishing lines. In the distance they could hear the sound of an animal tramping in the thicket. The sound lasted for a while. Soon Whimpey ran out of the woods. The boys chased him yelling, "Go on back home." It wasn't long before the dog knew he was not welcome company.

By the time the boys reached the bridge their feet and legs were covered with mud. They hung their feet over in the water to wash away the mud. The sun was still soft when they threw their lines in the river. Herbie was the first to land a catch. The fish were really biting. Within a couple of hours the boys' pails were full of fish.

"Let's go for a swim," suggested Clarence.

"The river is too high," said Herbie, "and I can't swim as well as you. Let's walk toward the road, and it won't be so deep there."

The boys grabbed their belongings and walked along the shore of the river toward the road. As they moved beside the edge of the woods, they heard footsteps on the floor of the forest.

"I hear something," said Cleotis.

"Oh, it is nothing," said Clarence, as he picked up a rock and tossed it into the thickets. The sound stopped. "You see, I told you it was nothing." The boys continued walking along the shore of the river at the edge of the forest.

The boys walked along in silence for a while and there was no sound to be heard except the patter of their footsteps.

"I'll race you," said Cleotis.

"It is too hot to run, and anyway we are carrying too much stuff," responded Clarence, who didn't always play fair. He walked several paces ahead of the others and yelled, "Last one there is a rotten egg." Cleotis took off. They both were far ahead of Herbie.

The boys ran almost a quarter of a mile. Cleotis easily overtook Clarence. When they could see the road, they decided to stop running and wait for Herbie to catch up. As soon as they stopped, Whimpey ran out of the woods.

"Oh, it was you out there in the thicket all along." The dog looked at him sheepishly and wagged his tail. "Come here, Whimpey." Slowly the dog walked over to him, still wagging his tail for approval. "Now you know Grandma is going to be angry with us." Whimpey jumped on Cleotis' shoulder.

"Don't try to make friends now. You are going to get me in trouble."

"What kind of a dog is that?" asked Clarence.

"He is just a plain old dog," replied Cleotis.

"He's just an old mutt. Go home you old dog. Get back home," yelled Clarence.

Cleotis didn't like the way Clarence spoke to his dog. Whimpey stood wagging his tail, looking at Cleotis with big sad eyes. But he stayed quiet. Clarence picked up a small branch and threw it toward the woods. Whimpey ran and retrieved the branch and brought it back to Cleotis. He took it and tossed it down the edge of the woods. The dog ran and got the stick again. Cleotis raised the stick to throw it again, and he saw Herbie coming to the area where they were.

"You finally caught up with us," said Clarence, balancing on Herbie's shoulder as he rubbed the bottom of his feet. "This sun is getting hot. Let's take a dip." The three of them took off their pants and shirts and headed for the shallow edge of the river. Whimpey had won Cleotis' approval, and he was right beside them.

The water was a bit cold. It was always a bit cooler after a day or two of hard rain. But the river felt refreshing. They did a few backstrokes and butterflies. They were busy playing in the water, but soon they decided that they had had enough. The boys came out of the river and sat on the side soaking up the sun. They opened the lunch sack they had brought along.

After the boys finished their lunches, they walked along the shore gathering shells and rocks. They threw a few and declared they were warriors. The boys threw rocks for about three quarters of an hour and took another dive into the river.

When they came out this time they sat on the bank throwing pebbles into the woods, watching as Whimpey ran back and forth. Before long, the boys started home. They had traveled far away from the path they had taken in the morning. They walked toward the highway to thumb a ride. They knew that they would find someone driving down the highway toward Folk Creek, the road that led to their neighborhood.

Clarence stood out on the highway and stuck out his thumb. Several cars passed them by, but soon a man came along driving an old truck. Herbie had just thrown a stick for Whimpey to run and get. Clarence yelled, "Come on! We got a ride." The boys jumped on the back of the truck. They were almost home before they realized that they had left the dog.

When they reached Folk Creek Road, they jumped off the truck and started walking down the road. They reached Cleotis' house first. He ran across the field to his house as the other boys went down the road to their house.

Grandma was in the kitchen with Aunt Myra. They were shelling peas. Cleotis wished them a good afternoon, and proudly showed them his catch of the day. He had fifteen fish in the pail, plenty for dinner and some to share. He went in the back yard and pretended that he was chasing Whimpey. He would throw a rock then go to the backside of the shed and run beyond the clearing whistling for the dog.

Cleotis had often taken his dog with him when he went swimming. Sometimes he got a ride home and the dog walked. Other times they walked back home together. But now the boy was worried because the dog would always come home soon. He looked beyond the clearing and thought any minute the dog would run out of the woods, but the only sounds that came from the woods came from a few birds. Cleotis saw the women come out on the back porch to clean the fish he had brought home. He knew that he would be needed to pump water for them to wash the fish, so he went and filled the two pails that were hanging on the porch. He quickly did that task and got far away from his grandmother. He knew that she would ask him where the dog was. He lay down in the big old hammock that hung from the old oak tree in the back yard.

It was suppertime before he woke up. His father had come home from the mill. No one mentioned the dog until after supper. Grandma noticed that the food she had put in the dish earlier was still in Whimpey's tray.

Cleotis knew he would have to tell his grandmother the truth. His father had given him the dog for his birthday. He was told that he would have to take good care of the dog. Now he would have to admit that he had caught a ride home and forgotten the dog. He felt terrible. The dog's absence was felt by all of them.

"What happened, Son? Didn't Grandma tell you not to take that dog away from here?"

"I didn't take him, Daddy. He followed us, and when I saw him I tried to make him come back. When we got down to the river, he hid from us in the woods."

His father only sighed. But Cleotis kept talking. "We walked down to the bend and took a swim and he ran out of the woods."

"Are you sure, Son?"

"Yes sir, Daddy."

"Now Cleotis, you knew the dog was over there when you got ready to come home. You completely forgot about the dog. Did you ever think about giving up your ride and going back to get the dog?"

"No, sir, Daddy, we were almost home before I realized I had left Whimpey." Cleotis felt horrible now. It seemed so careless of him not to go back and get the dog.

"Well, Son, it is almost dark, and if that dog is out there after a day or so he might be your loss, and somebody else's find."

"Yes, sir, Daddy."

"Go on and get your chores done."

Cleotis got up from the table and went out in the backyard to pump water for the night. He felt that he had let his father down. He wondered if his dad would give the dog away as he had warned when he had given it to him. He had told him if he didn't take care of it properly he couldn't keep him. Whimpey had been a newborn puppy when he got him, only six weeks old. Papa Dorcas had given him to his dad especially for him. Cleotis had been so sad when the family's old dog Rex died. Everyone wanted him to have a dog of his own.

After Cleotis had collected wood and piled the pieces high on the back porch, he brought in an armful to put behind the stove. The stove was still too hot for him to empty the cinders

and set the fire for the next day so he went back onto the porch.
Grandma was sitting in the front room putting patches on
some old overalls. He was glad that she did not call him to
thread her needles. He sat on the porch with his head down in
his lap. He hated for his dad to be disappointed with him.

It was dark before Cleotis went into the house. His father
was just getting ready to empty his tub of bath water out in the
backyard when he entered the door. He took one side of the
tub. His father asked, "Did you finish your chores?"

"Yes, sir, Daddy."

"All right, get your bath."

It didn't make him feel well for his dad to check on his
chores or tell him to get his bath. These were things he had not
been told to do for well over a year. Cleotis took the empty tub
back in the kitchen and dipped two pails of water from the rain
barrel. He carried them into the kitchen and put them in the
number three ten tub. He set the smoothing irons into the tub
to warm the water. After he finished his bath and emptied the
tub, he went to his room and turned down the bed.

His grandmother called. "Cleotis, come and get some
lemon pie." It was his favorite dessert. He did not have much
of an appetite for dessert.

Cleotis came to the table and said, "Only a sliver,
Grandma."

"You mean you don't want a big slice? This is your favorite
pie."

"But my stomach hurts tonight."

"Oh, cheer up. Whimpey will be back home tomorrow."

"Do you really think so, Grandma?"

"Yes, he misses you just as much as you miss him."

Her words made him feel better. He ate his pie, said good
night, and went to bed early.

When he woke up the next morning, his father had already
left for the mill. He dressed quickly and went into the kitchen.

"Good morning, Cleotis."

"Good morning, Grandma, did he come back?"

"No, not yet."

He walked straight through the kitchen and looked in Whimpey's dish. The food from the day before was still there. He walked down the steps of the back porch and behind the shed and yelled out. "Whimpey, Whimpey, come home, boy. Come back home, Whimpey. Come home, boy."

He was silent for a few moments. He hoped the dog heard him. He walked around the clearing as if he would see him run out of the bushes any moment. He sat down on the dewy grass. He could feel the tears began to well up in his eyes.

He soon heard the back screen door open. It was Grandma. She yelled out his name and called him for breakfast. He quickly dried his eyes on the sleeve of his shirt. She tried to cheer him up while they ate breakfast. But he still felt sad.

He thought that he might ask if he could go back out in the woods and search for Whimpey, but he was supposed to help with the gardening today, after he finished breakfast. He went in the shed, gathered the wheelbarrow and put in the pitchfork and the hoe, then headed to the garden with his grandmother. She had just finished feeding the chickens.

Herbie and Clarence came by. They wanted Cleotis to go to pick berries with them. He knew he'd be with Grandma in the garden all morning. They picked peas and beans and gathered the okra that was ripe. He also pulled the weeds and turned the soil for Grandma to plant a new patch of greens.

It was almost noon before they finished and headed back to the house. Cleotis put the freshly picked vegetables on the porch counter. He went into the hen house to collect the eggs for the day. As soon as he opened the gate he smelled a foul odor. He knew it was not rotten eggs.

Grandma immediately came into the chicken coop. She knew what the smell was all about. She started looking around.

"What is it, Grandma?" asked Cleotis.

"A skunk has been here, and something disturbed it," answered Grandma. They looked behind the hen house but they did not find a skunk: it was Whimpey.

Cleotis ran to pamper the dog, but Grandma commanded, "Don't touch him! He needs a bath." The bad scent was coming from the dog.

"What happened, boy? What happened to you?" They did not move from the spot: Whimpey just stood and whimpered.

Grandma smiled and said, "He has learned his first real lesson from the forests."

"What happened to him, Grandma?"

"He probably found the litter of a mother skunk and decided he was going to play with the babies – and the mother skunk sprayed him. Go get the rope. We are going to tie him to the fence until we can get him washed up."

Cleotis got the pail and a scrub brush. They finally got the dog cleaned. Cleotis felt a lot better as he sat down to have lunch with his grandmother.

– Sally Bill
July 6, 1995

Mr. Duck and Mr. Fox

Olivia S. Taylor

Mr. Duck was a hard-working farmer. He and his family had lived next door to Mr. Fox, who was also a farmer, for many years. Each one of them tilled the soil vigorously year after year. Mr. Duck always felt that at harvest time he would never reap all the seeds he had sowed, even though he worked late into the evening. One late summer evening as the sun was setting upon the horizon Mr. Duck saw Mr. Fox. He came across his field carrying a sack of corn.

"Mr. Fox, you are such a great farmer," said Mr. Duck.

"All in the touch; all in the touch," said Mr. Fox.

"You planted field corn this year as I remember. Didn't you?" said Mr. Duck.

"Yes, do say that I did," replied Mr. Fox.

"May I sample an ear of your corn?"

"Yes you sure can, Mr. Duck; here try this one," he said as he passed the Duck a fine plump ear. The duck tasted the corn and complimented the fox.

"This is great corn. Your field corn tastes as tender and juicy as my sweet corn. How do you do it, Mr. Fox?"

"Oh, dear neighbor, anything I touch just simply turns to sugar. It's all in the touch; all in the tender touch."

Mr. Fox continued his bragging. "Every time I plant field corn it turns sweet on me. It is all in the touch." The duck listened and looked strangely at the fox. "Take another piece if you don't believe me."

Mr. Duck reluctantly took another ear of the corn. He felt disheartened, for every summer he had tried to catch Mr. Fox stealing his crops, and every summer he had failed. But now he was determined.

Several days passed and Mr. Fox again crossed Mr. Duck's field. He greeted him as he always did. "You know that my field corn is getting sweeter and sweeter each day," he said.

The next evening Mr. Duck had decided that this was the last straw and he would catch Mr. Fox that very day. And tried as it may be, he did. He saw him just as Mr. Fox was plucking an ear of corn from Mr. Duck's stalk. Mr. Duck chuckled, "Now I caught you."

For a moment Mr. Fox looked very surprised. He looked up and asked: "What? You caught what, Mr. Duck?"

"I caught you, Mr. Fox, you old thief."

"I told you last spring, Mr. Duck, that I planted popcorn. Mr. Wind is like a miraculous force. He blew the seeds that I planted throughout this valley. And anywhere my crops flourish, I pluck – whatever I sow, I must reap," the fox said boldly.

Mr. Duck began to get angrier and angrier at the arrogant fox. But Mr. Fox was cunning. So in an appeasing voice he said, "Mr. Duck, now don't be so upset; for after all, you know I am a great farmer. Don't be so upset if a few kernels of my popcorn flew over in your field."

Mr. Duck grew madder and madder. "Mr. Fox, you will see me in court. We will go up before the judge tomorrow. Once and for all I will seek justice and peace." The clever fox heard the duck's emphatic statement.

"Now Mr. Duck, don't be so indignant. Haven't I been a good neighbor to you for more than ten years? We have lived side by side in peace. Haven't we been great neighbors?"

The Duck only looked at him and shook his head. "Now," said the Fox to the Duck, "don't be so pious now since you feel you caught me red-handed. Don't you believe that everyone deserves another chance?"

The duck screamed, "No! Definitely not!" – so loudly that it not only startled Mr. Fox, it frightened Mr. Rabbit and his family. Mr. Duck continued to shout: "No! We will go to court!"

The more the duck insisted on going before the judge, the more Mr. Fox repeated how great a neighbor he had been in past years. The more they argued, the more nervously the Rabbit family hopped about, completing their tasks of the day. When it was clear that it was pointless for them to argue, the decision became final: the next morning they would go before the judge.

The quarreling ceased, and Mr. Duck felt a bit shaken by his own decision. He knew that the valley had once been filled with ducks and rabbits. All were farming plots of land. The ducks once had a bit of trouble with the rabbits digging up the turnips. The ducks were happy when Mr. Fox first moved into the valley, for he settled the dispute between the rabbits and the ducks.

With the sanction of the ducks, Mr. Fox confiscated the rabbits' land. He made them tenants on tiny plots. Of course, these actions increased the size of the Fox's plantation tremendously. He earned a bit of prestige among the ducks because he solved the rabbit problem. This made him powerful.

Solemnly, Mr. Duck weighed all of the events that had taken place. Over the past few years in the valley, one by one, a duck had quarreled with Mr. Fox, taken him to court, and then quietly moved away. Each time Mr. Fox's land increased. Now he owned nearly the entire valley except the farm next door, which Mr. Duck's family owned.

Oh yes, when the valley was filled with ducks they all had their individual differences with Mr. Fox. One by one they came to Mr. Duck. They asked him how he contended with Mr. Fox. He told them all that he had gotten along rather neighborly. Each duck had to walk away quacking about Mr.

Fox, and Mr. Duck had always remarked what a pleasure it was to have such a good neighbor.

Now as the dusk of the evening turned into darkness Mr. Duck began to have second thoughts about his decision. But could he change his mind? No! That he wouldn't do. He did feel that although no one really talked about Mr. Fox, everyone in the valley really knew of his deceitful ways. Mr. Duck pondered his case that evening. He realized that he had never gone to court before, but he felt that justice would prevail. He knew what he had to do: gather some witnesses. This would not be a matter of just his word against Mr. Fox's word.

So Mr. Duck pondered: who could be a character witness? Poor, poor, Mr. Duck! All of his fellow duck friends had moved far away from the valley. They had even stopped sending each other greetings. There was hardly any way that he would be able to find a fellow duck tonight for court tomorrow. But Mr. Duck had forgotten: Oh, he had a witness! Mr. Rabbit and his family had seen the fox stealing from his garden. Now immediately after the thought had entered his mind he went dashing out the door down the path for Mr. Rabbit's house.

The house was on a tiny plot of land that was only large enough to hold a tiny coop and a small garden. But Mr. Rabbit was one of the few rabbits that still owned a plot of land. It was surrounded by a high fence with a big latch on the gate. Mr. Duck wondered if he would be able to get to Mr. Rabbit's front door. He did not want to yell, for he knew that Mr. Fox would surely hear him. Mr. Duck said: "Oh, if I can only unlock the gate."

What seemed to be a blissful thought now was a worrisome event. Mr. Duck thought, "Why had Mr. Rabbit built such a tall fence? If only it were half the size I would be able to enter." But just as Mr. Duck gave a sad sigh Mr. Rabbit came out of his coop and yelled, "Who's at my gate?"

"Oh, it is I, Mr. Rabbit. Your friend, Mr. Duck. Yes, it is I, your old neighbor."

"Why are you here?"

"I need to discuss a legal matter with you."

"Oh, really," yawned the rabbit.

"Do you remember the argument you had with Mr. Fox a few years ago?" asked Mr. Duck.

"Can't say that I do; can't say that I don't," replied the rabbit.

"You don't remember!" shouted the duck.

"Oh, I can't say that I do, but I can't say that I don't."

With much persuasion Mr. Duck made Mr. Rabbit remember the incident. Mr. Rabbit told Mr. Duck that if he really thought he needed him at a later date he would be there but he was too busy the next morning mending his fence.

Mr. Duck refused to feel defeated. As he passed Mr. Fox's house he could see that he was entertaining a group of foxes. Mr. Duck thought again that maybe he should try to find some of his old duck friends to fill the galleries of the courtroom in the morning. Mr. Duck had not shared the details of the argument with his wife. But he rushed into the house and asked Mother Duck to prepare a big lunch, for early the next morning. The whole family would go to the courtroom.

It was a brilliant sunny morning, and Mother Duck woke to see a beautiful sunrise. They hurriedly dressed and strolled down the trail. All eyes and ears were on them. Mother Owl, who would usually be sleeping, was at the front door of her house. The trail was busy with travelers going about their daily chores. They all watched silently as the Duck family waddled down the trail.

They finally arrived at the door of the courthouse. When they entered, they saw a few of the seats taken. They went right up front. Mr. Fox was seated across from them. In a short while, in came the judge; he asked everybody to remain standing until the jury all came in. Now many others had arrived. Everyone was seated at the judge's request. When Mr. Duck observed the courtroom, he saw that the judge was a fox and the bailiff was a fox. The jury was comprised of twelve foxes, and most of the audience were foxes. Now only a few ducks

wondered what would happen to Mr. Duck's complaint against
Mr. Fox in a den of foxes.

– Sally Bill
July 1982

Gabriella M. Belfiglio

A Selection from
Unraveling the Yarn

Gabriella M. Belfiglio

Unraveling the Yarn is a series poem[1] tailored from traditional fairytales. I am fascinated by the illusive boundary between poetry and prose. Poetry is intimidating for many in a
way that a novel or short story or memoir is not. So many
times in my life I have heard: "Oh, I don't *get* poetry – I'd
rather read a story." The two are not exclusive!

While reading Italo Calvino's tales, which are based on traditional Italian oral stories, I was intrigued by his magical details and moods. I was reminded of a place and weight of language I often encounter in poetry. After reading Calvino's
"Rosemary," I was inspired to rewrite it as a poem. "Rosemary"
is about a plant that is human. It is a haunting tale, like so
many old children's stories. This experiment of merging fairy-
tale into poem ignited the spark that eventually lit the fire of
Unraveling the Yarn.

I started to read the narratives of the Grimm brothers: Jacob
and Wilhem. The more I read the more enchanted I became.
So much of their original tales is bizarre and gruesome, but by

---

[1] A series poem is made up of individual poems with a common thread.

the time most of us get a taste of their stories, they have been watered down and sugar coated. The memories of childhood stories, juxtaposed against the original Grimm tales, provided a framework for my own versions.

These poems form the collection, *Unraveling the Yarn.* I have selected several to share. I invite you now *not* to be intimidated by poetry, but instead to find the stories inside, between, and outside of the lines.

The Princess and the Pea

It's not so much that my bed was uncomfortable—
more that I was overtired from the storm and lonely
in this strange house, not to mention I was afraid
I might fall off the tower of mattresses under me.
And as I lay awake I heard through the walls the queen
and king arguing—something about what vegetables
to serve at dinner. When I finally fell asleep,
everything was in green. Sets of round green eyes
staring at me, a string of emeralds circling the queen's
thin neck. Even the drops of water from the faucet dripped
the color of grass into the large orbed pool of the sink.

Envy

At first I enjoyed the little house.
So different from my massive castle with
its walls full of mirrors and frigid stares.

But soon I got tired of doing all the dishes,
making all the beds, cooking every meal,
and I felt   so lonely.

The little men were gone all day and
once home they were exhausted and grumpy;
all they would do was sit by the fire, smoke their pipes.

Every day it was the same.
So when the old peddler woman came
with shiny new laces, I could not resist.

She reminded me of my sweet nursemaid,
who each morning would wrap me in beautiful colors:
ebony black to match my hair,

blood red to match my lips,
sky blue to match my eyes,
and snow white to match my skin.

The second time she came, I knew it had to be
another trick, but I wanted her attention,
and as she held the ivory comb in front of me

I couldn't recall the last time someone brushed my hair.
As she picked through my knots and curls—
I felt loved.

Days, weeks, months passed.
I dreamt of snowflakes like feathers,
a needle pricking a pregnant woman's finger,

the lung and liver of a slaughtered boar,
and always large eyes,   glaring.
The third time she came,

I was ready. She held the apple
so round on the platter of her hand.
I raised it to my teeth, my final thought: *at last.*

Aschenputtel

After the wedding, things started to fall apart.
My limbs were abandoned in the deep
vastness of my new berth.
I missed my snug bed by the fire.
The King's son only came to my chambers on clear nights
when the moon would blaze fire in the window.
He would arrive rigid—fierce—erase me inside his body.

Every time I tried to visit my mother's grave,
the King's son would stop me—
want to know where I was going, insist I not go
alone. At the palace it was worse,
I found I could not keep still.
It started with a little broom—sweeping up the fair
petals that would fall from the flowers round

my room—wee drops of snow
forming a sheet against the marble floor—
but soon the King's son caught me
on my hands and knees
scrubbing the courtyard stairs.
I could not help myself:
I got tired of sitting all day—static as stone.

I thought it would be better if I had a baby
to care for—but after our first I never had any time
to myself, and since I gave birth to our second,
I see how he looks away from me toward
all the pretty younger girls.
Besides, he always wants me to wear
those tiny golden slippers—

but my feet have swelled since the babies
and I can barely fit into   those cursed things.

The Briar Speaks

It was our period of glory.

    Everything became so quiet—no galling chatter

of humans, no jarring barks
                   of dogs, not even the buzz of a fly.

Only the subtle hum of our parents—sky and earth,

stretching   our   verdant vines,   plush flowers, and

      prickly thorns

   between   them   endlessly.

Oh! And our roses—petals soft as the feathers on a goose
        thick as the bark
        of the old oak,

   to speak of their colors does nothing.

   How can one explain the shades of sunrise?

Not pink, not orange

but a pool of both.

Fibers reflecting light,   whirling a

feral brilliance.

After the kingdom re-awakened,
we were once again tamed. Cut back.
Torn apart. Thorns carefully discarded.
Thousands of our precious flowers
scattered throughout the courtyard for
the princess' wedding day. Trampled on.
Left to fade.

Menarche

A cape made from the finest red velvet. Thick and gleaming.
Softer even than the luxurious fur of a leopard.
Her cape a giant rose petal.
Deep carmine like the viscid wine
her father drinks every night.

Everywhere the girl goes—she wears it.
To see the cape is to see the girl.
Folks got to calling her Red,
because each time she passes a blaze
is reflected in their eyes.

After Red finishes all of her daily chores,
she escapes to the forest. In a clearing,
surrounded by a spiky cerise wall of larkspur,
sure no one's watching, Red unhooks
the rings of scarlet thread that fasten her cape,

tenderly, frees the tiny ruby buttons,
resting against her slender neck
and lays the weighty cape onto a patch of green.
Delicately she touches it, first around its edges.
Soon moving to its center,

pushing harder and harder into the soft velvet.
Red's ache to be close to her cape grows.
It appears to her in the dark of her dreams.
A crimson river. She plunges inside—
her body all flow.

One day, Red's mother orders her to bring
her sick grandmother some supplies.
Red packs the basket herself:
Juicy slices of ripe tomato, smears of gooey rhubarb jam on
wedges of bread, and strips of fresh beef, newly slaughtered.

All morning Red's mother hovers over her
directing every move. "Don't forget to
turn right at the fork in the road, my plum."
Her mother nudges out the door to Red.
"I Know The Way Mother," she shoves back.

The sun was barely rising in the blushed sky.
The clammy air radiates heat.
Hungry, Red follows a trail
of wild strawberries off the path,
popping the sweet gritty treats into her mouth.

She soon meets a strange figure—a hairy fellow
with a smile stretched wide across his face.
"Little girl," he whispers, "what are you doing out here alone?"
"Little girl," he continues before she can answer, "from which
    way
did you come?" His pink tongue wets his swollen lips.

"Baby girl," he coos toward her, "Where are you going?"
His nefarious gaze seems to pry her
wide open. The bleeding bush of gladiolas
behind her begins to tremble.
Maybe it's just the wind, she thinks.

Red hides the luminous blooms she's gathered,
still wet with the morning dew, outside the heavy door
of her grandmother's house. The smell inside hits
even before the door is open, seeps out
of the cracks between the bricks.

It is sour, stale, akin to mildew, with something sweet,
lurking underneath. Red's grandmother is all huddled up
in that tall musty bed of hers—waiting. The first thing
she asks is, "What took you so long, child?"
Next: "Did you wipe that dirty clay off your feet, dear?"

Her mother's mother will soon want
to know what Red has brought her.
The old lady will ask her granddaughter to slice the meat
into small pieces—"Take that knife there on the counter,
and honey be careful now," she will insist,

"don't hurt yourself."
It has already been cut.
By the time Red returns to her parent's house
most of the petals have fallen off the flowers.
Now, in her hand, there are only naked twisted stems—

seeds exposed, palpable, awaiting.

Cinderella Washington DC 2004

There is no wicked stepmother. No weak father
who discards me—

> *The Prince asked, "Haven't you got another daughter?"*
> *"No," said the father "there is only a puny little*
> *kitchen drudge that my dead wife left me.*
> *She couldn't possibly be the bride."*

And just forget about the prince, right off.

Only a woman back from the ball—a drag ball—
women on stage dressed up like mini men twisting
hips, thrusting crotches full of cloth or plastic.

There *is* a fairy godmother. She is tall and blond,
like in the movies. She finds me in sneakers
and baggy jeans. A face tired from classes and
loneliness. She puffs me in sparkles—pulls from
her bag of tricks a slinky evening gown.

Before a room of strangers I bare myself.
I slip on the dress held up by strings thinner
than capellini, my prickly hip bones,
pliant tummy and wide thighs become
outlined in a delicate layer of sweetheart red.

She put on the dress with all speed, and went to the ball.
Her sisters however do not know her, and thought she
must be a foreign princess. They never once thought of
Cinderella, and believed she was sitting at home in the
dirt, picking lentils out of ashes.

I only have enough money for one drink,
which I consume too fast, willing my body
to relent like clay that starts stiff but
quickly softens with kneaded touch.

Cinderella danced till it was evening
and then she wanted to leave.
She slipped away so swiftly
that no one could follow her.

I retrieve my heavy bag of books and clothes from
the corner of the smoky club. The cold outside
creeps under my long skirt, encompassing me.
My jacket pocket holds the number of a woman

I will never call—the dark ink sinking
into the torn white napkin. I rush to the subway,
grateful that I left my sneakers on
beneath the gown.

Once down the tower of stairs
I find out I have missed the last train home.
The squeals of the subway have silenced
and I stand on the empty platform, at a loss.

And here the story ends.
No lost shoe. No royal wedding.
No happily ever after.

Princene Hyatt

To Cousin Allene Moody-Harley
Dillon, South Carolina, 1930's–40's

Princene Hyatt

Dear Allie,

I was thrilled to spend my 75th birthday and Mother's day with you and yours. Sunday, May 13th, 2007, was perfect for celebrating; several days of unseasonably cold rain had disappeared. Blue sky with bright sun and gentle breezes lifted my spirits for the occasion. Dinner in Lumberton was exceptional in many ways – thanx to Anna.

Your children are always such good company; they inherited the Moody sense of humor. Also, fortunately they were born into a family where kindness and caring is practiced. All the effort you and your husband put into making sure your twelve children graduated from high school really paid off leading to higher education. It is good to see them pass along to their own children the same guidance received from you and K.D. Your grandchildren will be able to create a lifestyle of their choice – rather than settle for whatever comes along.

I loved the family update quiz! It was very impressive, all their accomplishments, including pictures and reports from newspapers. I expect to see a lot more in the future, especially if *second mother* – Big Sister Patricia has anything to say about it.

Before I was allowed to visit your house, I was totally fascinated by the twelve Moody children.

As an only child I was extremely lonely and sad. I was a burden placed on folk who did not deserve huge responsibility dumped in their laps. Ma and her oldest sister – who the family called "Sista" shared the old family house. Both were already on *overload* before I was born.

Ma had been widowed when she was seven months pregnant with her seventh child, my mother Sue Lacy. Sista, who had no children, told me when she last saw her husband he was "totin' a jug o' White Lightnin' over his shoulder." Life had been a lot less than easy for descendants of former slaves.

Yet, by some miracle there was love of family, friendship and lots of laughter going on at your house. Friendly exchanges and joyful moments very seldom happened at Ma's. She did not tolerate noise in her house and disapproved of anybody who did. After she beat me, she quickly shut me up – with the lie – "I din' hurtchu, stop all dat noise!" The place was filled with Ma's insanity. Even the air couldn't move; it just sort of hung heavy and stagnant from the ceilings of the big, overstuffed house. Only when necessary did one speak – except Ma – who bitched and moaned constantly, about everybody, everything and nothing.

Sista cooked at a boarding house. Every night we waited anxiously, quietly, listening for the sound of her footsteps on the porch. She brought leftovers from supper and the local newspapers home from work.

Thankfully, she also brought what I needed most–spoken words! She always read out loud, "Jo Jo Says." A sort of philosopher/spiritual advisor, Jo Jo was a monkey. I recall this entry:

> *No room in the inn – poor guest turned away*
> *Lord forgive our sins – abide with us today.*

Every detail of life in the white folks' world seemed like such
big, important news to our very narrow, very boring, demanding existence. Who said What to Whom, and When – was a
stage show for me! I visualized the whole scene–faces, places,
body language – every minute detail!

In reality – if I dared put together a few words – just to com-
municate, I was promptly told, "nobody is talking to you."

In contrast, Allene, your house vibrated with activity!
Voices big and small were free to speak.

On holidays your older siblings drove home from the North
to visit. Sometime there would be two cars – filled with cama-
raderie. Your cousins, friends, and neighbors all gathered to
enjoy bid whist and each other. Ma was annoyed with voices
expressing themselves. I suspect she was really jealous. She had
no friends. I was excited with all the activity and stayed as close
to Dargan Street as possible.

If Ma saw me enjoying anything, she made work for me to
do – like the time you were all playing ball in the street. Ma
was on the Ninth Avenue side of the front porch. I hoped it
would be safe to stoop out of her sight, on the far side of the
house. I could at least learn the game, or so I thought. While
pretending to go in the smokehouse, she caught me watching;
and made me take Topsy, the cow, grazing on the opposite side
of the house away from the game. Normal, joyful activity was
forbidden. Her favorite comment was, "dem ol' laze yun'uns
oughta be workin!"

I took my frustration out on the helpless animal, jerking her
head with the chain – like my problem was her fault.

Pain must go somewhere –
that was the only way I knew to express it.

My grandmother, who I called Ma or Mama, and your father were sister and brother. They were so very different. Ma
made a show of being religious by keeping up appearances in
church.

Your family made no such pretenses. Ma was a closet alcoholic, her brother David's drinking was no secret.

I remember your father was a specialty cook and butcher as well. One winter, your brother Albert was home to help him with Ma's hogs. Together they were a comedy team; they never stopped joking and laughing! Ma couldn't shut them up like she could me, so she made an effort to lighten up, to enjoy the jokes with her brother and nephew. I was so glad to be there when joy and laughter replaced the ever-present gloom that lived in Ma's backyard. I felt so-o good, like a living, breathing member of the human race!

You will recall, Allie, times were hard back then. Many were hungry. Ma had so-o-o much food with only two of us to eat it. Aside from her profession as midwife, she was also a farm wife; highly skilled in all areas involving food. While she no longer had a large family to feed, her old survival habits never changed. In addition to her own garden she would barter for any open land in the neighborhood. Ma loved to fish. She dried and/or salted certain kinds for winter.

She picked berries to make jams and jellies, canned fruit, cured pork, banked sweet potatoes, made wine, churned butter – you name it! She had much too much food and no need for it.

Canned items aged and were no longer edible. Cured pork went bad, sweet potatoes rotted, fresh butter turned rancid, veggies dried on the vine. Pigs and chickens were often fed with excess.

Neighbors came over sometime when they needed fresh eggs, buttermilk, or whatever. If they brought a nickel or dime to pay – Ma gave and gave – yet, she never offered, even to her beloved brother – and his large family across the street.

What I heard in church was about feeding the hungry
What did Mama hear – I wonder????

One summer day just after school closed, Miss Ruth Jackson walked over to ask Mama if I could work for her. Like most working southerners – she came home for dinner at 12 noon. Her mother, Miss Annie could have been at least a hundred years old; she might forget to cook. So, at age eleven, I had my first job. Three dollars a week was good pay! Sue Lacy was paid two fifty a week for cooking and washing. All of a sudden I was grown! I had a grown up job for the summer, earning grown up money!

My very first pay turned out to be a down payment toward my freedom. Sue Lacy claimed motherhood and ownership. "Mama, Print-cene's *my* child and oughta be bringin' ME hur money!"

"Wha chu ever dun fur uh?" Ma asked. "I brout ur tuh dis worl" was Sue's answer. They went on and on for several minutes. As Ma put my three dollars on the kitchen table, she declared, "Here, tak hur money and tak hur too! Um don' trinnuh raise hur up to be 'somebody'! Go hed on – um done widhur! Lethur be a tramp lik 'er mammy!"

That's when I was allowed to visit your house, Allie. Sue couldn't care less where I went, as long as I brought my money home to her – and stayed out of her sight.

Finally – I found out how to get my mother's attention.
She often sang about greenback dollar bills.

I loved going to work. There was a lot more to see three blocks down on Main Street. The Jacksons were friendly people. For decades Miss Annie was the neighborhood seamstress until her eyes gave out. She and I picked peas, beans or whatever from the garden together. We shelled them for dinner while gliding ourselves along in the big, old, wooden, double contraption on the front porch.

I had watched others cook and basically knew how. What I didn't know was how to measure, or guesstimate. Quite often I made too much biscuit dough. I threw the extra out the kitchen window for the chickens to eat so nobody would know. Every day I walked two or three blocks downtown to buy meat or something for dinner from Piggly Wiggly. On the way back I treated myself to ten cents from the grocery money for a double dip at the drug store.

"Life was so-o-o good!"

Before the summer ended Miss Ruth asked me if I ever saw her mama let anybody have money. "Money goes awful fast," she said.

That was so kind – the way she handled it. Many colored
people had their lives destroyed for petty theft.

I cut back some on the ice cream. Peach, strawberry, orange, and pineapple will always be my favorites. I still look
forward to enjoying them every summer!

Visits to your house, Allene, made my existence across the
street bearable. Looking back, I'm sure I wore out my welcome, but it was never mentioned. You and I were always
friends. We never allowed nonsense to make a difference between us. Do you remember making me a broomstick skirt –
black polished cotton with white eyelet trimming? You were
always the smart one, doing everybody's hair, helping neighbors
with homework. You even played basketball while still earning
top grades.

Bet you don't remember teaching me French: *Bonjour*
Mademoiselle, commen je suis contente de vous voir, comment
allez-vous? Je vais tres bien, merci, et vous? Tres bien, merci –
vous avez une mine superbe!

I loved learning new things!

Our recent week together was great fun as usual! Revisiting
the past is always a pleasant experience somehow. Your memory is better than mine, maybe because you never left the area.

I was shocked and saddened to find you living behind locked
doors like we do here in the North.

Drugs absolutely destroy the quality of life. It's hard to believe there are no cab drivers anymore.

Tell Deborah THANKS for me. I have no idea what I
would have done without her and Pat to drive me around.

Love to all,
Princene

P.S. Give my best to Ruth Tadlock and family.

To Eubulus Latham Marsh
Assistant Principal
Mather Academy, Camden, South Carolina,
1945–1951

Princene Hyatt

Dear Mr. Marsh,

The pretty southern town, the middle class private school, seemed worlds away from my beginnings in September 1945. I was not welcomed. Emotionally disturbed children are very seldom, if ever, welcome anywhere – especially when they are obviously from the bottom of the socio-economic barrel. I always pretended not to notice how people looked past me, to avoid eye contact. PRETEND was a survival tactic. Fantasize to escape painful reality. PRETEND it never happened, perhaps it will go away. Pain must go somewhere. It has a physical presence. It shows up in many disguises.

You may remember me. I sometime visited your house with your wife and children. I didn't have to be invited – I just showed up at the door. I had no social skills and was a loner. Aloneness is instilled from birth in many dysfunctional families. Socialization is forbidden, for fear of exposing family secrets. Besides, if given a choice, who would choose to spend their leisure time with a loser? On more than one occasion fellow students told me to stay away from them – they couldn't socialize with me. I looked mostly like an orphan who was left to fend for myself against the world.

This letter is to let you know what a major role you played in turning my life around. Our regular teacher, Coach McGirt, I think, was absent that day; you covered the period by speaking to the class. The subject was what to expect at college.

To paraphrase: Philosophy would be especially challenging to young minds who would need to question their own belief system. Did they, or did they not, believe in the existence of God – as most of us had been taught?

Well-informed, well-spoken students had a rather heated exchange with you regarding principles of being, truth, logic, etc. I was shocked! However, I was a curious child who once asked my aunt, the Sunday school teacher, "How do you know there is a God?"

I was maybe five or six years old and my own existence was in question.

Fast-forward to 1976, 25 years after high school – I enter intensive psychotherapy looking to put an end to my unhappiness. I am bringing my friend Eva up to date on what has happened so far in my quest. I hear myself say that I internalized what Mr. Marsh told us years ago:

You can do anything if you want to badly enough.

I have also said that while I was exposed to a well-rounded academic education, I was too overwhelmed to absorb nearly as much as was offered. Yet, miraculously, when something was said that I needed to hear, I was listening.

Thank you so very much for planting the seed.

Sincerely,
Princene Hyatt

P.S. You were right about philosophy – it does challenge the established.

To Catherine White
Mather Academy
Class of 1946

Princene Hyatt

Dearest Catherine,

You were the first RAY OF SUNSHINE to touch my pathetic thirteen-year-old life at Mather High School in 1945. While others laughed at, bullied and avoided me, you befriended me – allowing me to enter into your circle of friends and roommates.

When fully realizing my sad state of existence, relative to the group, I began making up lies that I thought would make me seem just a little bit "less of a loser." For example, your father was a Captain and, I believe, Chaplain in the army. My uncle was also in the army; his rank was Private First Class. A staff member was writing to her husband when I noticed Staff Sergeant on the envelope and rightfully assumed it was a higher rank than PFC. I used that lie to seem just a little "more than mud."

You were so much fun for all of us – your roommates, friends and me, the "outsider." You taught us to dance. I had been forbidden to dance when I was maybe three years old.

Remember how the floor turned white in the center? We danced so-o much!

Most importantly – you taught me songs to sing. You owned stacks of sheet music; and knew every word of every song, and its history – ever published in the English language. Life would never be the same again once I was exposed to jazz, pop, blues, classical, opera and so forth. My world expanded with every song. What a wonderful experience! When school was over for the summer, and I was back home on my way to work, I sang non-stop – like I would burst! For whatever reason nobody shut me up!

After you graduated Miss Wallace, Miss Wigham, Miss Bryan and others were saying that I, too, had a special soprano voice. It was much like yours. But, also like you – I had been much too traumatized in early childhood and lacked the necessary confidence to share my voice with the world. Perhaps I will in my next lifetime.

After high school I moved to New York City and contacted my father for the first time. He was a tenor, and his agent led him to believe he was about to become world-famous. It never happened.

Kindness gives the downtrodden a faint glimpse of hope – a shimmer of possibility. Thank you for the enormous lesson you taught me by not further trampling on a troubled teen in an unfriendly environment, a highly rated boarding school sponsored by women of the Methodist Church.

One favorite motto of yours was:

> *Give to the world the best that you have,*
> *and the best will come back to you.*

I sincerely hope this happened for you and yours.

With love and gratitude,
Princene

Note: My plan was to find Catherine, take her to lunch, and say all of the above in person. When I inquired, I was told she had passed on.

To Gloria Conyers
Mather Academy
1950-1951

Princene Hyatt

Dear Gloria,

In the mid-nineties while waiting at the train station in Florence, I noticed several young people wearing tee shirts that read: CONYERS FAMILY REUNION. I started thinking – I could look you up and explain just how I came to destroy our friendship. It was not intentional. Friends are treasures. Who are we – who would we be – without our friends?

I was supposed to be the "lookout" – listening and watching for signs of oncoming traffic. As I stood looking out the window, my mind wandered off – as it often did – to some other time and place. I didn't hear or see Miss Carson approaching. When I did hear her, I was crippled by a panic attack. I could not utter a single sound. As I struggled to speak, to warn you, she walked past me and saw you two. When I gained some sort of mobility I walked out behind her – which looked as if I was as surprised as she was to see you and Charles in each other's arms.

You trusted me to look out for you. I let you down. It was a very sad day in my life. Although I had known about my impairment since the third grade, I could not admit to you or anyone else that I was mentally incompetent. I chose instead to cover myself with a ridiculous, impossible lie – that I warned you. I did not! I could not!

> *Real truth was not even a vague notion in my life at that time.*
> *At this time, truth is everything.*

I can say now what I couldn't say then: I was so-o relieved and overjoyed that you were not sent home over the incident. (Faculty suspended me when they were told I kissed a guy, although they didn't catch me in the act.)

Looking back, I'm sure it was common knowledge on campus that I came from a mentally ill background. Our family doctor, one of my many mentors, was the first and only one who ever had the courage to tell me the absolute truth about my family history of insanity. I am deeply, deeply grateful to him for my progress in recovery.

Hoping life has been good to you and yours.

Sincerely,
Princene

To Mary Ellen Phifer
Chairperson, Education Committee
Brooklyn C.O.R.E.
Early 1960's

Princene Hyatt

Dearest Mary Ellen,

Forty years ago you were widely known and highly respected in Brooklyn's Congress of Racial Equality where you headed the Education Committee. You knew the Board of Education's rules and regulations thoroughly, much more even, than their own principals. You constantly used that knowledge to fight for the rights of our children.

You were a single parent, caring for six sons – including twins – all by yourself. Then, quite unexpectedly, concerns for family brought you further challenges, adding two more children to your immediate family, for love and care. Those who knew and loved you were very concerned, they couldn't believe you would get involved in this monumental undertaking, but you did. That's just how remarkable you are!

While Mary fought battles in New York City schools, her
sons kept watch in the streets.
When young male children were picked up by police, her
boys ran home to tell their mother.
At any hour of the night in all kinds of weather this work-
ing mother of eight presented herself to the local precinct to
inquire – to question, "Officer, what is he charged with;
why is he being arrested?"
Law enforcement knew her well! Once I recall an officer
shook his finger in her face, shouting – "NOW DON'T
YOU START!" But Mary's vigilance had already started
and could not be stopped!

What an enormous message of caring this sends to young
children as they accompany their mother on a mission, in her
nightgown to confront "BIG BLUE." To speak for those who
have no voice – from nowhere. Talk about above and beyond!

Mary, you are the Good Samaritan I learned about in Sunday school. Never, even in my dreams, would I expect to meet
a real live human being of your stature!

I have come to know the Phifer Family quite well. Your exceptional qualities were passed down to your children and are
reflected in their lifestyles. They trust you because you are
trustworthy. And just because you brought them into this
world you do not consider them your property, to be traded in
at will, nor slaves – i.e., "do as I say, not as I do." You respect
them as individuals. In return they respect you. Love is very
present in your home, Mary. I feel it whenever visiting with
you guys.

After your children grew into adulthood, you remarried.
We loved your husband Randy – just as we love you; he was a
sweetheart; we miss him. Once, back in the mid 80's, I made
your favorite Italian spaghetti dish and invited the two of you
for dinner. I took the liberty of letting you know how much I
admired and respected you both, as truly devout Christians. I
was not; and, used that opportunity to inform you that I did
not belong to any organized religion. Why?

I had been brought up by hypocrites, who preached one thing, yet practiced quite another. I did not choose to be who they were; nor did I choose to stand under the same banner labeled CHRISTIAN with child abusers and molesters, racists, war mongers, rapists, and others I could name. YES: they were all good Christians in the Bible Belt where I grew up. All one need do was announce: "God called me last night, he told me___ ___ ___." (You fill in the blanks.) Such proclamation gave one status. Divine Right was a power play to be used, whenever. Although the announcement was suspect to most, they pretended to accept the revelation to one's face, then laughed and ridiculed them behind their back. These were the Christians I came to know in church where I went every Sunday from the time I was "potty trained," to learn how one conducted one's "good Christian" life – or so I thought.

What kind of message does such behavior send to very young children? It was not only disturbing; it was dishonest. I was filled with questions and no answers. Was it at all possible that the concept of Christianity was completely misunderstood? Could it be that biblical language was confusing, therefore misleading? I wonder. Or, was this one of many experiences I could have lived without? I'm sure it is. Very sure.

I was very impressed with the experience you recalled, Mary, regarding a long distance bus trip you took with your five-year-old. You could have saved a few much-needed dollars if he had been a year younger, but then in your son's mind there could have been questions such as: *Why am I four today, if I was five yesterday?* Children need clarity, not confusion, in order to grow up knowing, for sure, who they are. I applaud your decision to pay his full fare as charged.

Truthfulness can never be overstated in my opinion. It is freedom for the complete being: mind, body and spirit.

I was not fortunate to learn that lesson at an early age, like your children. I was fully adult – on a journey to reclaim my authentic self – when my truth was uncovered and identified. It was buried in the family plot – in several places – each under six feet of crippling lies.

Congressman Major Owens and Borough President Marty Markowitz are not the only ones who "sing your praises," Mary Ellen. I've never spoken to a C.O.R.E. person who didn't "think the world" of you. All my friends have to listen to me brag about – my friend Mary – who I first came to know as a dedicated SUPER MOM with a HUGE HEART. We became personal friends quite by chance at Sears cafeteria where we continuously ran into each other having lunch on Saturdays.

I was real happy when you invited me to visit in your new North Carolina home. I was born and grew up just next door, in South Carolina. One would think it was a foreign country. The culture is as different as night and day. It must be something in the drinking water.

I appreciate the role model and family you are to me, Mary. I never had these positive influences in my early life. You are one of my biggest supporters, having bought several pieces of my artwork, while also lending me a helping hand in any way possible. But I am proud to know and boast about "my friend Mary" – because of your extraordinary character – your tireless, fearless dedication to the struggle for social change.

So, in March of 2007 – Women's History Month – I honor my friend – Mary Ellen Covington-Phifer-Kirten as my personal, real live, phenomenal WOMAN OF THE YEAR.

With All My Heart,
Princene

Note: Presented to Mary Ellen in person at Brooklyn Society For Ethical Culture on March 25, 2007.

To Robert Michaels
Significant Other From 1965 to 1973

Princene Hyatt

My Dearest Bob,

We closed the Nitecap. You and your friends took me to an after hours "watering hole" where we had additional, unnecessary drinks. That should have been a signal – "CAUTION – proceed at your own risk." You dropped me off at my place in a cab. We kissed goodnight. It was no longer night. It was a new day, the beginning of an eight-year relationship between you – me – and booze.

Two years later, in 1967, we moved in together. I became aware that you were never without a drink and a cigarette within your reach. Your habit of always making two drinks – no matter that I said, "none for me," was a clear indication that you needed a drinking partner. It was hard to watch you ignore your health. When I mentioned the subject your response was always, "look what I would miss if I give up my drinking and chain smoking – got really healthy – then got hit by a truck!" Drinking with you was way, wa-y more than my mind, body, and spirit could handle.

Why was I a participant for so long?

I was born into and grew up in a situation that demanded sacrifices. My teenage mother worked as housekeeper and cook for her widowed mother. She was not paid, although there were boarders in the house. She had no choice. She traded her labor for a place to call home for herself and her child.

My maternal aunt had plans to adopt me. She bought me everything. I was an investment. My grandmother said, in her dialect, "You so lucky tuh hav people look afta you, take care o' you. Pleny people don' hav nobody, no hom – nothin'!"

What price would I pay for being taken care of?

My aunt would tell me, "Listen and obey what grown people tell you. Don't you dare sass me. Say nothing – except thank you. Stand up straight. Look at me. Don't get dirty. Stop squinting." How many choices does a toddler get from such demands?

(Behave like a DOLL. Don't ever go anywhere near your own feelings, thoughts, opinions. Give up everything that could possibly resemble your true self. Sacrifice one hundred fifty percent of your soul. Do exactly as you are told.)

NOW, after doing exactly what you're told during your formative years: STAND UP, SPEAK OUT, CHOOSE WHATEVER YOU WANT AND NEED FROM LIFE!

Some might argue, but you're no longer two, you're thirty-two. No matter – once you've thoroughly learned a behavior, you own it. And you are very likely to repeat it should similar situations occur in your life. It has its own permanent place in your psyche.

I was first attracted to you because you were very funny. I love to laugh. Our neighbors and friends loved your quick, witty, colorful, comments, along with your generous supply of alcoholic beverages.

No one ever loved me as much as you Bob, but at the same time you were destroying me. Alcohol is a downer, it makes me feel physically drained and psychologically down. It takes away my joy!

PARAGORIC, an over-the-counter opium-based product used to control children during my childhood, had the same effect on me as a toddler. It not only robbed me of my energy, but it sapped my true feelings as well. Can you see how you fit perfectly into the blueprint created by my folks?

Do you remember knocking on the bathroom door, asking, "Is everything was all right, Babe?" I had been out of your sight for too long. You were quite possessive, jealous of everybody, including my girlfriends. You would interrupt a visit or stop me from socializing without you whenever possible, always needing to share my space, hold me close.

Just like my aunt, you were very generous, Bob.

Aunt Annie had those same needs – to smother, hold on tight, afraid I might notice I could breathe on my own. And maybe even discover my own wonderful worlds to embrace – without her.

We were friends a long time, Bob. We honestly shared our severely crippled lives with each other. You were a good person. I loved you yet, was never in love with you and would not marry you for that reason. I said as much and would not let you believe otherwise.

Since we went our separate ways I've often thought of you and have surely missed the fun times of our relationship. When we met I didn't know the first thing about how to live a meaningful life. I didn't even know the right questions to ask. What did I need to be fulfilled? What was happiness? Had it knocked on my door and introduced itself, I would not have recognized it – and I would have said, "try next door."

I now know considerably more about who I am, and I would not trade my new consciousness for anything I have ever seen or heard of on this planet. I needed to learn to love myself, listen to and honor the dictates of my body, not abuse it. I needed to feel good enough to enjoy my life and the many simple pleasures that appear out of nowhere: on the street, in the park; like the laughter of a happy child, the smiling face of a stranger, like a playful puppy, brilliant colors, flowers, trees, music.

It has been probably twenty-five years since I last drank alcohol and maybe twelve years since I won my battle with nicotine. For three decades I've searched for self and found true feelings and real needs. I became a counselor, a teacher, a fabric artist and lived long enough to write about it. I need to be proud of who I am!

It is my sincere hope that you are enjoying the happiness you deserve.

Love you always,
Princene

To Carol Westfall
Artist/Professor/Mentor
Teachers College, Columbia University
1977-1978

Princene Hyatt

Happy New Year, Carol!

Congratulations on your very successful career. I have followed your work since becoming familiar with the Internet. I remember your spending Christmas vacation in India, studying their wonderful textile methods. You have earned and deserve it all. ENJOY!

Soon after I registered at Columbia University in 1975, I became aware of some special somewhere – place? person? subject? Something in that academic setting was reaching out to me; I had to find it! Whenever I walked thru campus I felt the same presence – picked up the same energy. A fellow student introduced me to Teachers College. The Graduate School offered interesting "hands on" courses.

Nothing really SPOKE to me until one evening, Spring 1977, we all sat waiting for our instructor. She rushed through the door like Santa Claus – loaded down with beautiful handmade baskets and bags filled with all kinds of notions. There were wonderful wooden beads in many colors, and threads, and raw wool, and yarns and needles of all sizes and shapes for every conceivable task. There were vegetable dyes, and "this and that" to keep a class busy and exciting! Following her was a young woman, an advanced student, Theresa, who was equally loaded down with "what have you" – for creating unique handmade items!

> *As a fiber artist, Carol presented herself as such. She was wearing a long, wrap, batik skirt with a white peasant blouse, a very colorful silk headscarf and dangling earrings. She wore a most unusual large, rectangular silver ring, in which sat a flat stone that appeared to be baked, brown mud or maybe chocolate? It was so-o striking, in a class by itself – just like its owner. (Why didn't I ask her about her ring??? I was so-o disconnected!)*
>
> *I had found that special somewhere – place, person, and subject!!!*

The class was all-consuming, fast-paced, I could barely keep up, but then – I was always a "slowpoke." Field trips to New York City art gallery exhibits introduced me to the world of Art and Design. It was completely foreign and totally fascinating! I had moved to the Capital of my world immediately after high school. There was always opportunity for expanding horizons, but this was different – it stimulated my enormous curiosity.

My final project for the class Fabric and Fiber was three yards of batik from recycled cotton. It was not a wise decision. My tiny kitchen could only comfortably allow me to indulge in hand sewing; it was hardly ideal to mix dyes, melt and apply hot wax, air dry, iron wax out on newspaper non-stop for three days, then start all over again.

Twenty-four hours before final showing – my finished product was a disaster, a non-entity. Colors could barely be seen – they were so-o pale! I was beyond devastated!

As usual, when I came face to face with crises I took to the streets. Grabbing my jacket I ran down three flights of stairs and around the corner before I remembered to breathe. After wandering aimlessly for some time, I bought a package of brown Rit Dye. Up to this point I had used only vegetable dyes. How did I know to choose this particular item? It was instinct – it worked – somewhat! At least my colors of light blue and mauve were visible to the naked eye. My piece was terribly boring; I didn't know it at the time. I had no understanding of that ancient, very ambitious craft.

Several students were told they had artistic potential; I was not one of them, and wished I had been. Yet, I was proud of my efforts. I learned something important about myself; I enjoyed working with my hands.

Carol, when we first met I had just taken the first step toward turning my life around in one of the new psychotherapies of the '60s and '70s, (which – initially – made me even more confused). Today, some thirty years later, I am proud to report I am richly rewarded for my efforts. I know what you tried to tell me about my work all these years. Having seen my limited skills in spring of '77, you were certain this new effort in Autumn '78 was not 10x10 patchwork squares for the quilt we agreed I'd make. They were fabric collages telling my life story! You always called my work a "gift"!

I applaud your insight, honesty, and knowledge.

The Independent Study was a much-needed extension to my therapy. While I learned to speak about my painful past in group sessions, at the same time I began to share my life with others thru creativity. Emotions with tremendous need for a voice found a way to express themselves – to speak and be heard – thru recycled neckties. (I was not allowed to speak freely as a child; "children should be seen and not heard" was a common belief where I grew up.)

Interesting – neckties like girdles are restrictive by design.

Your reaction was a complete shock to me on that final night of class. I had mixed feelings being the center of attention – having the class hear your evaluation and A+ you gave me. I had tremendous fear of compliments; they had been turned against me in the past. Yet, at the same time I was elated! My wish had come true! I was going to Art School!

Until life stepped up – with other plans.

I was not able to take your advice and graduate from Pratt – School of Art and Design. I only studied there for one semester. Years later I earned a B.A. in a completely different concentration. I was terrified of success, from early childhood trauma. I sold several pieces against your better judgment. Your advice was to KNOW the work before selling.

My therapy is a work in progress; without it I would always be severely crippled. With it, I will continue to heal. I can't tell you Carol, just how proud I am to find myself in this place where I find myself – at this stage of my life. I just don't have the necessary verbal skills.

Thank you, Carol for encouraging me over the many years since we met. Thank you also for putting up with my CRAZIES. I am well aware of being the pain you could have lived a hundred years without. Remember the caftans/cover-ups I made? How telling – or not telling – that was!

At midnight New Year's Eve I walked down to Brooklyn Heights Promenade to greet 2008 along with fireworks. In 1988 I gathered enough courage to show my complete body of work there by the River, in a juried exhibition. It marked another turning point in my life. My friend Janet hung the work and sat with me for support. My friend John was the photographer. It took me ten years to expose my work to whatever feedback came my way.

None of this could have happened without you, Carol.

Wishing you and yours the best of health and happiness in 2008 – and always.

Gratefully,
Princene

Morning Glory
(Title of Book Cover Art)

Princene Hyatt

The artwork that appears on the cover of this book was created during my happy period when my hopes were high, pending exposure to the Internet.

Notes in my journal from this time read:

> *This AM I finished my fun piece: I call it* Morning Glory. *How would I have survived without the beautiful surroundings – on the outside – I have no idea. There was constant talk of flowers among our neighbors. I am very, very pleased with this piece.*
>
> *– March 1996*

Wire fencing enclosed the backyard and garden. In summer it was a delight, loaded down with lovely, climbing flowers that opened every morning. There were other tall beauties: hollyhocks, gladiolus, and sunflowers the size of dinner plates. In addition to flower, I am reminded of the very big, very old grapevine. It had a base of black, crusty limbs that would fill a small room and was enclosed and supported by heavy, grey, metal pipes and poles. I very often spent time underneath, in the shade, amidst heavy sweet smells of ripening purple grapes, trying to entertain myself. I had all my stuff and my imaginary playmates. No warm, breathing, feeling, human beings, just lots of THINGS intended to impress the neighbors and me.

Yes! I was bought and sold at birth.

Unconditional love, if indeed there was such a ting, certainly did not exist for me. I desperately needed all the flowers, fruit trees, greens, beans, figs, pecans – all the growing, breathing, aliveness in the yard. They were the only real truth. They were all I had in my whole wide world to brighten my day and accept my existence. My journal reads:

> *After hanging my new piece* – Morning Glory, *I thought it was my lovely ribbons and hair that Ma destroyed.*
>
> *– April 1996*

My very first memory of hair is how my head hurt and how I cried when my mother, Sue Lacy, combed it. She kept saying, "I ain' hurtin' you!" When I kept on crying – she hit me on my arm with the comb. She said I was tender headed with thick hair. The next thing I remember is how it hurt to have it rolled up to make Shirley Temple curls. I had to sleep in curlers all night; they made my head sore. Next morning, Sunday, my mother brushed my hair out over her hand, then rolled it into big, fat curls. Afterwards, I always climbed up on the dressing table to look in the mirror. I patted my curls softly. They were pretty.

Neighbors passing by kept saying, "She got pretty hair, Sue Lacy." She always replied, "She got hair like her daddy."

Little colored girls couldn't wear curls very often; their hair stayed plaited for the most part to keep it neat. One Easter Monday when I was maybe three or four I convinced Sue Lacy to tie my hair in ribbons. She tied pretty ribbons at the base of all my curls–which left them loose. I thought I looked like a BIG girl with my hair loose. I was happy!

But happiness was not allowed in Ma's house if she had anything to do with it. She was hoeing in the garden while keeping watch over me. Ma saw me enjoying my ribbons by slinging my head from side to side in typical small child behavior. She came in for a cold drink of water and said, "brime da sussors so I 'an cut– cho hair." I was stunned, shocked, scared out of breath!

Remembering the story of Samson, from Sunday school or somewhere in church, I was absolutely terrified I would lose all my strength. At that young age, I believed whatever was said in church was true and applied to me. As I ran around like a chicken without a head, looking for scissors, I kept saying to myself, "Oh no, Oh no, I'll lose all my strength! Oh no!" I didn't dare say nothing to Ma.

Aunt Annie came in through the back yard. Ma didn't notice. Seeing my hair all over the kitchen floor, Aunt Annie had a fit. She hollered, "How com' u cuttin' off all 'er hair?"

Ma was stunned. She gasped, then quickly lied, "She cain't have no brains wid all dis hair!"

"It'a gro' bac," she added as she gently stroked my head, pretending she meant me no harm by cutting off my hair. After all, it was for my own good.

Rita REB Wilson

Kin

Rita REB Wilson

The joy of sisterhood offers hope in the time of despair,
Especially when our young sisters are hollering, "act like you
    just don't care."

Allegiance with sisterhood gives glowing expectations,
it is the center of being in good relations.
Sisterhood is kinship and it binds us with love and forgiveness,
So, when lyrics blast, "act like you just don't care,"
Know that love and forgiveness erase despair.

The joy of sisterhood offers faith when doubt wants a home;
it's a challenge to evict doubt, put a strong mantra in place....
    "Be gone, Be gone!"
Connections for common causes will sometimes be unspoken;
The relationship stands steadfast for positive proclamation,
Honoring the young and our ancestors that helped to build this
    nation.
Standing on the shoulders of those before
keeps the sisterhood strong and in the "know."

Reach and Touch

Rita REB Wilson

You reach for my hand and touch it with kindness and appreciation
You're glad that I'm here,
It electrifies a connection, we're glad we are here.

You reach and touch me with a warm sensation, it triggers excitement
With a comfort zone,
It engages delightfulness, you make it easy for me to be with you.

You reach and touch me where words are lackened,
The vast or huge megabytes can't be measured,
You ignite fire that I hold and treasure.

You reach and touch me with love and tenderness,
My mind gallops off for a future caress.
It's grand and splendid when you reach and touch,
It simply means so much.

Your reach and touch crystallizes music for my ears,
Be it Aretha's *Call Me* or Stevie's *I Just Called
To Say I Love You*
I hold your reach and touch very near and dear,
I'm in your arms, they have comfort, they have relaxation.

I wanna stay close, the connection is magnificent and blissful.

the look on your face

Rita REB Wilson

the look on your face

tells me my behavior is in bad taste.

i was just laughing at Sister Lee,

i didn't know you could see me.

she was sleeping and slobbering at the mouth.

forgot all about that she was in god's house.

now i'm caught laughing at her, got you upset,

i'm in trouble, this is something i regret.

the look on your face,

sends a message that i'm saved by grace.

i was just sleeping during the sermon to the young,

i did wake up before the last song was sung.

no use sitting in the back pew,

there were ushers and aunt janie to keep you on cue.

caught sleeping, yet quite ready to respond,

could tell what happened and what went on.

the look on your face,

made me know that i was in a good place.

the love was there without the say so,

you were happy when i became the editor of "The Echo"

the look on your face kept me in line,

taught me to be gracious and refined.

never lost it and perhaps not use it often,

i send gratitude for the here, now, and past,

i got much for a future that will last,

even if i don't use it often,

i still holdfast.

Olivia S. Taylor

The Frozen Flower

Olivia S. Taylor

It was a frigid Monday morning at the end of April, not March. Mable Morrison stood outside of her home on the corner of Chestnut Street, waiting for the bus that would take her to the Morningside Senior Citizen's Center. *Spring had sprung well over a month ago,* she mumbled to herself. *It is supposed to be spring, not winter.* But there was an ice storm that had traveled down from the Arctic across western Canada into the Midwestern Great Lakes region. It was so hot a few days before that everyone was in their shirt sleeves, and the Lake Shore walk was crowded, with many folks strolling along in their shorts. Mable thought to herself, *it seems as though the heavens had opened up late Friday night and every form of precipitation had fallen to the earth over the weekend.*

The terrible weather began with a strong gust of cool wind. By mid-afternoon on Friday there was a big downpour of hail. The lunch crowd had to run for cover to get back to their work sites. By three o'clock the heavy downpour that came after the hail had turned into freezing rain. The center usually closed an hour early on Fridays, but the rain came down so hard it was difficult to drive the van and avoid the areas where there was flash flooding. The heavy rain caused their trip home to be delayed.

The group was reminded when leaving Friday, that the art teacher would be there every day of the upcoming week to assist in getting ready for the spring art show. Everybody was asked to be sure to come and be an artist.

That winter, temperatures had been unusually mild: only five inches of snow all season, the lowest number ever recorded. However, Friday's forecast had warned of five to six inches of snow. This Friday in late April the predicted snow did fall, mixed with the sleet that never stopped. The inclement weather lasted until Sunday morning with temperatures remaining in the teens and twenties.

The usual neighborhood boys came around on Saturday afternoon. They cleaned and cleared the Morrisons' sidewalk and the walkway leading to the house. When Mable walked out Monday, she carried a plastic bag with rock salt to toss ahead of her. She had done the same thing when her next-door neighbors took her to church on Sunday.

Mable Morrison said to herself: *I can stand any kind of weather, but this is a bit much of Mister Winter in Spring.* As she stood waiting for the bus, she began to feel very cold and pulled up the collar of her dark-brown tweed coat. She stared down the street and waited a little while longer, then decided to go inside to thaw. As she started back into the house, she caught a glimpse of a small, yellow, frozen flower out of the corner of her eye. She paused briefly to observe it before she went back into the house. The flower had been crystallized with the sudden drop in the temperature.

This weather, she thought. *Maybe the bus got stuck. I wonder if I should check the phone messages; maybe they just could not make it after all.*

Mable let herself into the living room and went for her chair beside the small round oak table, which held pressing notices, her mail, and the phone. The red signal was not blinking, but maybe a voice had slipped through. She played the messages anyway. The only things on the machine were the two saved messages that she had received Sunday afternoon while she was still at church; one from the senior center that stated: "Yes, we will be open on Monday. Your pick-up may be a little delayed due to weather conditions."

The other call was from Cora Dixon, her dear friend, who had made a decision to move out of state to a retirement facility but had returned home after six months. Her friend Cora's voice sounded a little frail, but she would try to make it to the center tomorrow, and she asked that Mable return her call after church.

When she got home from church, there was no need to call the senior center, but she definitely returned her friend Cora's call. It was not just a conversation. It was like a visit between two old friends. Mable sat in her warm tweed coat and laughed out loud as she reminisced about Cora's words. Cora told her that she began to wonder for a while why she should be taking care of a house. The idea of moving away to a sunny retirement complex was the ideal situation.

"After last year's bitter winter," Cora said, "I was determined that another winter would not catch me here. Life has been wonderful here for me. It is cold, but not hard to get around."

"We are able to get public transportation whenever we need it," replied Mable.

Cora grunted: "Well, that was quite different in my retirement village. If you didn't drive, you were at the mercy of someone to give you a lift or hire an expensive cab to take you to and from. There was no public transportation."

Having placed her house on the real estate market, Cora really began to wonder out loud: "Am I thinking with all my marbles? Here I am stuck with a maintenance fee, a mortgage, and maybe now a car note, not to mention the quarterly fee for garbage and grounds. The last time I sat waiting for a ride to the supermarket, the real estate agent called with bad news. He regretted telling me that after six months he was unable to get a buyer. He asked: 'What do you want me to do, maybe lower the price?' I only paused for a few seconds. I cancelled the sale of my home immediately. It took me all of a week to be back to Lakeshore. When I got home, I practically kissed the ground I walked on. I knew that I was ready to really retire but I had not decided to resign living."

Mable gave a belly laugh, as both of them did the day before. "We have convinced our grown children that we can live alone. Without moving in with any of them we might as well enjoy these old barns," they both agreed.

Mable smiled and reminded herself: *Don't forget the apron to use as a smock you left here accidentally on purpose. Ms. Director won't like it. She might be tempted to ask with her big beautiful smile. Was this a senior moment or a private time for selective amnesia?* The young director of the senior center was an innovator. Who else would assist mother Dunbar with a sweet sixteen birthday party for her 96th birthday? "Everybody celebrates you at 75, 85, and surely at 95. But who will remember you at 96?" the old lady said. "Let's give them something to talk about."

Signs of the times and the weather were not going to be the only thing that Ms. Sweet Director's seniors had to talk about. They went roller-skating, dancing to the oldies but goodies, fishing, walking on the lakeshore often, and even camping. She dared them to be bored but they could get on board. Now they must become computer literate.

Mable took off her coat, rose from the chair and stared at the old Bing Bang clock on the wall beside the window. She sat back down in her chair as if some force drew her back. She looked at the phone again and she thought: *I remember when you used to ring out of the cradle; now you hardly ring at all.* Soon her mind went back to her friend, Cora Dixon. She thought back: there was hardly a thing that the two of them did not share: births, birthday parties, graduations, all types of family celebrations. Additionally, they consoled each other after the deaths of both husbands in the last 15 years. *I remember when we first went to work in the County Clerk's office. We were so isolated being the only ones. We became instant friends. Now we have been friends for almost fifty years. I can't think of too many times we were really mad at each other, except once over something trivial for a month, yet we agreed to disagree and go to see a movie together. However when I found out she had picked up and moved out of town without even mentioning it to me, I felt sad at first, angry, frustrated and a bit lost. I do recall the day she finally called to say that this was a decision she had to make on her own, undisturbed. Then I recollect she had the heart to ask: "Are you angry with me?" Then she had the nerve to inquire, "Did you get another best friend yet?" That Cora, she knows how to get a laugh.*

Suddenly the smell of the beans that Mable had left in the crock-pot fumed the air. She was sure she had turned the pot on low and the beans would finish cooking while she was at the center, but the smell forced her to the kitchen. When she looked, she had not moved the knob from high; the beans were practically done and she turned the knob to simmer. "Nothing like a fresh pot of pinto beans on a cold Monday night," she whispered tasting the beans.

Mable walked across the kitchen floor and checked to see if she had unplugged the coffee pot. She started back to her chair. As she passed the dining table she spotted the program for the order of service for yesterday, Sunday's eleven o'clock service, entitled "Passing the Torch."

Mable grumbled to herself. *In single-digit weather I went to church yesterday to give my entire program book with all the lessons outlined to the new Sunday school teacher. She didn't even show, after I had worked hard on it all weekend. I looked around in the Sunday school classes. The only one that had any significant numbers was the senior class, the old timers. When church started and the Devotion ended, or as they called it today, Praise and Worship Service, I looked around again and almost all in attendance were the old timers. It seemed to me like the good young reverend should have changed his sermon yesterday to: "Are We Ready to Receive the Torch?" but no, he never questioned if the young hands were going to be present and ready to take the torch. I guess I'll tuck this away for safe keeping,* she thought, as she put the program away to the back of her Bible.

She walked back to her chair, but before she sat she pulled back the curtain and peeked out the window. The sun was shining bright, but she knew it would be late in the afternoon before the ice would melt away. Mable stared at the phone and wondered why the center hadn't called her; the delay had been almost an hour.

She fumbled through some papers on top of the little round table beside the chair as she said to herself: *Bills, bills, and more bills. I will get to you, this evening.* But mixed with the bills she picked up a special invitation and she chuckled as she read it.

Special invitation to enjoy a special sweet sixteen party at the age of ninety-six. It was the January 28th celebration of Mother Dunbar's ninety-sixth birthday. *Who would think of having a sweet sixteen-birthday party at ninety-six years old? But she told us all she wanted was for us to come and we must come with a date! It could be your husband, your friend, but must be a special person in your life all the way down to your great-grandchild.*

Just as she walked back to the window with the invitation still in her hand, the phone rang. Sure enough it was the center director. "I apologize for the delay; the bus should be there within twenty minutes. The roads are very bad." She was forewarned to wait until the director telephoned before she went outside. Before she hung up the telephone she reminded herself to bring her smock and join the art class. Mable thought, *I don't really think I want to become Picasso today.*

She hated to admit it but the only reason she was anxious to get to the center was to see her old friend Cora Dixon. *The nerve of her to bounce away without even a word! And to sneak back in without a whisper. Well she moved away to avoid the bad weather. She must be a ground hog because she has brought bad weather with her. Look like we gonna have winter clear up to summer time.*

It was too funny when Cora said that the real estate agent called her, saying he had no luck in selling her house. It was the happiest news she had heard. The agent was shocked when she told him: "Good, good, take it off the market right now. I'm going to keep my house." She made her way back home.

Mable sat for a few minutes gazing around her neatly clut-
tered rooms as she thought: *Be it ever so humble, it is all mine.*
Then she gathered her belongings, put on her coat, and took
the portable phone from the stand and walked out the door. It
would only be a couple of minutes before it rang. She walked
to the side of the house and again looked at the frozen flowers
only to notice there were two others that she hadn't seen before.
She thought back; it had been a spring morning many years ago
that she and her grandson had dug up a frozen flower and took
it to his kindergarten class. She stood staring at the frozen
flowers. When the senior bus pulled up she didn't even see it
turn the corner.

The ride to the center was rather smooth. Everyone was
busy with the chatter of the weekend and the ferocious weather
the area had experienced. The director had set up an icebreaker
with the art teacher. Instead of a round of discussion, everyone
would pick a color that best described their mood. The art
teacher asked everyone to participate, and if they would choose
to paint she would appreciate it. If they were angry, think of
the color red; if they were sad, pick blue; if they saw themselves
among luscious vegetation, save green for later; if they felt
sunny and bright, pick yellow.

Mable Morrison looked around the room. Everyone looked
eager to start, but she was hesitant. The art teacher was very
encouraging. "There is a sun inside every one of us. We all are
a source of energy. We must always be able to take it in and
give it out; we've just got to stay on the path."

The art teacher laid a sheet of paper in front of everyone
with three big circles, and she asked everyone to use the three
primary colors – red, blue and yellow – to fill in as they felt.
Mable could hardly pick up any of the three colors because she
was filled with mixed emotions today. She had only got a
chance to give a glance and wink at her friend Cora Dixon
seated at the far end of the table, but she noted Cora's big outer
circle was painted a big bright yellow.

Mable picked up the yellow but it landed on the small center
circle. Then she picked up the red and tried to put it in the

middle circle, but by impulse it did not fit, it landed on the big outer circle, and instead the blue fit in the middle.

Mable didn't know if she could explain why there was so much red on her painting, but before anyone was called on to explain their painting, the art teacher had a bag of tricks for them. She separated them. Some were at easels, others at different tables, quite privately. Everyone wondered what was next, but before anyone could ask they were all instructed to pretend they were in a beautiful flower garden and use their circles to change the path and go any direction they wanted in the garden.

Mable thought about her big red circle and questioned herself. Was it directed at Cora whom she was so anxious to see, or was she angry at herself? But she didn't let her mind stay there, neither on herself or her friend Cora. The image of the frozen flower filled her vision. She remembered as if it were yesterday: the morning that her grandchild saw a beautiful yellow flower in a crystal on the side of the house. He wanted to take it to show and tell. The problem was: *how would we keep it from melting?* They decided to put it in a little container in the freezer for show and tell the following day. Mable smiled as she painted a big yellow flower and enclosed it in a block of ice.

– Sally Bill
April-May 2007

The Voice from the Old Shack

Olivia S. Taylor

Once there was a strange pair of boots that belonged to an old fisherman. The boots had been the only thing in the fisherman's wardrobe that didn't look like it belonged to a ragamuffin. After the death of the fisherman his boots were left on the back porch of his deserted shack.

The fisherman's life had always been a bit mysterious. No one really remembered when he moved into the old house by the river. He knew all the people that lived in the small fishing village, and they all knew him. He had no family left. His wife had died years ago, and they had never had any children. No one knew his real age, but everyone said he was as old as the waters. The elderly veteran of the tidewaters was known to be a very hospitable character. He was known for his generosity. He always shared his food and everything else with any and everyone, but he never shared his boots. Many travelers and neighbors enjoyed his company within the walls of the fisherman's shack. It was said that he kept a huge pot of coffee brewing on the hearth 24 hours a day. He told many a fish tale in his day. When he did, he always ended his tale with a loud laugh, and said, "You know, I want to be buried with my boots on."

It came one day that the old fisherman dropped dead, one week after he bought a new pair of boots, the finest pair of boots anyone had ever seen. Everybody looked at him with envy because they wanted the boots. The neighbors saw to it that the old man had a proper funeral, but they did not put his boots on his feet as he always said.

He had welcomed everybody to everything he had in his old hut. He had jars and jars of old coins. He had left a jar to be shared with everyone in the village. He left an old widowed woman a jar to be shared with all of the children in her care. His nets and his fishing rods were to stay in the hut for any old beggar that passed and needed a fish from the river to make a meal. His boots were willed to no one. All of his wishes were carried out, except his boots were not buried with him. They placed them in the corner with his poles, tackles and gear.

But too many people had the idea of returning and taking the boots when no one was looking. It would be only a week or so after the fisherman was buried that a farmer in the nearby area decided to take a break from his field. He came to the old hut and put on the fisherman's boots. The next morning as soon as the dew had dried off the grass the farmer was found dead in the bottom of a boat drifting in the river.

The boots were removed from the farmer and put back in the corner. Several months passed by, then another man went into the cabin and took the boots. He did not get off the porch before he dropped dead. In the course of three years, more than ten people had been foolish enough to put on the shiny boots, and all of them now rested in the graveyard.

On the third anniversary of the fisherman's death, all of the people in the village began to feel afraid to go out on the water to fish. Some declared that they heard the fisherman's laughter coming out of the shack. But soon a wise old man led the people of the village to the porch of the shack. Some of them carried magic potions and lucky charms.

The wise old man took the boots and turned them upside down. The rattlers and fangs of a rattlesnake fell out of the boots and everybody jumped. This time they did not put the boots back in the corner. The people of this small fishing village took the boots down to the graveyard and buried the boots next to the grave of the fisherman.

– Sally Bill

The Ghost of The Old Oak Tree

Olivia S. Taylor

In the community of Weedville there had been a tragedy in the year of 1887. The accounts of the event lived on in the minds of every man, woman, boy and girl from that day on. On the night of November 13, 1887, a group of hooded riders rode into the community on the main road and burned the home of a family. The people of the town awoke to the yells and the screams. They ran from their homes to try and rescue the family, but it was too late. The sounds of a crying child could be heard in the cabin, but no one could push past the flames to make a rescue. The fire engulfed the entire house within a quarter of an hour. The firefighters left, and the undertaker came to take the bodies to the funeral home. The people went back to bed, but no one could sleep, for every time they would lie down to rest they could hear the child screaming.

The neighbors all rose out of their beds to go and investigate. But no one was there. There was not anyone in sight. They could only smell the smoke, and the stench of the charred bodies hung in the air. The screaming at night continued for a week. Then the screaming turned to crying, and after several weeks the crying turned into a sound, such as a soothing sob. This went on for years.

One cold harsh winter, several men knocked the remains of the old house down, and people in the village used the wood in their fireplaces to heat their homes. The grounds where the house stood were barren. The only thing that stood on the plot of land was an old brick chimney. After several years an oak tree began to grow where the house previously stood. It grew bigger and taller than any other tree in the area. As the tree got taller and the branches got broader, a crying child could be heard again in the area. News of the haunted tree traveled far and wide. But the cries became soothing as a memory for the people who lived in the area.

The oak tree grew older, and moss began to hang like whiskers. It provided shade for the passerby who needed to rest when working or walking in the beaming hot sun. The tree became a comfort zone for everyone in the valley. But if any stranger dared enter the area after dark, the tree would creep and wail, holler, and growl.

– Sally Bill

The Biscuit Party

Olivia S. Taylor

It was another Friday night, and Daddy was late again. Soon Dottie Mae and all six of us sisters and brothers would go into the big kitchen and wait for Mamma to light the fire to heat the huge oven in the big old cast iron stove and announce that we were going to have a biscuit party tonight. Mamma made biscuits almost daily, but she was too busy fixing Daddy's lunch and getting breakfast ready to have the bunch of us children at her heels. Yet there was nothing like a Friday night biscuit party, for all of us would join her in the kitchen.

We lived on the outskirts of town, across the tracks, just outside of the city limits. Electricity had reached our area, but there were no gas lines. Some families had large butane gas tanks, but most still heated their homes and cooked with wood and charcoal. Our home was far enough away from town to still have chickens and a few ducks running around on one side of the backyard and a luscious vegetable garden on the other.

Everyone had been sitting on the big front porch watching the sun set upon the horizon and disappear behind the large clump of trees in the woods. Mother called for us to do our last-minute chores. Eleven-year-old Dottie and her twin sister Joddie Mae had to get all of the chickens into the hen house and lock the gate. They fed the special corn to the two chickens in the coop that Mamma had put up for Sunday's dinner.

Nine-year-old Joseph helped me gather armfuls of the stove wood that I had cut for the evening fires. The two youngest – Chet, a boy of seven, and our five-year-old baby sister Clara – mainly chased each other around. They made sure that old Lamp, our dog, had fresh drinking water in his pail to last through the night. I would always feed him later, after dinner.

Now that all of the outdoor chores were done, I made sure that there was plenty of firewood stacked beside the stove. Mamma was still standing at the ironing board pressing the clothes that she took back to the lady for pay on Saturday mornings.

Joddie called, "Everybody in the kitchen."

Joseph could not wait, and he announced, "There is a biscuit party here tonight."

When there was a biscuit party everyone had a ball. We had great fun doing a special task. Joseph would always climb up to the top shelf of the cupboard and get the large brown clay bowl. When Joddie got the sifter Chet would count out the cups of flour. Mother would hold the sifter while Clara turned the handle. Clara counted by ones, but Chet showed off by counting by twos, threes, fours, and fives. The last cup they held for later.

Joddie and Joseph were at the big round table. They were putting butter on the pans to get them ready and sprinkling flour on the table to roll the dough. After Chet helped with the sifting, Dottie got the baking powder. Chet always liked to spell the words: b-a-k-i-n-g p-o-w-d-e-r. Then he would close his eyes and show that he can spell without looking, and he spelled "baking powder."

I reached up and got the salt. Then Clara said, "I bet you I can spell salt." She closed her eyes and said, "S-A-L-T."

Now Mamma had to put in the liquids. She said, "We needed the can of M-I-L-K," and Chet told Joddie to bring a cup of W-A-T-E-R. Mamma started the mixing, and everybody gave a stir. Finally she took away the spoon and began to knead the dough with her hands.

Soon the dough was ready to roll. Dottie had the rolling pin ready. While she rolled Mamma would always start the singing. "Put on the skillet; we rolled out the dough. Mama's going to make a little shortening bread."

At our Friday night biscuit party we children got a chance to cut out and design our own biscuits. Mama would place them in a pan and put a dishtowel over it. She'd let the biscuits sit a few minutes to rise before putting them in the oven.

Dottie had laid out one pan of biscuits. She liked when she could lay them in fours and sixes. She made her designs: six rows of four. The other pan she would lay by fives: five rows of five.

After all the biscuits were cut out Mother would collect the leftover scraps of dough and roll them to make one large johnnycake. She would take out a jar of special preserves. When she asked, "Tonight, will it be peach, blackberry, or apple?" Everyone yelled: "Peach!"

While we looked and waited for the biscuits and johnnycake, we sang songs and played "category." Clara, who was learning to count by fives and tell time, watched the clock to time the baking; it was almost five when Mamma put the last pan of biscuits in the oven. Chet counted the minutes of the clock: "1-2-3-4-5." He knew that he had to wait another 25 minutes for the biscuits to be ready. He watched the hand move to one, and he knew that there was five minutes; when the hands moved to two he knew it was ten minutes; when the hand touched three it was fifteen minutes; when the hand touched the four it was twenty minutes. It was at this moment that Mamma looked at me and said, "I want you to go and meet your daddy – you should be back by the time the johnnycake is ready."

I was thirteen, the oldest son and the oldest child of six children. Some times on Friday Mamma could not wait for Daddy to come home, and she would send me into town to meet him. It was about dusk when I put on my jacket and dashed out the door. I had mastered the trip. I knew I could walk to town in about ten minutes. Much to my surprise, just as I turned the last corner, my father came walking down the main strip with a rather steady stride. *Only gambling tonight,* I thought. I waited somberly. Within a few minutes we greeted each other.

Our walk home was dreary. No matter how I found my father, when we started our walk home he always whistled. Tonight it was dry silence. The darkness had rolled in swiftly and a winter chill had accompanied it. There was no moon tonight. After we crossed the tracks, the paved streets turned into dirt roads. The absence of streetlights often forced us to travel with flashlights. I knew my trip would be made in a jiffy so I carried no flashlight. If Daddy had one in his lunch box he did not bother to use it.

When we were about three streets away from home a heavy downpour of rain started suddenly. I had forgotten to put on my cap. The rain struck at an angle. The heavy frigid water appeared to be falling on my cheeks instead of my head. I took the sleeve of my jacket and wiped my cheeks. As my hand moved across my face I felt two streams of warm water. I raised my head a little, to hear my father say, "Son, why don't you pull the jacket over your head?" I did as I was told. The dusty smell of the earth began to fill my nostrils.

We quickly reached the ditch on the corner of our street. Only small narrow streams of water were flowing. It had not swollen and overflowed its banks. Therefore we did not need to jump or wade. We did not slip but crossed the ditch very easily tonight. Yet I remembered so vividly the evening about six months ago when Daddy fell in the ditch. Some boys stood laughing at us while I tried to get him up. It was a while before a neighbor came to help. But tonight his steps were steady.

The front porch light was on when we arrived home. We could hear the laughter floating from the kitchen as we crept into the front room. Daddy did not leave an envelope on the mantelpiece as he usually did; he put his lunch pail down there instead of carrying it into the kitchen and went to the big bedroom. I hung my wet jacket in the hallway and walked into the kitchen.

Everyone asked in unison, "Where is Daddy?"

I answered somewhat emphatically, "He has gone to bed." I sat at the table where Mamma had placed a cup of hot chocolate and a piece of johnnycake. I looked down at the plate; the stream of warm water that had swollen up as I walked home began to flood my face. The laughter that filled the room was no longer there. The same somberness that overtook the walk home filled the atmosphere in the kitchen. I heard the voices asking, "What is the matter? Don't cry," but I could not stop the stream of tears from flowing.

Suddenly, our baby sister Clara began to cry out very loudly as if a red-hot cinder from the wood stove had struck her. All eyes turned toward her. She looked at me and said, "I know what's the matter with you, Simon." She stared at me for a moment then buried her head in her armpit. She said, "I'm sorry. I am so sorry, and I won't do it any more." She rushed over to my side and began hugging me, still saying, "I am so sorry, Simon, don't cry, eat your johnnycake." It seemed as if my tear ducts had empted and become the source for everyone else's sad eyes in the room.

I looked at Clara and asked, "What are you talking about, Baby Sister?"

Through her tears and sobs, she cried out, "It was me that pinched off your johnnycake, but don't be mad at me." We smiled. Then Clara held up her little finger with her thumbnail, "See, Simon I only took a little fingernail full." We all burst into a big roar of laughter. She did not quite know how to take our laughing. She hugged me tighter. Then she looked up and said, "The next time we have a biscuit party you can have my johnnycake."

I made a double deal with her that night: if she would stop crying and share my johnnycake with me I would share hers next time. Clara sat beside me as we finished the pastry and cocoa together. I never missed the fun at another biscuit party.

It has been almost 20 years since I was in our hometown on a Friday night. It was a family reunion for Mamma's 65th birthday. I thought it would be a wonderful time for my children to see my old neighborhood where I grew up, so we took a drive south.

As we neared our town, Interstate I-10 cuts completely through the main strip of town where I used to go meet Daddy. The railroad tracks had been almost completely tarred over. All of the dirt roads were paved and the ditches had been filled and tarred. When we reached our street all the fields where we used to play ball had become lots for houses. Many families whose homes had been taken to make way for the interstate had moved further out, but now this area was considered within the city limits. Daddy died the year before the interstate completely demolished the entire main strip. Death spared him a bit of grief.

There are no butane gas tanks anymore. Instead there are lovely flower gardens where they once stood. The front porches that dominated the houses on the block had now become a part of enlarged living rooms or parlors. Now families gather, but not on their former back porches, which have now been enclosed and made into dens. I will not be able to show my children the real neighborhood in which I grew up, but I will always cherish the memories of the biscuit parties. Mama only bakes biscuits now on Saturday mornings and johnnycakes on Sundays when the grandchildren are over.

My siblings and I still never ask for a sliver of cake or a small portion of anything: we simply ask for a fingernail full.

– Sally Bill

Princene Hyatt

my early world

Princene Hyatt

I come from a Long line of Sickness
Generations of Violence and Fear,
Pretense and Prostitution,
Incest and closet Alcoholics.
Generations of Hating Self
Hating life, All life.

I look back into Unspoken Feelings
Of Shame, Blame, Guilt and Terror.
I look back in Sorrow at Secrecy
– surrounding the HORRORS –
At the dawn of Every day.
I relive the Bone Crushing Pain.

I step back into Crippling Aloneness,
Silent Emptiness, of my early world
In the BIBLE BELT.
I was Raped and Ridiculed,
Molested by a NUN and (2) Old Men.
A world filled with Ignorance, Envy,
And LIES.

LIES created to support, protect and defend
Sadistic Behavior–while quoting what
"THE BIBLE SEZ"

Wonder how different life might have been
If Someone could have cared?
If Someone had known – How To Care.
Or, at least – how Not To Hurt,
Even if one Could Not Care
In my early world.

Appearing in the Personals
Who Am I?

Princene Hyatt

I am not keen featured, not curly headed, not caramel colored,
  not pretty eyed.
I am unorganized, undisciplined, undiplomatic.
SLOW – what others do in two hours takes me at least five.
SLOPPY – getting clean clothes mixed with wash.
Stubborn to change – as in Taurus The Bull.
Super-sensitive and much too idealistic for the real world.
I am neither emotionally nor financially stable.
I am not a professional SOMEBODY.

I am tall and small and filled with joyful, ageless spirit, artistic
  vision and character defects.
As a late bloomer I am phenomenal, which makes me extremely
  proud – On a good day.
My perception is acute, my curiosity enormous, my imagination vivid!
And without your permission – I could show off my loud,
  corny, country, southern self. And cuss and swere!

True friends make me very happy!
Good food is my bosom buddy.
Truth is beauty! Truth is freedom!
So, don't ask me – if you're not ready for my truth.
I speak from my center – not some intellectual place.
I am brave, bold, boring, timid, simple and fun-loving. I have
    tons of courage.
And scared!
Yet nothing scares me more than a hypocrite!
I am soft. I am hard. I cry as easily as I laugh.
I have much to share and do.
I also need.

                            WHO ARE YOU?

Rita REB Wilson

Karmilita's Claim

Rita REB Wilson

The term or celebration "Coming of Age" has significant meaning according to the culture or ethnic background of the celebrant. A celebration at twelve years of age could be First Communion or Holy Baptism. There are also celebrations of manhood when the young man is able to drive a car, change a tire, kiss a girl.

For a young female, celebration can mean buying her first bra, a sixteenth birthday party, debutante ball, introduction to society, or just a plain old party. Also, it is based on the circles that a family includes or how much money is available to host a celebration.

For a male teenager, the celebration would most likely be different than for a female, coming from the same economic and cultural background. Of course, special circumstances and conditions would merit the celebration to turn into an outstanding event or one of modest means.

The young male of thirteen would probably be encouraged to score with a young girl. Also at this time opportunities for a young male could include traveling, exploring ideas for the future, learning about nature, getting special training in the community and/or doing community service.

The teenage girl at thirteen would have probably had her menstrual period and/or she would have been admonished about boys and what not to do with them. Also, coming of age meant that emphasis was on school, fashion, beauty, charm school, the debutante ball at sixteen, along with other gala or intellectual activities. Or she could have been left to do whatever she wanted to do, just as the boys were left to do so. As the saying goes: "boys will be boys."

Actually, the main idea for both sexes is to celebrate the transition from childhood through the in-between stages to adulthood.

The celebration is usually an event where people gather for a ceremony first, a party afterwards, and performances of rituals honoring and focusing on the one being celebrated.

Not this time. One day a young girl, Karmilita, broke the news that she did not want any kind of celebration. All she wanted was truth-telling about her life and where she came from. Her request had been tabled when she was celebrating her 13th-year birthday at her dad's church. No one understood, or they pretended that the child was just spoiled. "That child has everything that a child could want. She has too much, if you ask me, and I don't know why she's obsessed with a question of where she came from," said a church member.

Teenage years were difficult for her as time set the stage for adulthood and curiosity, especially when the rumors, the secrets, and malicious talk exhausted and depleted her self-esteem. Time seems long and hard, and getting along with parents was done by staying away from them. That was a part of what Karmilita did for about two years. She spent less time with them and more time with her music. Her dad diagnosed her condition as mild depression and made an appointment for her to get counseling, and of course she rebelled and would not go. When she was approaching sixteen, she took a driver's education course and established a better relationship with her dad, so that he could help her prepare for a permit.

On her 16th birthday, Karmilita handed her parents a notice from family court that she wanted to know who her birth parents were. She left them to sort things out. She did not want a traditional celebration; she wanted to know the truth about where she came from. She looked like a white child and her parents were not Caucasian. She'd told them months before that she would have a celebration for them on her birthday and it might surprise them, if they were not willing to share with her about from whence she came. Afterwards, she went to practice with her music group.

Her father became irate; her mom was more than emotional: she needed Prozac. Dad was fit to be tied up with duct tape and a rope; mom needed a couch and more medicine. Karmilita wished that she had a better plan for her folks, but she didn't have one. Yet, she was less burdened as she walked to the community center to play music with her friends.

Her parents were appalled and insulted that she had gone to such measures to involve authorities and filed papers as though she were being treated brutally. "Karmilita has lost her mind," said the Reverend to his wife. After she had wept and was comforted by him, she said: "Honey, we are due to give her an explanation or have a talk. She's approaching adulthood, and we promised her that when she turned sixteen we'd answer whatever questions she had."

He replied, "I had no inkling that she would go as far as to take us to court."

His wife interrupted: "Did you get any indication when you took her out for driving lessons?"

"No, there wasn't any indication or discussion at all; she was quite happy that she'd finally learned to parallel park. She was excited with the anticipation of having her own car; so excited that she left her purse in the car. Anyway, I'll get ready to have a meeting with her tonight. I'll cancel all of my appointments for the evening, because I will not go to court! This is a family matter that is pressing, and I'll not have you upset and I'll not have my good name plastered in the newspapers and in other media. Who does she think she is? I'm prestigious and known in this city; I can't have my reputation tainted by going to court with my daughter because we haven't answered her questions. Be sure that she's available tonight."

Karmilita was born to Rev. Dr. Moses Micford and Dibby Cress Micford: a loving couple. They were outstanding citizens, professional people, and the child was a blessing for them. They were delighted to have this angelic child. She really looked like an angel: she was very beautiful from birth, and had a good temperament as a young child growing up. She was precocious and well-behaved. A nanny and household help assisted in raising her, yet the parents were right there for their child. She was their pride and joy. However, she had no resemblance to either parent. The parents were dark-skinned, and the child was very fair-skinned with light silky hair and hazel eyes.

Her contrast in appearance to her parents wasn't an issue until she entered third or fourth grade. That's when the parents began to pick her up from school or attend meetings at her school. Prior to that time, she was usually picked up by the nanny or some other household help. Her classmates started to tease her and the child complained to her parents. Her parents just suggested to her to "ignore the teasing, they're just unkind little children who are jealous because you're pretty and smart. So what, that you don't look like me or your dad; you're still our little munchkin."

As time passed on, Karmilita would sometimes hear adults or children whispering and making comments about her. It didn't make her happy. Sometimes she cried alone.

She managed school very well and she was active in the after-school music department: she loved to play the flute. One afternoon she was getting her instrument from the closet when she overheard the music teacher saying to another teacher who worked at her mom's school, that she wasn't her father's child. She started to cry. Her mom taught at the high school that was nearby. Karmilita left her school and walked to where she found her mom. She stopped crying and composed herself before entering her mom's classroom. She flopped down in a seat near the door and blurted out to her mom, "Would you ever cheat on dad?" Dibby dropped her marking pencil and ran over to hug her daughter, but she pulled away.

Dibby was a dedicated and loyal wife. Her marriage to the Reverend came about at the right time, though unexpectedly – right for them as a couple, unexpectedly because she was grief-stricken. She sought him out for counseling after she had had several deaths in her family.

First there was her sister, Libby Cress Gold and her husband David Gold. They died in a plane crash. Next, was Dibby's first husband, Alex Dalton, who was a judge; he dropped dead during a criminal case hearing. Afterwards, Clement Cress – he was dad to Dibby and Libby – died of a heart attack. They had different mothers. As a result, Dibby needed to have counseling and recommendations for a life coach to help her deal with the tragedies.

The Reverend had lost his wife several years before and he had decided to lighten his schedule and not carry the workload that he once had. He no longer had a private practice as a psychologist. His main concentration was on his ministry and his congregation. He was more than happy that he had made such a decision when this hourglass-shaped, attractive woman came into his office in need of help, and something else too. He was glad to have her there and glad to send her off to someone else's couch for counseling, "cause she needs other care that I can certainly provide. Whew!!! Lord, I've been waiting," he said to himself.

Dibby and Moses developed a relationship after a year of intense counseling for her condition. She took a leave of absence from teaching and worked on herself, and she dealt with family matters left by her sister, her first husband, and her dad. She had a huge job ahead of her, yet she was a quick learner when it came to business. She healed gradually from the traumas that life had dealt her.

She was happy to have Moses in her life; he met her criteria: drop-dead handsome, almost old enough to be her dad, he had means for her to live in the fashion to which she had been accustomed. He was high-ranking in his profession, he loved children though he didn't have any. She also felt adored by the man, and the thought of how lavish he lived was inviting to her in her pursuit of wellness and happiness. Because of her inheritance from her late husband she could live a good life on her own, yet the icing on the cake was the Right Reverend and his ability to contribute to her lifestyle. He was ready to make such commitment because he was a man of the cloth and should not be single indefinitely.

After a short engagement, an elaborate church marriage ceremony and reception, the honeymoon was spent on the French Riviera and in Johannesburg, South Africa, surrounded by the beautiful savanna. It was wild and wonderful with time to plan the future.

She shared with him intimate details of her non-traditional family life. He wasn't surprised because he knew her father's accomplishments and reputation. Her father had his way in the community with women and projects for the better things in life. He owned property; he contributed to community centers for the aging and youth. He was an outstanding man about town. He was the cat's meow for some women and he was dedicated to a soul mate, Freeda.

Also, Dibby's ability to take care of the reverend and look good as his wife were plus signs favorable for him. He could handle her family losses; he had endless information as to where she needed to go for counseling because it seemed as though she mourned her sister more than she did anyone else.

She and Libby were very close; they were born five months apart from different mothers. They grew up in the same household and went to the same boarding school and ascribed to some of the same values. They both dated and married successful older men. Libby's mom was white, Dibby's mom was African American, and the mothers both agreed to allow their father to raise them in his household with his live-in girl friend, Freeda.

Dibby's dad was as good as he could be, given his lifestyle and circumstances. He had five children and was not married; he was a real estate tycoon and the ladies took advantage of his "ladies man" way of life. Freeda was his mainstay, very supportive of him and his children. She handled his business and while doing so she allowed advantages for her family members. He was a good provider for his children and their moms; he had good relationships with all of his children, including the three boys that did not live with him. His girls were exposed to the very best of upbringing because they lived with him and Freeda. She made sure that the girls went on holiday trips excursions, and took classes and seminars that taught courses on self-esteem, girl power, character-building blocks, "how to marry well," and above all how to manage their inheritance. When Freeda sent the girls to these different educational courses, she also sent her two nieces from the Bahamas for the same experience. Therefore she had to eventually introduce her nieces to Dibby and Libby because her nieces knew of them, yet they didn't know the connection to her.

Freeda was left, after Dibby's father died. She was given the charge to arrange appointments for the will to be read to the five Cress children and the selection of charity cases. She had her nieces set up as a charity organization, which made them eligible for Mr. Cress' donations for the next ten years. Freeda was the executor for his personal estate, which was to pay the bills that were left behind, while his daughters and sons reaped the benefits of cash money without any responsibilities to pay anything due or contribute to his final resting place. She knew what she was doing as she put things in order for herself and her nieces. She thought to herself: "That Ms. Dibby has her father's inheritance, her sister's inheritance and her own inheritance; she's a very rich woman, and she has married well because I taught her."

Dibby also inherited something that had no monetary value: life itself. She inherited frozen embryos. Libby and her husband David had decided to stock embryos until they were ready to start a family. They died before using any of them. The beneficiary of Libby's estate was her sister who was married to an older gentleman, the Reverend, and they still wanted children... therefore the fertility bank had her sister and brother-in-

law's pre-fetal product waiting to be implanted, part of the inheritance.

Proper procedures and pleasing results brought forth the
wonderful one: "Karmilita." She's taking them to court, if
they don't explain who's the donor.

Lacey and Zipper

Rita REB Wilson

The morning was rainy, with a slight chill. It was mid-September, and the rain and air felt good, especially after the grueling almost 100 degree weather in August, which resulted in a heat alert. The rain was refreshing with a comfy chill. The soaked young woman lingered on the outside of her cottage with arms opened, embracing the wetness, expecting the dryness inside.

Lacey McGee was an author of short stories, and she would often drive to certain nearby areas to write. This time she drove to Orient Point, Long Island; she'd reserved the same cozy cottage each time she went there. It gave her privacy and quietness. Even though, she could write under almost any conditions, she preferred to reward herself by leaving her tiny Brooklyn studio apartment at least twice a year. Or sometimes she would travel with her parents during their vacations...she vacationed with them to write, even when they traveled to South Africa.

Her parents often invited her to accompany them; it was their way of supporting her craft, even though they were concerned that she didn't have a real job. She was educated, smart, very intelligent and had her view on how her life should be lived. Her parents' theory was: get a professional job and write all you want while earning a decent living wage. Eliminate the hassle of looking for work that is flexible, and dependent on exhausting savings, doing physical labor and having grueling hours.

She worked for two catering companies to afford her lifestyle to write. Also, she was published and was paid for more than a few of her short stories. Her novel was also on the back burner; she had appeared at the Spoken Word Cafe and was asked to return. The rewards were worth the hard work she spent so she could write and perform. She enjoyed her life, though it was not in the tradition of her immediate family. Her Dad was in management for city housing authority; her Mom was the tailor for a notable department store in Brooklyn, and her brother was an attorney on Wall Street. She was head waitress for two catering companies. She was happy, though not financially stable according to others.

She was an attractive young woman who didn't work at any particular look except her own. Her own look just happened to have had a Venus or Serena Williams statuette. She was 5'11" barefoot, with a dark complexion and a non-chemical geri curl look. She shampooed and conditioned her hair, and the rest was by chance of a ponytail or the playful look, be there style. She went to the gym, she walked, she rode a bike. She was a good-looking young woman without intent; she didn't add the nails – that certainly could've been used since her nails were nubs. The hair needed management, yet some fellows found her perfect and beautiful, mostly non African-American guys. She didn't know for a fact why, yet she thought that she knew why her fellow brothers had less interest. She didn't think it mattered, but she thought that some brothers hadn't gotten past the dark skin issue. It wasn't an issue for her, just an observation. She got much play from other males and females too, life was good.

She and her brother had great parents: they came from a good lineage of southern entrepreneurs, educators, working-class people. Lacey was grateful to her parents for their support, yet she was happy when she decided to decline their invitation to go on a cruise.

"Mom, I'm not feeling a cruise or vacation time with you and Dad – take Zipper, he'd love it."

"Girl, you can't tell us who to take, we can go with 'just the two us.' You gotta' tell your Dad. I'm alright if you don't wanna' go with us on the cruise to the south of France. We'll miss you dear."

"Mom, you know how Dad is, so just tell him and I'll deal with the after effects. Is that too much to ask?"

"O.K., I'll be the one to disappoint him 'cause of your request, and I'll serve him with a hot reward...I'm your Mom, and I'm your daddy's Mama."

"Thanks Mom, but you're giving me too much information."

"Lace, I wish you would reconsider taking the cruise with me and your Momma, but if you got other plans, go ahead. Yeh, I'm disappointed, me and MM (Mama McGee) will do just fine without you. Her sorority sisters all like me, even the ones whose husbands ain't dead," Dad said.

"Dad, you and Mom are great parents, loving, caring, supportive and all that good stuff and I appreciate you so-oo much, I love you so-oo much. Problem for me – and Zipper too – you share too much information. We are glad that you have a healthy life, happy with each other, glad that the sorority and church sisters find you handsome and appealing. Ask Zipper, he doesn't want to hear about y'all neither, act normal for people your age."

Her dad interrupted, "Lace lemme tell you something, you and Zip got here 'cause of the same stuff you talkin' 'bout now. Why you actin' 'bout us now? You've seen us like this all of yo' life. It ain't nuttin' new for me, you, your bother or your Momma...get over it and laugh like you did when you were kids."

She changed the subject and asked, "Are you and Mom coming to see me perform at the Lighthouse in Williamsburg?

The seats have cushions now; you don't need to bring the pillow from the car."

"Yeh, yeh, we comin', but don't set us up wid' that boy who thinks he's a girl...he's a nice person, and I'm not homophobic. I jus' don't wan' him sittin' with me and yo' Momma."

"Dad, that's wrong, you are homophobic. Today is only Saturday you don't know how you'll feel next Saturday and, face up, that's your favorite expression."

"Okay, I maybe a little homophobic, 'specially when that boy smacks his mouth mo' than you or your Momma ...that's jus' me, I ain't quite there. I had reservations about two very famous basketball players, don' have it now but that's just me."

"That's just me," she thought. He gave the same response when he talked about her and her social life.

"When you gonna' find a husband so you can make some babies? Yo' Momma and me could stand some gran' babies. Yo' brother ain't got nobody, thought you had somebody, but you ain't got nobody neither. Ya'll gettin' old, we're older and expect gran kids...it's on you 'cause Zip got much more time than you, that's jus' me, you don' have much time..."

She interrupts, "Dad that's an unfair statement just because Zipper is male. He might have more time than I have to make you a granpa, but you need to have a talk with him, he might surprise you."

"Lace, you know that males have more capability to make babies than females, they can do it into their seventies or eighties." He started to speak as though he was at work, without chopping his words. "Look at Jimmy Durante – he did it, I know he did. He was before your time; you don't remember, but he did."

"Dad, I'm not going to continue this discussion with you, still love you though."

"That's just him," she thought as she touched his Tiki Barber bald head, kissed it and headed out.

The refreshing mist of rain had turned into a downpour by the time she entered her cozy cottage. Shedding her drenched clothes, she noticed the blinking light on the phone, which in-

dicated that she had messages. Her cell phone would occasionally not work whenever she was in this area. Therefore she used
the land phone for contact and the internet. She called her
brother and her ex-boyfriend, Lem; neither were available. Her
message to each one was the same: "If it's not life-threatening,
and no one needs blood, I'll talk with you when I return...I'm
busy." Of course Zip calls her anyway to tell her he was getting
engaged.

Raindrops started to sound like pellets on the roof; her mind
went into the reflective mode. She acknowledged a few things
that she really felt proud of, such as her education, her writ-
ings/published work, her performances, good or bad, and her
work. She had wonderful family and friends, a high honor and
important to her. However, she would've been negligent if her
mind had skipped over her social/romantic status. The fact that
she had turned thirty-eight, she wasn't sad or unhappy about
her place in life...yet she was feeling guilty about her non-
concern. Maybe she should feel disquieted...think about the
next two years to reassess rather than waiting for forty. Okay,
okay, I know where this is coming from, she said out loud to
herself as she stopped pacing and sat on the bed.

"So Zipper is getting engaged: what does it have to do with
me, and why am I asking this question? I need to call him and
congratulate him and his fiancé, whomever she might be."
Maybe her Dad had spoken to Zip. "I don't believe he did,"
she thought. She knew her Dad's theory had validity, yet he
doesn't recall her Mom's family lineage with two women having babies late in life. Mom had a grand aunt who had a baby
girl at 63 years old with her husband who was 71 years old, so
what happened to their clock, time span for her fertility and
reproduction? Also, a female cousin had a baby for a younger
man of 41, she was 61, their child functioned well with a slow
growth. Lacey was from the same lineage, yet not so close to
60.

Lacey was getting off track from her purpose of being in her
special place to do her special writing. In this very same cottage
she had written stories that had gotten published, and also a few

non-sellers. This is the space for her to re-start her novel or re-write it...(light bulb thoughts for the latter). Her mind started to race in an organized way, "an outline, a description of characters, what should the reader come away with? Beginning, stuff in between, ending, gotta' do a re-write," she decided.

The first step was to walk between the raindrops to her rented car to fetch her frozen foods and drinks for nourishment. She returned to the cottage drenched and started to shed her clothing in the entrance area. Window curtains weren't drawn, she saw two peepers, she thought. The two were interested in coming in out of the storm; she complied, after understanding what they wanted.

Ollie and Molly had walked to Orient Point; they were headed back to the house where they were staying when the downpour occurred. Instead, they sought shelter and it happened to be Lacey's place where they ended up. After becoming acquainted briefly, introductions, the twins talked about Lacey's cozy cottage. They were soon picked up by the owner of the house where they were staying. Lacey was left to get busy with her work... re-writing, writing, there is always a story to be told.

Her second step was to get busy reading the novel and creating an outline, which she didn't do when she began it a few years ago. She read, made notes and finished the outline; the rain had stopped, the sun was peaking, it was time for a walk. More than four hours had been spent on the project and walking always rejuvenated her mind and spirit.

She dressed herself in tights, shorts and deck shoes; her sneakers were still soaked, though her windbreaker jacket was dry. The hood on the jacket was convenient because her hair had taken on a mind of its own. It would often take on a wild or an artistic look after a good soaking. A few of the short locks had the tendency to stand up and out for attention, rather than lie down with the longer locks. Therefore a scarf, a hat, or a hood would put them in place.

The air was fresh and pleasantly cool. She walked for about 45 minutes before heading back. There were two people coming towards her, and as they came closer she recognized Ollie and Molly. They had a brief chat about the sunrise, the tides, and possibilities of the fishermen's catch, since the three had a view of people with fishing poles. They departed, and Lacey went on her way to her cottage; she knew that there was a short story to be written. She made notes, yet she forbade herself from starting a new story just now.

She continued reading the novel, making changes, additional notes...more in-depth development of characters were reminders of her initial insight to write this novel. It was becoming more than she anticipated. Perhaps, the publication of the short stories had an impact on her train of thoughts for the moment. Regardless to what it was, she was on a roll with this project; though her mind wandered, "maybe I need to think about marriage and children – call Zipper at midnight."

It's past midnight when she called her brother. "Hey Zip, what's happening, are you asleep?"

He answered without a greeting. "No, not sleeping, but I'll have lunch with you on Tuesday when you return. No threatening crisis here. I saw your number, so I picked up to schedule a lunch or dinner with you on Tuesday; I'm free. Think about it and leave me a message, see ya." All in one breath, and CLICK!

"She must be there with him, and who is she? And he doesn't know whether I have a crisis or not, he didn't even ask," she thought.

Her brother was good looking, a Wesley Snipes kind of look with naturally curly hair and a Mike Tyson body, just over six feet. He was a successful attorney, smart and intelligent and basically a good catch, by most standards. Her parents were proud of him and she was too. He had many female friends, he had brought three ladies to family gatherings on separate occasions – which one was it? "I'll not find out tonight, I mean this morning, it's morning already...I gotta' get to work."

She enjoyed the chirping of crickets and the sound from the Long Island Sound; it was blissful for her. Her surroundings were perfect, the cottage was similar to her studio apartment in

Brooklyn. Walk into the vestibule area, hang up coats or outerwear, leave the footwear. One large room with table in center with two chairs, kitchen area on the wall with bay window, sleeping area to the left with small window, the right had a full bathroom with a tiny window. Brooklyn apartments didn't have as many windows, her sleeping area had no window. Also, the decor and colors in the cottage were always seasonal and coordinated. Her apartment was eclectic; the two places had similarities in terms of the setup. She read and made notes until after 5 am; drowsiness began. She resorted to sleep, with the plan to be out walking by 9 am. She kept her schedule and during the walk she waved to Ollie and Molly. They responded by motioning for her to join them.

She stopped and yelled, "Later, later at two o'clock, right here."

The girls gave thumbs up and said "Okay, okay."

Wow, the story was jumping out at her, "hummed" she said, though she did not let her thoughts wreck the mission. She had to rewrite her novel, *Phamous in the Dark;* the book title was changed to *The Paths of Phamous.* This project was extensive, especially after reading other information that actually coincided with her format. She must take this excitement back to Brooklyn, minus the crickets and the sounds from the Long Island Sound. It was essential to continue with the enthusiasm and be driven to work on the book every day until it was completed and ready for the publisher. "I'm lovin' it, and I'll do like Dr. Wayne Dyer did, sell from the trunk of Mom's car – of course Dr. Dyer had his own car, not his mother's car," she thought.

Reading and writing in this cottage gave her enjoyment and granted quick thinking. While working in her apartment gave her pleasure too, she had delayed thoughts. Her creativity wasn't as quick and as clear as when she read or wrote at home: that's why she must put forth the effort to maintain enthusiasm.

"Oh gee, it's time to meet Ollie and Molly. I'm late; hope they didn't leave," she hurried. She didn't cuss or use bad language like she had heard from the streets or on very rare occasions at home. She decided that it was empty language; therefore she didn't use it. Her brother's vernacular would often change, depending on the boys or environment. Why was Zipper in the picture? She went to meet the girls; she saw two people at a distance with a young child running back and forth between the two. She didn't think that it was Ollie and Molly, yet it was them. They came to the cottage to check on her after their walk – they had a little boy with them. He was the cutest little black child. He was so happy to run and play by himself and play with Ollie and Molly. He laughed and talked with Lacey as though he knew her. She was cordial with the little child and impressed with his friendliness, yet she wondered where did he come from. They did not have a child when they were scampering out of the rain and they couldn't have left him alone.

The young women and the child said their goodbyes. Lacey resumed her work on the computer, yet she thought of her brother and his engagement: "Who is he going to marry? I shall see him when I return to Brooklyn on Tuesday – I'll still not know who he'll marry," she said to herself.

"The boy has this sudden interest to marry someone, and he has not talked to Mom or Dad: something must be going on, I need to head back to Brooklyn to get heads up on this matter. Or was he doing this to get more attention from Mom and Dad?"

He was such a whiny guy, especially if he thought Lacey was getting too much attention from their parents. He was the more successful one from a career/monetary perspective, yet Lacey was the one to have happiness and contentment with the help from him and the parents. So, Lacey was thinking that she must check on him in person, interrupt her schedule, leave Long Island on Sunday morning instead of leaving on Tuesday at daybreak. So, she walks the waterfront where the fishermen were on Saturday before daybreak, dips her feet in the water and wishes each one a hearty catch. She decides to write for the rest of the day and she decided to make a point of waving goodbye to Ollie, Molly and the boy. She did that and notified the registration office that she would depart early and inquire for the possibility for a two-day credit or any credit for early departure.

The return drive back to Brooklyn took less time because of the traffic and the hour of her departure. She was back on 7th Ave. in Park Slope at Karina's, near her brother's address for breakfast in less than 2-1/2 hours. She called Zipper; he met her for breakfast. He asked,

"Why are you here?" He asked. "I thought your return was scheduled for Tuesday."

"Yes you're right, I'm here earlier. I need to know what's going on with you, why are you getting engaged so quickly. Is it because Dad and Mom want grandchildren?"

"No, it's because they have a grandson, his name is Oliver and his Mom's name is Ollie and her sister's name is Molly. I had hoped that you liked them, they're nice people. I was a sperm donor, and I recently learned that Oliver was the results. Your ex-boyfriend, Lem, and I have children, he'll give you details."

Kim D. Brandon

Excerpt from *Seven*

Kim D. Brandon

The excerpt that follows is from the novel Seven. *The journey in* Seven *is one of forgiveness and one of self-discovery when family secrets and outright lies forever change the ground on which you are standing.*

Chapter One: Mom's Retreat

My mother, Synovia, waited until she was forty-seven to become a base-head. I was seventeen.

On a cold gray morning in January, wet globs of snow landed and clung to tree branches just long enough to form sacks and then slap down on my head. I had been summoned to the dean's office for an emergency meeting. My head was freezing cold and spinning. I could feel the snow melting on my scalp. I could hear my mother's reminder, in my head. "Sophie, darling, where is your hat?"

"They tell you if a parent is dead immediately and put you on the next thing smokin' back home. My mother is not dead. She is not dead. If she were, they would have told me yesterday and not scheduled a 9 AM appointment. Right? You damn right." I said to myself just loud enough for others to hear and give me that crazy-girl-walking look. "Cause if your parent is dead, they tell you right away and put you on the next thing smoking. She is not dead!" This became my mantra, as I stomped along hoping that the gods would be kind.

Dr. Dwight kept me waiting for over twenty minutes. It wasn't fair: my life was in his hands, and he was late. My heart was pounding. I was wet from a combination of snow and sweat. My hair recoiled and fluffed itself around the last remaining drops of water that didn't run down my face. I was more of a mess than usual, given the circumstances. When he opened the heavy wood framed smoked glass door, he stopped to look at me. I felt tiny, almost invisible. He had all the power. He was wearing his usual suit and tie deal with no flair and no flash. He was tall, thin and reserved. His steps were calculated. It was like he had to conserve every movement. I wished he would smile, but he didn't. He was way too young to act like a 90-year-old man.

He drank me in and then said, "Miss Tracey, this way please. Please have a seat. My apologies for keeping you waiting for so long; it couldn't be avoided. I have been trying to reach your mother for some time, to no avail. So I just sent off a letter to Mr. Tracey, your father. You see Mr. Tracey is a friend of the college. Why, he provided funding for…" His eyes lit up like a seventh grader with a secret crush. His voice trailed off in my head as he sat behind a giant desk that looked like it was there since they created the building. From his desk you could see half the campus from the floor to ceiling windows that framed his every action. It was impressive. He was still talking about my mom and reaching for a manila folder, opening it and flipping the papers about. He was trying to reach my mother – that was good news! She was alive. I could feel the tears of relief forming. I fought hard against crying. It was the tiny tremors of my bottom lip that preceded the water works. I didn't have a tissue, and the dean didn't notice I needed one, or he didn't have any, either. You would think that a dean would have a supply of tissues.

So, why this meeting? I thought. *Why scare the hell out of me? Why make me think my mother was dead?* I tried to remember everything my mother ever said about manners. I wiped my face with the back of my sleeve and waited for Dr. Dwight to finish his sentence. I even placed my hands in my lap.

"There is a problem, Miss Tracey. Your mother, well she has not honored the checks that she wrote to cover your tuition and board. Actually, the last two payments have been returned," he said, extending the checks out for me to take. A soured pout covered his mouth like he had been sucking on lemon peels. I took the blue paper checks and looked at them. Maybe he could deposit them again, I thought. I still hadn't said anything. I always clam up, like a giant rock, when I'm nervous, and then imagine what I could have said later.

"I am very sorry, but as this is your first year, we need to address this immediately. We have already let this situation go on for too long, hoping that the situation would be rectified before we would need to take this action. Well Miss Tracey, we need you to contact your family and arrange for payment. If we don't receive a cashier's check in one week, then your registration will be cancelled and you will have to withdraw from the college. It was a courtesy to your father to extend your grace period and to open our door to you at all. You certainly didn't have the grades." My average was a solid B and besides no one twisted his arm to accept me. He had said too much. The balance between admiring my dad and dealing with my bad-check-writing mom got the best of him.

"Yes, sir," I said, my stomach flipped over and I dropped my head. "What was going on with my mom?" I thought.

"Miss Tracey, please tell your mother that we are an institution of higher learner, we are not a charity. Good morning." He started looking through a pile of papers and selected one to read without looking up or motioning for me to leave. I was dismissed. I stumbled out, making every effort not to fall over my feet, as I was prone to tripping, falling face down when I'm under stress.

On the walk back I thought of a great comeback. "Just get the money from my dad you blockhead. And by the way, this same institution of higher learning should set higher goals than sarcasm. Good day to you, sir. No: Good Morning!" I imagined myself standing over him dressed to the nine's, turning on my heels and walking out. This comforted me on the walk back to my room.

I called home, and the phone was out of service. I tried to remember the last time I spoke with my mother. It was only three days ago. She called, in the middle of the night, around two in the morning and said, "Sweet Face keep your head up, don't let nobody take you for granted. Hear me?"

I should have been worried then, but I wasn't. I was always a slow-to-boil kind of girl. See, I never worried about my mother. She was one of those women who made things happen. Not in a bragging, show-off kind of way. It was just her thing. She was PTA president twice when I was in grade school, again when I was in seventh grade, and two more times while I was in high school. She always said that she wanted to support the institutions that support me. She organized trips and auctions to raise money. She even auctioned off a financial planning lunch with Dad. She should have bid on that one. It could have been like a date for the two of them to get reacquainted.

She was always asked to help with bake sales and little fundraisers, and not because her lemon squares were perfectly shaped and dusted with snowflake-shaped powdered sugar puffs and then individually wrapped in cellophane. It was because whatever she baked was going to appear in the same blue plastic Rubbermaid shoeboxes and taste out-of-this-world good.

Mom had a way of making things happen and then giving the credit away. She did it with a wink at me. Like she and I shared a powerful secret, that the folks she gave credit to needed it more than we did, and it worked for us. So I had every confidence in her taking care of us.

My mom was white-white and my dad was African-American. They adopted me straight from the hospital. And lucky me, I kinda of sorta looked like both of them. All my time was spent with my mom. We were a team.

My father, on the other hand, was a high stakes mover and shaker. He called himself a banker, a senior vice president; he didn't work in a branch or anything like that. He said his customers were other banks, whatever that meant. He left for work at 6:20 every morning and didn't come home until minutes to eight every evening. Then he'd read trade papers like *The Financial Times, The Journal,* and some Asian forecasting newsletters. By 10:30 PM, he would shower and go to sleep. It was years before my mother realized that we should not wait to have dinner with him. By the time he settled in for dinner, he was distracted and not good company at the table, anyway. His mind was always calculating something. So my mom ate dinner with me and had a late desert with him. That is, if she could pin him down to one place. See, Dad was mobile; he usually started eating in the dining room and would finish his dinner standing up watching the evening news in the den. He always yelled "Another good meal, Syn!" when he was done. It was something, and my mother took it. She'd try to turn it into a conversation until she saw that he wasn't listening. Food wasn't that important to Dad, even though Mom had traveled to the ends of New York for the perfect ingredients to buy for his dinner. Her soul food was even good. She could smother fried chicken with mash potatoes or potato salad with the best of them. But, he would have been happy with anything. So her endless chatter about basil vs. fennel in a dish was lost on him.

My mother adored my dad, but Dad lived for the bank.

I think I was twelve the last year that he invited me to his office on "Bring Your Daughter to Work" day. Each year girls of all shapes and sizes would be paraded around the building like convicts on parole. The tour included stops for everyone. The mailroom was a career option for girls who aimed low. They implied the supply room was for girls who aimed just a little bit higher. None of the tour guides had anything nice to say about the folks that worked in their basement. They were downright insulting right in front of the supply room manager, who I could tell had whipped out a brand new light blue lab jacket just for this occasion.

Then there was the computer data center and the trading floors for those who were easily impressed. After the tour and after shaking hands with every manager that said, "I worked my way up from blah blah" and "stay in school, blah blah blah," we girls were led into a large conference room for a buffet lunch.

There was enough food for over one hundred girls, but you got the feeling that you weren't supposed to eat much, because the only plates were the size of coffee can lids. My father was prone to embarrassment, so I decided to fill one plate to the very top and not have seconds.

I had already stuffed my purse with an assortment of paper clips from the supply room. Some even looked like they were made out of solid gold. They said we could take something, and I did. I was amazed by the cases of paper clips and I could have all I wanted. My mother's over-the-shoulder purse bulged from the tiny boxes.

I knew my father wanted to show off his daughter, and unfortunately, that happened to be me. So I stuffed my assortment deep into Mom's purse. I hoped that Dad saw the long-term math skills that an attraction to paper clips might conceal.

"Girls, if you see something you need for your briefcase, go ahead and take it," they said. There was a table covered with a red tablecloth, a balloon centerpiece with the bank's logo on every balloon, and office supplies in pretty baskets. There were folders with legal pads and stamped envelopes. There was even a little newspaper, fixed up to read like a trade paper, and it was all about us. "New VIP's Arrive Today!" One story that included every girl's name and who they were related to at the bank. The story ended with a giant list of details we should know and finally a special thank you for a long list of people who make the day possible. Old dad was at the top of that list.

I took the newspaper and a folder because everyone else did, and because I didn't want to embarrass the commander-in-chief. I hated being in his work world. It felt like I came second or third to the people here, the meetings and important phone calls that kept him from ever hanging out with me.

In the conference room there was an odd array of women in red power suits. The suits talked about themselves. It was like a bad career day because everyone had the same damn career, and there weren't any demos or prizes or donuts – only gourmet food that one of the suits mistakenly thought would be better than donuts, pizza, and cheese doodles.

There must have been an article in some financial women's magazine that said you must wear a RED POWER suit or short of that a red jacket with a thick gold necklace, not a choker. Most of the women were wearing red – from crimson to dark orange. Some wore short tight skirts and jackets with way too much make up. I planned to ask my mother about this "woman in red thing" when I got back home. Even the receptionist, who was real old, had on a granny red suit with a white lace collar on it. Her rayon skirt was way too big and came down below her knees. Funny, it was the women without red that made a mark and impressed me most.

I never saw myself following in my dad's shoes. As a matter of fact, I didn't really see past middle school back then. At school I was a member of the Ashley's. There were four of us. Ashley McFadden was our leader and the trendsetter. As long as we followed the rules we could stay in the club. I was on probation for not maintaining my makeover and for constantly forgetting to look down on other girls. I knew that my days as an Ashley were numbered, but in middle school it was better to be in any club than to hang out all alone.

There were so many big mouths who gave us career advice. I started a paper clip bracelet on the sly. By the time the last red suit had finished speaking, I had a double-looped necklace that hung down to my legs in a roaring twenties style.

My dad was the final speaker. He was important around the bank. Heads popped in to hear his address to the girls. Folks started taking his picture, like he was a celebrity or something. The room erupted with flashes, and then he took questions. Hands flew up eagerly to show that they, now, wanted to wear junior red suits and spend their lives at the bank. And power, money and red suits with high heels were in their immediate futures.

My dad, Mr. Tracey, SVP of blah blah and blah marketing looked past the eager hands at me like I was some kind of a corporate plant – I'd open my mouth and financial wisdom would flow out. Young and old all looked at me, too.

"Young ladies, you have spent the day with my associates; I hope you all have been tuned in to their talks. So, if the front office is in your future, is your plan to start as a branch manager…?" The question went on too long for me personally, then ended with "something something Home Equity or Foreign Trading?" My dad attempted to pass the torch to me. I fumbled and blurted out, "Marketing and trading."

He looked at the small boxes of empty paper clips in front of me, then at the bulge in my purse and the chains around my neck that were now down to the floor. I could see the disappointment on his face. He recovered quickly, almost too effortlessly. He called on the girl in the seat in front of me.

"Can you start in the branch and then transfer to another area, Mr. Tracey?" she asked.

"Great question, and yes, we encourage our team to learn all of our products and services. In the end it benefits our consumers," Dad said, lost in a thought. I knew he was distracted cause no one answered his long ass question but he let it slide.

I was glad I had chosen the small paper clips to work with; they were more pliable. And besides, I think that my dad would have flipped if he saw chains hanging from my neck that were almost three times bigger. No one snapped any father daughter pictures, Dad didn't introduce me to anyone, and I kinda melted into the scenery. I put the clips away.

Later that night dad came into my room and sat on my bed. I wanted to pretend that I was sleeping, but I didn't notice him knocking until he was in the room. He never came into my room, much less sat down on my bed.

"Sweet Face," he said. "You don't have to do what I do or even like finance and things. But you need to decide what you want to do. What do you like? You have any ideas, child?" He waited for a reply. I wasn't prepared for a "what do you want to do when you grow up" talk.

I tried to think of what any of the red suits had said about their jobs when they were young. But nothing came to mind. Then I remembered that my mom had always wanted to become a teacher. *What did she want to teach?*

Nothing came, so I blurted out, "Dad, if I could do anything it would be to teach arts and crafts to little tiny kids." Darn, I wished I had said science or math to high school students.

He looked down at his buffed fingernails and then stood up and kissed me on the forehead. His body dwarfed my bedroom; he really was a giant of sorts.

"Good night, baby. Dream big dreams, Sophie," he said almost whispering.

My dad never invited me back to the bank again. This fact was not lost on my mother. Neither Dad nor I ever mentioned the paper clip incident. After a long while, Mom stopped asking or yelling about him bringing me into the office anymore. Mom had loads of these wars, that neither Dad nor I cared about. She had a way of seeing things the way she wanted and her perfect visions of our family drifted away slowly, but not without a fight.

Dad left Mom the following summer. It hurt me, but not like it hurt Mom. It broke something inside of her.

* * * * *

I called my Aunt Lucky, my dad's sister. She was stupid rich and cursed with terminally bad taste. There was a life-sized stuffed white polar bear in her living room. He was even taller than Aunt Lucky and he was standing on his hind legs with his teeth showing. Her home had this safari-meets-whorehouse décor.

"Hello Aunt Lucky, it's me, Sophie."

"Hello there. How is my little old Sweet Face doing? How is school?"

"Aunt Lucky, I need to get in touch with my mom right away."

I was always surprised anytime Aunt Lucky answered her cell phone. She loved having her maid Jeana pick up and screen her calls. She wasn't ready for cell phones, but still liked the idea of having the newest phone in her high-end hand bags.

"There has got to be a way to have Jeana answer my cell phone while I am on the go," she used to say. Aunt Lucky had her view of things and didn't bend. It was her way or no way at all.

She didn't like my mother for some reason and was glad when my father left her. She never seemed to consider the fact that my dad had left me too. My mom was the one that cut off my visits to Aunt Lucky's house. She felt that "old big mouth" was a bad influence for me, as she was way too militant. Militant was my mom's code word for "we are not dealing with racism again today. It is just too much work." As usual, I agreed with my mother and never pushed to see my aunt.

"Aunt Lucky, do you have any way of reaching my mom?"

"I could call her for you. Have you tried that, dear?" Her voice said "hell no."

"Yes I did; the phone isn't working."

"Well, that's interesting. What do you suggest, dear?"

"Maybe you could go to my house; it's really an emergency."

"You mean me go to your house, dear?"

"Yes, Aunt Lucky – my mom could be sick or something. I need her to call me today. What if something is wrong?" I wanted to whine, but didn't think it would help.

"What! Wait! Wait! First, I will not visit your mother. I will hold my peace, for your sake. And besides, I am having work done downstairs, and my trainer is on his way. Things are just popping here. Maybe I could send my driver. Look, it sounds like you are calling me with some drama."

I didn't want to mention the bounced check, but it was now necessary or I'd have to call my father, I thought. Aunt Lucky was very tall, driven, and she did have a big mouth. I would still rather deal with her than get my dad involved.

"Aunt Lucky, Mom missed a tuition payment, and if she doesn't send it immediately, I will be put out of school."

"Sweet Face, call your father. He can take care of it. Or were you thinking that I should pay it? Why are you calling me?"

"I need to know if my mother is okay, and I thought you might help me. I just need to speak with her, that's all."

I couldn't call Dad. He had a new family now and two small children of his own. I knew that Dad loved me kinda sorta, and my being adopted didn't make him more or less than the limited father that he was. The problem with Dad was that he was becoming a Super Dad to his new kids. He was involved with them. He had never-ending stories about them that he loved to share with me. *Of all the people in the world, why did he need to tell me?* After I graduated from high school, I stopped talking to Dad. I would rather drink gasoline than hear another of his proud papa renditions.

As a child, I remembered how my mother would always group us together when asking for Dad's time. I remembered her saying we would have to become customers in order for Dad to remember either of our birthdays.

We didn't open accounts, so he never remembered any of our important celebrations. Before their split my mom would say to Dad, "Oh, honey, by the way, you gave me diamond earrings for my birthday last week."

Dad would whisper, a technique he must have come across in personnel meetings. "You should check with me first, Synovia."

"Like hell. If you can't think to buy your wife a present, then I will buy anything that I want."

I was glad when their divorce finally happened. The only change I noticed was that the arguments that started the same time on Saturday mornings and continued through dinner on Sundays ended – the pressure was off. Oh, and yes: no more pro golf marathons on cable. There was no silence requirement being demanded as he cranked the volume to full blast on golf games. The commercials would come on and shake the house. Mom didn't retreat to the mall or to movies or anything. She loved being home when dad was home. I bet he wanted to have some time alone, by himself, on the weekend. Unfortunately, Mom insinuated herself into every room that Dad was in. Her life folded into his, and even I, a former Ashley, knew that Mom needed other interests.

"Syn, why don't you go out for a walk or something?"

"I am just looking for some adult conversation, Boyd."

"What about what I am looking for, hon?" he snapped back.

"What about what you're looking for? You used to look for it right here. Do I repulse you, Boyd? Have I gotten old?"

"I am not going to dignify that with an answer."

* * * * *

I guess he found what he was looking for with the help of his sister. She introduced them.

Dad remarried someone much younger the very next year. Aunt Lucky set him up with a friend of a friend. The new wife, Tia, was some Jack and Jill girl who grew up with all the right connections. They got pregnant quickly, so that told the whole story. At first, it didn't seem like it bothered Mom or me that Dad had sired an heir.

The problem was that I still couldn't call him because of the way he was with his new children. He goes on and on about them not connecting that I am still his child, too. The thing that hurts most is that I can't ask him why he is making so much time for them. The tears come when I think the difference is in the blood. This is the hurt that I couldn't even share with Mom.

I didn't call my dad; Aunt Lucky finally agreed to help me. Later, she called and said that her driver waited at our house for an hour, then left a note.

I didn't hear from my mother the whole day. So I packed my stuff and asked the dean if I could return after working things out with my dad. The dean's eyes got a twinkle at the mention of SVP blah blah.

"Yes, we will hold your standing, Miss Tracey. Do let your father know that we will work this out together."

"Hold my standing" – was that some kind of message or a code? I was so worried about my mom that I didn't even have an imaginary "put the dean back in his place conversation" in my head.

I should have flown home, but the bus was cheaper and didn't require completely emptying my checking account. The problem was speed. Sitting on the bus for five hours was torture. Different scenarios popped into my mind, and none of them were good. I got back home around ten in the evening, and nerves had taken over. The house was a mess – no one had kept up the front of the house, and sparse holiday decorations had sagged. There were still two deer-shaped moving statues on the lawn. Their bodies were traced with white lights. Only the smaller deer did not move his head and neck up and down. He was broken so he twisted his neck just a little and it looked like he was saying "NO! NO!" *A bad omen, if I ever saw one,* I thought to myself. I stepped over the mail and opened the door.

The house smelled of stale air and old food. There was a lot of unopened mail pushed into a pile under the desk in the front hall. So my mother had been here recently. Someone had to get the mail from the box and push it under the desk. I went back outside and checked the mailbox. It only had a water bill with FINAL NOTICE typed across the front in red.

That didn't help, not really. I looked up and down the street hoping that a familiar face would stroll by and help me check the house. If she was in there, it was not good news either. My stomach ached, and I took a step back inside and then took another step.

I wanted to scream and run back out. But I needed to find Mom. So I kept going. I started in the kitchen. There was more of the same in there – no upkeep. I was home for two days over Christmas. Mom seemed a little jerky. Even the whole story about her visiting her cousin and needing me to return to the dorm was questionable now. Things were kind of okay. Right? I didn't notice all this mess then.

I thought I might check the whole house for notes then get on the phone to her friends. No notes. A nagging voice started to whisper to me: *Your mother is dead. She would never live in such squalor.* I went upstairs and opened her bedroom door. And in the pitch black room with drapes and shades successfully managing to block any ray of sun or moon light, I felt completely alone, and I was frightened out of my mind. *Was my mother in there?* I fumbled around for the light switch. *Would I be the one to find her body?* Ideas started popping into my head. *Leave now! Go get Aunt Lucky! I'm not ready for this! I can't do this alone!* I stepped back towards the bedroom and fell over a lump of clothes or something.

"Sophie, is that you?"

"Mom?"

I could see the light switch now and got up. I turned on the light, and there she was. She looked like a ghost. She was pale. Her silky blonde hair was all but replaced by an uncombed swirl of yellow straw with gray roots. Her Pooh Bear T-shirt told the story of someone who had completely succumbed to real or imagery demons. I couldn't tell if she had just been sitting in bed in the dark or if she had been sleeping.

"Hi, Mom," I said grabbing her neck and hugging her hard. *Oh my God!* There was less of her, and she looked lost and very old among her fifthly wrinkled sheets, the dirt and clutter. There were empty Pepsi cans, Cheese Doodle bags, and Snickers bar wrappers everywhere. She had made ashtrays out of everything, from shoes to the edge of her nightstand.

"I've been looking for you. They put me out of school. Why didn't you tell me that you were ill? They put me out of school. I didn't call Dad. I was going to call him today, if you weren't here. I had to find you." I wanted to stop talking and listen to Mom, but I couldn't yet. And the worst part was that my voice was getting louder and faster. I was starting to come apart, holding on to what was left of my mother in a sea of filth. "I took the bus home by myself; I didn't know what was going on. The dean said that your checks were bouncing, and..."

"Sophie, stop."

I took a deep breath, and tried to collect myself. This made the tears flow. I continued to hold on to her. Her breath was strong and rancid as she pushed an arm between us, pushing me away. That failed, so she rested her head on my shoulder, like she was exhausted or something.

"Sophie, we are in trouble, baby."

"What happened? What kinda trouble? Are you hurt? Can you stand up? What kinda trouble? What is...?" I was off again and could not stop the questions.

"Shut up!" she whispered in my ear. It stopped me cold in mid-thought.

"I'm sorry, baby, but you gotta listen to your mom. Your dad is taking his time with the payments. He is spending every dime on that witch. We are about to lose everything. Our house is the next thing to go. You should ask him for some money." I got up and opened the drapes some more and cracked the window. "Only don't let him know that I need it. You hear me, baby?" I heard everything.

I started picking up her room, and she got up to find the telephone. Her legs weren't steady at first, but she was motivated. She was up, and her bare bottom was exposed. Skin was sagging off of it. That was all I could take, and I headed for the door.

"Call him, Sophie, use the phone downstairs, damn it."

Once out of her room, I fell against the wall that led downstairs, just to catch my breath. The situation was tragic.

I went downstairs. In the kitchen the base for the phone was without the handset. I decided to press the large gray and black numbers. I realized that I didn't remember my dad's phone number. I hadn't called him in seven or eight months. The number was not locked into memory, nor was it a mindless dance that my fingers would play while gliding over the number keys. I walked over to the refrigerator and saw the yellowed note. It was old emergency numbers. It was written during our lemon square days by a woman who took care of all the details of our lives, but who was no longer around.

I rubbed my forehead on the refrigerator door and wept. All our joy had been sucked out of this place. I looked around the butter-colored kitchen. · There were dishes everywhere – all dirty. Dried food and a trail of ants were at home on the floor. Something about the mess and the smell felt weeks old.

How could this happen to us? My hand shook as I dialed my dad's home. Silent tears fell and increased with every number that I pressed.

"Hello, this is Boyd." He sounded like a giant voiceover.

"It's me."

"I'm sorry, I didn't catch your voice. Who's calling?"

"Me. Sophie." I hadn't said my name on purpose; I needed him to know my voice and that I was in trouble. He was such a jerk.

"Sophie!" He screamed like he had just scored a touchdown.

"Dad."

"Hello there. What a pleasant surprise. Let me get rid of this other call. Don't go anywhere." He clicked off.

"Okay, Soph, you have my undivided attention. What's up, sweetheart?"

"Well…" I must have paused too long because Dad started in on the new family.

"Tia and I were just talking about you. We are throwing a birthday bash for Joy and want you there."

"My mom is in trouble. She might be sick. She is not eating or cleaning, and the bills aren't paid. It looks like the water and phone will be shut off soon."

"Where are you?"

"I'm home."

"Good, I spoke with Lucky. I got the phone turned on, just in case you came home. I also left a message for your dean."

Something wasn't right. Why didn't he come and check on Mom? And why didn't he expect that I would be calling him? However, I was not surprised.

"I got put out of school 'cause Mom didn't pay any bills. What's wrong, Dad?"

"I'll take care of everything. Don't worry."

"Dad, can you come, and soon?" I was falling into despair and Dad was the only support I had. It was more out of desperation than pulling together a plan.

I looked at the phone a long time. It was working! I had called before I left school, and there had been a service interruption message. I hung up as Mom came downstairs. She was wearing a pink terrycloth short set. It was her attempt to clean up for me. But I could tell that it was the only clean thing she had.

"Did you call?" she said, pulling her hair into a ponytail.

She turned on the TV and plopped down and started watching a hair transplant commercial.

"Sophie, damn it – did you call? Is he bringing us some money? We need dinner and stuff."

"Yes, I called. Did you know that your phone was turned off?"

"Meet that ass out on the porch, Sophie," she said, looking around at the place. "I don't want him in my house. Can you make me something to drink? Tea?" She lifted her bony legs up and spread out on the couch.

She continued, "You know what I think? I think they take the "after" shots first and then pull the hairs out, and *voila!* It looks like they got the cure to baldness – but it is all crap. Sophie, when is he coming? How much did you ask for? Cash, I hope."

I didn't move.

"Sophie, I am talking to you. Wake the hell up. You always flake out at the wrong times." She was angry, and I just didn't know what to say. "Sophie is a flake, a flake out expert. A flake out expert! When is he coming?"

I watched her – taking everything in. I was frozen with fear and disappointment. Who in the hell was this woman? My mother would never live like this.

"How much money, Sophie?" she screamed.

I moved a damp towel from a dining room chair that was in the living and sat down. "Five hundred dollars," I lied. I just said anything to shut her up.

"Good, good – did you say that the phone was back on? It was out of service for a while. Go outside and wait for your dad."

I sat on the porch in the cold and waited for him to come and straighten everything back out. I knew he could get Mom to do anything. After about twenty minutes, I realized that Dad didn't say when he was coming. The thought of going back into the house with her was not a pleasant one. It beat freezing to death. Mom was already asleep on the couch. I slipped up to my room, and to my surprise, everything was the way I'd left it – kinda clean. I relaxed on my favorite pink and green "bed in a bag" ensemble, and in no time I was asleep.

Dad came in like the big alpha male. In 24 hours he had forced Mom into a 90-day treatment center in Connecticut. He had connections, and Mom had to go – even though she pleaded with us to let her do it on an outpatient basis. Getting her there was very traumatic. The alpha male arranged for three men to come and scoop her up like she was a lost puppy. I should have known that something was up when Aunt Lucky herself picked me up at the house and took me shopping. At 4 PM she and her driver were outside waiting for me. Dad said that he would stay with Mom while I took a break. I didn't realized what he was up to, so I welcomed the break. We actually had a nice time. I got new boots, a brown leather jacket, and red suede gloves from Lord & Taylor, all gifts from my aunt.

We had an early dinner at Doc's, a seafood restaurant with white table linens and waiters in short black jackets. The fried seafood platter was heaven. Aunt Lucky was funny as hell, and we really started to click. She talked about various people in the restaurant. She could spot everything from a dead-beat date to a fake-Prada-bag-carrying-has-been actor. I should have known that studying other people would lead back to studying me eventually.

It was Aunt Lucky's opinion that I looked like a young woman without means and with suppressed potential. It was the Ashley's all over again. I promised her that I would consider her offer for me to get a head-to-toe make over. I didn't take offense to her need to change everything about me, because this was my auntie with the stuffed polar bear. I even had to omit that I was looking a little frumpy.

I was wearing my favorite green and white T-shirt. It said, "Recycle or perish?" I paired it with faded black jeans, old silver flats, and a black headband to keep my hair under control. My nails were chipped, and my skin, especially on my hands, was extremely dry.

"Thanks for checking on Mom, it means the world to me. She will be back to her old self in no time."

"Anything for you, dear," she said, as if sending her driver around to my mother's house had been personally taxing.

"What did my mother ever do you?"

"Excuse me?"

"Why don't you like her? Just give me one reason why you hate my mother so much." I was no match for Aunt Lucky's wit, but her looking down on my mother, especially now, was wearing on my nerves.

"Only one? Narrowing it down to just one is going to be difficult. Suffice it to say that I didn't like the way she treated you."

"What are you talking about? I had a great relationship with my mother, Aunt Lucky."

"What do you have to compare her with?" Her phony sweetie-pie voice was replaced by her I'm-about-to-lose-it voice. "She paraded you around like you were her badge to sainthood. 'Look at me; I am trying to manage and teach the child to be normal at the same time.'" She put her hand out in front of her like she was playing an imaginary piano that someone was pulling away. "I only suggested that she allow me to take care of your hair and your wardrobe. She had you, my brother's child, running around here looking like Sophie Orphan Annie. Do you know that she never even combed your hair? Never. It was too hard for her to manage. She let it mat up, and that is why it was all cut off and you cried for a week. You cried for a week, and no amount of lemon squares or the designer clothes that hung off her back could stop you from crying. It broke my heart. She spent Boyd's money like it was coming out of the bathroom faucet, and you looked like her bohemian love child. I told that mother of yours that you needed to learn how to be a black woman in this world. She said that everything wasn't black and white. Boyd's dumb ass gave her a free hand with bringing you up. And look at you, you're not half black, half white – you're half raised."

Aunt Lucky was telling the truth. I had forgotten all about having my hair cut off and how I had wanted to wear pretty things. But I was my mother's little recycling project. She got all my things from her friend's used clothes shop, A Moment in Time. The clothes fit, and they were always clean, but they never made me feel special. I wished I could have ripped this dumb shirt off. But that would show my hand. *There were times when I wanted more from my mother. So what?*

All of my mother's shortcomings sailed back to me. I remembered feeling that something was wrong between my parents and that my mother would take out her frustrations with my father on me. I used to hope that my dad would be kinder to her, so that she would be more patient with me. When I didn't feel close to either one of them, I would escape into my fantasy world. That was how my daydreaming started.

"A penny for your thoughts," she said almost apologetically.

"Aunt Lucky, I'd like to go now."

"I've said too much. Let's make a deal right now. If you don't want me to talk about your mother, then don't bring her up. Do we have a deal?"

She put out her hand for me to shake, and I just couldn't do it. Aunt Lucky had opened up way too much history. I couldn't get my brain around all of what she had said, and I remembered. I couldn't really shake on anything related to it. So I put out a limp hand to move the moment along.

We got back just in time for me to hear my mother's screams as she was dropped in the backseat of a black limousine by my father's goons. She was hollering, "Boyd!" at the top of her lungs.

One week later, he had me neatly tucked back in school. On the way back, Dad volunteered to drive me. I got my own credit card and a monthly allowance. Dad explained everything and told me when he noticed Mom's falling apart, and how things had to be now with our expenses. I was to take charge of my finances, and between the two of us Mom would not be allowed to touch any money. I felt like one of those giant inflatable rats used by striking employees. I held the purse strings now. He even suggested that I leave Mom and live with him or Aunt Lucky. I was a rat for considering leaving her. I could see that he was through with Mom, but I wasn't. She needed time in rehab, and then she would need me.

Before returning to school, I spent the week home supervising the Handy Maids during the day and sleeping at Aunt Lucky's place at night. Getting our house in order was my obsession. If I could pick up the house, my mother would recover. The Handy Maids came for three days, and in the end the house felt normal. But my world felt like it was spinning apart. I charged their service to my father's account. I even got my father to get current with Mom's gardener and he took care of the outside of the house. Everything was pruned and ready for spring. I left instructions to take down all the Christmas decorations and pack them away in the garage – no matter how broken or worn.

Staying with Aunt Lucky, at her estate, was a scream. She wasn't the happiest or the nicest woman I had ever met. However, Aunt Lucky was brilliant at keeping the nature of her fortune a secret. All I knew is that, she didn't work for it, it wasn't old money, and it wasn't from a family inheritance. I wondered if my father knew where her money was coming from. Dad had money, but Aunt Lucky was rich. She ran the servants crazy. She changed some of their names, especially if their names were not easy to pronounce or remember. Like she changed Talara, her housekeeper's name to Lori. Behind her back they called her the "unlucky buffoon."

I don't know what was worse, the bear towering over us, or the super rich food made from scratch for every meal in my honor. Everything was in some cream sauce or something: even breakfast. I hated it. All Aunt Lucky had to do to impress me would have been to give me Captain Crunch cereal and turkey hot dogs.

Dad arrived early Sunday morning in jeans, a white bomber jacket, and designer sunglasses. I could tell that Tia was dressing him now. If not, it was his own attempt to look younger while out with his babies. We had driven about an hour while he talked about drugs, drug addiction, and drug addicts. It was hard to tune Dad out, because he had this annoying habit of touching you every time he wanted you to get his point. His preference was your arm, but he would settle for a shoulder or a hand if they were closer to him. He tried to make it sound like my mother had ended their marriage to pursue her new fullblown drug habit. The hole in his story was that he now had two other children: one was turning five. He had been gone for years. Mom seemed like things had gotten out of control recently. So I didn't believe his lies, but with my mom committed to a treatment center, I didn't dare stand up to him.

When he ran out of sage advice regarding my mother, he talked about his children and how he was an involved parent. He talked in detail about spending a Saturday painting the set for their winter recital. We were sitting in his brand new silver gray Range Rover when he said, "I love parenting." He touched my arm. "My children are my world, Sophie," he beamed. I felt excluded from his world.

"Maybe those children are your world." My heart was beating wildly. I couldn't take any more of his "I found the light and it is in my children's eye" stuff.

I discovered my voice. "Why not me? Why?" It was out – I had managed to listen to his shit for two hours, and now it was out. "What about the all-important Bank?"

"Sophie, I got a second chance," he said, reaching for my hand. "Missing all that time with you is the biggest mistake of my life. But, I got a second chance, Sophie, and I am here if you need anything, honey." He continued looking at the road, taking quick measured glances at me. My mind raced. *If I need anything, is that what he said? If he knew that my mother was on drugs, then why did I have to find her and then call him?*

"See, I thought that giving you and your mom the best of everything was my job. That is what the men in my family did. My dad worked fourteen-hour days. Spending time with us children – well it wasn't what fathers did. My dad wanted to get us out of the slums and into good schools. He succeeded, Sophie, so I wanted to give you more than he was able to give me – a bigger house, a first class college education, a future where you are calling the shots." He smiled as if he had just explained a tough math problem to a fifth grader.

"I don't know you, either. Dad, how many sisters and brothers did you have?"

"We were three total, honey. Danny Jr. and Lucille – we called her Lucky, cause she got blamed for everything Danny and I did wrong. The name stuck. And then there was me. Why?"

"I was alone, Dad. It was just me and Mom and sometimes it would have been nice to... well, never mind."

I started to cry and looked out the passenger side window to hide my tears.

"Funny, I thought that you would stay little forever, or at least until things settled down at work. Then we would have some great times. But I was the merger and acquisition king, and before you knew it I was running the show. It wasn't until you left for college that I realized it was over: you were a young woman who didn't need to play games and go to amusement parks." I could feel him looking at the back of my head. "I am not proud of the void I created in your life, Sweet Face."

I started to feel sorry for him. I wanted to steer the conversation back to my needs, but I just sat there.

"I've been given another chance with Joy and Zee. And another chance with you."

"Your children are lucky to have you," I said.

"They are your family too, Sophie. Joy is your little sister, Zee is your little brother, and then there was your other brother."

"Another brother? How?"

"Never mind." He started speeding and changed his focus on getting the car moving faster.

"Dad? You had another son? When?"

"Sweet Face, let's change the subject."

He had revealed something and began to sweat. It made me nervous, and now I was exhausted. It was as if someone had sucked the air out of the world. *Who was the other brother? Where is he now? I didn't have to be alone all these years?* I was never one to plan and plot. But I was determined to find the answers, and I would not stutter this time.

Chapter Two: The Other Brother

I had to find out who this brother was. I made a short list of what I knew. Was he my father's son? I didn't know that for sure. My dad knew more than he was telling, and if my father knew, then my mother knew something, too. I had to get to my mom while she was still in her drug haze. I had to see her soon, before my dad warned her about his little slip of the tongue. This meant leaving school for a short trip back home. On Friday after fourth period, I got on a bus heading home. I wrote out notes and questions that could trick my mom into the truth. Finally, I realized that it was not the questions. She simply needed to believe that Dad had told me everything. That would be enough to get her talking.

It felt good to be at home. I spent the night in my room, and on Saturday morning I headed out to see Mom. During my visit with her at the Life Changing Treatment Facility, I asked her about my brother and told her that Dad had told me all about him. She sat there with seven long pretzel sticks, holding each one like it was a cigar and then chopped them like a beaver with her teeth. The pretzels weren't about eating at all; she just needed to crush something with her teeth. She was dressed in regular street clothes, her uniform: Calvin Klein jeans, a white tailored blouse, and a red leather belt. The clothes were out-dated and hung on her bony body. The belt had a new hole put in and wrapped around her one and a half times. Her little butt was all but gone. But it was her face that had stopped me cold: her sunken checks and her empty eyes. They bulged out and darted all around the room searching for something, like an opportunity to get out.

"He did?" she said after a few moments. "I thought we were going to tell you together. What all did he say, Sweet Face?"

"About my brother?" I couldn't really lie to my mom.

"Yes, sweetie."

"We talked during the drive back to school last week. But he didn't let me know his name or how old he is." I was kinda telling the truth.

"Okay, it's just like your dad to start something and leave it to me to finish it – just drop the damn thing in my lap again."

Again I wondered what she meant – but knew it had something to do with his leaving her. *Bastard – he must have had an affair and fathered a child. I had another little brother.*

She lit a cigarette and puffed without inhaling.

"His name was William; you were three, and I wanted him. We got the call that he was born and available. We didn't plan or even think that it was a possibility, and yet there was Mrs. Helen Silveright on the home phone, our beige slim line kitchen phone, asking me if I wanted a son. I called your father and whispered to him that you had a new brother and the Flower Bright Agency wanted to know if we wanted him to join our family. I had to repeat it to your dad four times. He could not get his mind around it. I told him, 'Mrs. Silveright told me over the phone that Sophie's birth parents had another child, and they placed him with the Flower Bright Agency. We must let them know now, or they will call the other family.'"

I didn't breathe, didn't move a muscle. I didn't understand. "He started screaming. 'Yes! Yes! Yes! We have a son. Well I'll be a monkey's uncle,' he said. That was one happy man." She had been talking rapidly and had come to the end abruptly. She looked around the room again. I wanted more. This story was not what I was expecting.

We were talking about my birth parent's child. It hit me like a freight train. I needed to get my mind around this information.

"What did Mrs. Silverwhatever say?" I asked, hoping that she would continue.

"She said that Shelly – they never gave us your birthmother's last name, they just said Shelly – had given birth to a son and had placed the child with the agency. Those were her exact words – funny how I remember that all these years later. I always had a great memory – photographic they call it. I was a real whiz in school, especially in social studies. Ask me anything, go ahead. Go ahead, hon. I was pretty too," she said looking at an older gentleman, in a navy blue suit, who was visiting a much younger woman on the other side of the room.

"Mom! What happened?" I was becoming impatient and hoped that she didn't realize that I was in total shock.

"Well it turned out that we got to meet the baby, but then there was an interview. We went. We were not selected. So, in seven days after learning about William and meeting the boy, we had lost the chance to adopt him. It was a pain like none other. I had made a place for William in our house and in my...." She looked around again. "Nevermind! Well, anyway, it was a loss that I didn't share with anyone. No one understood that you had a brother and that you could not see him. Once we recovered a little, I mentioned to the agency that I wanted you two to know each other and that I would follow any guidelines that they felt were appropriate."

She stopped and checked her pockets for something. Not finding it, she continued.

"Mrs. Silveright told me outright that William's new family did not want to confuse things for him. So, I never saw him again, and that was that. He should be sixteen or seventeen years old by now."

"Why didn't you tell me?"

"Why? You can't touch him or see him or talk with him. So after weeks of consideration, I determined this course of action to be prudent." She sounded just like my dad. She checked her pockets again.

"What did he look like?"

"Like a little you. He had big curly hair and the sweetest little face."

I started to cry. Big sloppy tears that I didn't know I had, and nothing Mom tried comforted me. "Now, now, Sweet Face, we can't have that today." She looked around like I was causing a scene and said, "You want to look up these people or something? There is the adoption registry. Maybe he or Shelly is in it. I'll help you honey. But please stop crying – I just can't handle it right now. I thought this was going to be a happy visit. Now tell me about school."

"These people?"

"I'm sorry, I was feeling a little over-protective of you and locked up at the same time. Sorry. Look I haven't been myself lately. Okay?"

"It's okay. I'm sorry, Mom. I had better go."

"It is just that this is the very first conversation that you initiated about your birth family in your entire life – ever, seriously ever. So forgive me for being weird about it. Look where I am, for God's sake. I'm an emotional basket case. Your father has me locked away like this for no good reason."

She chomped the last pretzel.

"I'd like to meet them; just let's wait until I get out of school, and you are out of here. Okay? I don't want to handle anything that could upset me. Let's just let me think about all of this for a while."

"I know, and I am proud that you are asking about it. I can help you."

"Only when I am ready. Okay, mom?"

She nodded her head slightly and looked at me for a long moment. I noticed that she needed a color touch up, her eyebrows needed threading, and she just needed some general grooming. *I guess the first thing was to stop the drugs, then get beauty treatments.*

As if reading my mind she said, "First we take care of the inside and then the outside."

"Okay."

"Sophie, write the agency, honey. Tell them that you want to meet your little brother. I could be out before you get the reply, and then we can track this kid down. You hear me?"

"Sure," I said, knowing that if I didn't lie, my mother would start writing these people. "And Mom..."

"Yes, Sophie?"

"You need to be in here. I found you, remember?"

Her face bristled. She was disgusted and offended. She stood up and walked away from me. As she headed back through the door, where she had first appeared, she screamed. "You believe your father's lies. I was sad and under the weather. You all act like I got a serious problem. Well I don't. If you can't be positive, then next time stay home. I don't need this shit."

Just like that, she was crazed and yelling. Everyone was looking at her. It was a mistake coming here. Some doors are better kept closed.

Chapter Three: Fern

Except for my repeating fantasy of being in the world with William at my side, a little brother to adore, I didn't advance the search at all. I didn't write one letter or make one phone call, nothing. My senior year was difficult: the workload was overwhelming, and I needed to land a job after graduation. Since I didn't plan for a career, the possibilities where slim. I had to keep one eye on my mother, and I was seriously dating. His name was Harry, but he wanted to be called Wise. He was the struggling artist type, with parents who always bailed him out of any trouble or any adult responsibilities. His needs always seemed to overshadow mine and I was being way too kind and indecisive about seeing him at all. Once I opened up one of those black and white composition books and wrote: "Why I am dating Wise?" I put Pros on one side of the page and Cons on the other. All I could come up with was that he was selfish and that he was cute. So I planned to move back home when school ended, and if I was lucky Wise wouldn't bother to visit me.

My mom still clung to an addict's view of money and trying to get over on people – mostly my dad. She had forgotten who she used to be and how powerful she was. She lived for Narcotics Anonymous meetings and her job. She was now working as a relief cashier at Kmart. She was making barely enough money and still expected my father's handouts. My goal was to help my mother restore her confidence. This was easier said than done, as she loved the perks of working at Kmart. The main one was the items that magically jumped into her bags. She would open shit and dump the contents right into her bag. She would come home with her giant handbags full of tampons, AAA batteries, Oreos, Jordan almonds – anything little and strange that she could have purchased or gone without. After a year, she was fired for arguing fiercely with a customer, and all her perks stopped.

By the summer before my senior year, my mother had managed to stay clean for eighteen months.

She was clean, but her thinking was still a little skizzy. Her goal was always to find ways to use me to get money from Dad.

One day she had a plan for me to trick my father into giving her new car money.

"Sophie you give me the money. We wait a few months, buy an end-of-the-season refurbished mark-down, and no one is the wiser. You get a brand new car, and I get four grand to help with the house, ching-ching." She saw that I wasn't excited about the plan and added, "We would split the diff."

Her plans never worked – she was not good at it. I spent weeks avoiding calling my dad – until she cornered me and handed me the phone with him on it. I said everything that my mother wanted me to say. Dad knew a guy and the two of us went car shopping. I got my first car, a blue Ford Focus, and Mom got nothing. The only good news was that the longer she was clean, the fewer capers she needed to attempt.

The funny thing about finding out about my brother was that I discovered that adoption suited me. My parents made it an everyday word like silver or purple, and my mother was so cool about who we were – that I was cool about it too. Growing up, my mother got me. She understood my need to tune in and out and sometimes stay out longer than most people thought was normal for a young girl.

By the time I graduated from college, the chasm between my dad and me was even wider. He wanted me to choose between an MBA and an internship with the bank. I couldn't decide. I needed to keep an eye on my mother, who looked like she was getting her self together ever so slowly. I was always worried about her slipping. I also needed to get rid of Wise. I wondered if I was the only young woman to date a man for two years on and off just, because I felt sorry for him, or something even more nebulous, like it was better than no relationship at all. I had promised myself that I would drop Wise after I finished school. I didn't want the drama of a big break-up.

I was about to graduate. My mind wasn't on the future, or leaving Wise or anything like that. The only thing more joyful than the graduation itself would have been to have William at the ceremony. I had a fully developed young man in my mind after all this time – tall wiry, well spoken, and handsome. He even got all my jokes. I had planned to share many laughs and good times with my little brother. The only thing was that I had never written the letter so the chance of William coming to the ceremony or being a part of my life was zero.

The funny thing was that as much as I wanted William to enter my life, I wanted Wise to leave as badly. It was time for me to give Wise his walking papers. I would be moving back home soon, and I wanted to do *me* for a change. Wise was one of those relationships that ended right after college. Loads of people must have been in them, because break-up trauma was happening all over the place. The sad thing for me was that I didn't think Wise would be anything but annoyed at the inconvenience it would cause him.

I sat on my bed and opened my red leather journal and wrote, "Getting ready for my life" across a clean page. "1. Find Little William, he should be a teenager by now. 2. Find a way to support myself. 3. Just leave, Wise won't care." An hour later I had written down everything I remembered about the conversation with my mother regarding William. The other items on the list would have to wait.

I was ready. I seriously wanted to find William. The thought of that empty chair during graduation awoke in me a need and was a reminder that time was running by. I was working as an after-school counselor at a YMCA center to earn some money of my own. Working with all those school-aged kids was fun. Hanging out with the teenagers gave me the courage to put my plan in action.

I got home from the YMCA after 7 P.M. Wise wasn't around, so I decided to call my mother and get her on board. My heart felt like it was going to jump right out of my chest as I dialed the house.

"Hello," she said.

"You promised to help me find my brother, remember?"

"Good evening, Sophie"

"Mom, will you help me?" I tried to calm myself and regain some control. I kicked off my shoes and started to remove my earrings.

"Sophie what's going on?"

"You said that you would help me find William, my brother. Remember?"

"Help you? Help you how?"

"You said that you would help me find my brother." I was about to cry. All I needed was for her to say yes. My blood was starting to boil, and for the life of me I didn't know why, exactly.

"Have you been drinking? Where are you? I can come and get you."

"Mom, I am not drunk. You said that you would help me find my brother William."

"I did? When? Who told you about William? Your dad told you? That son of bitch, I wanted to tell you." She didn't remember any of it. *How could that be?*

"You did. You told me. You were in treatment, and I came to visit. You told me that you and Dad tried to adopt William from Mrs. Helena Silver something or other. Remember?" I was screaming and disappointed. Our conversation was so meaningful to me that I had thought about it almost everyday for years. It divided my life into B.W. and A.W. – before William and after William. But what was so pivotal to me was bleached away in my mother's drug rehab haze.

By the time I went over the whole visit word for word, supplying the details of the scene even down to her Calvin Klein jeans and her wrinkled white top, she vaguely recalled the conversation and agreed to help me anyway.

"Let's start with the adoption registry," she said. "Sophie, I am so proud of you."

We talked almost every evening about our next steps. She was going to recovery meetings and spouting their slogans. Her favorites were "be careful of what you ask for" and "no pain, no gain."

We began our search first with the online Adoption Registry. We searched for Shelly and William in census data and other public records. Nothing! But one week later, Mom had a brainstorm.

"Let's write her a letter in care of the adoption agency and ask her for a meeting or ask if she could tell us about William."

"Write who?"

"Mrs. Silveright."

"Mom, you said there was another family. Who was the other family?" I didn't want to mention that she told me while in treatment again. She never brought up her stay in treatment, so I tried not to say it much either.

"What?"

"Think back; when you got the call about William, you said that you had to make a quick decision or the other family would get him?"

"That is right. Mrs. Silveright said that the other family would get a call if we didn't decide right away. Wait a minute – I got the impression that Shelly had just delivered and they were completely surprised by this baby. They were scrambling to figure out where to place little William."

"That is my point, Mom. We weren't the only family. I think Shelly had another child before having William."

"Sweet Face, we just don't know."

"They called you because you had me, Shelly's daughter. Did they call you every time they had to place a child?"

"No, they didn't."

"See what I mean?"

One week later, I was spending time with my mom. We had a folder with three pieces of paper at this point: my birth information sheet, my hand-written notes of Mom's account of William and the conversation surrounding finding out about him, and a pamphlet for the adoption registry. At the top of my birth information sheet was the contact information for the agency.

Without thinking too much, I grabbed the phone receiver off the wall and brought it over to the kitchen table. I laced the curly old phone cord around my wrist and dialed the agency. A woman answered.

"Good afternoon, you have reached the Flower Bright Agency. How may I help you?"

"Who are you calling, Sophie?" Mom asked.

"May I speak with Mrs. Silveright, please?" My heart was pounding like imminent death was approaching. I put two fingers over my lips for Mom to be quiet.

After a long pause, the woman spoke again. "I am sorry, but Mrs. Silveright retired a few years ago. Would you like to speak with Mr. Roy Nickerson? He is now in charge of African-American adoptions."

I managed to say yes, hoping that it would buy me time to collect myself. Little beads of sweat collected on my forehead. "Mom, Mrs. Silveright retired. I am being transferred to Mr. Nickerson; please speak with him."

I gave her the phone before she could say no. I was out of breath and beyond nervous. Mom leaned in close as the cord was still around my arm.

"Hello, Mr. Nickerson, my name is Synovia Tracey. I adopted my daughter with the help of Mrs. Silveright..."

My mother was going on and on with useless details about me. I gave cut signal by running my fist across my neck. She turned her back to me and listened to him for a while.

"Yes, yes. I understand. My daughter is interested in meeting her birth family and we were hoping to have your agency forward our information to them. Yes, yes. I understand. That would be wonderful. Really? Are you kidding me? About twenty-three years ago, right... Just finished college with honors... Certainly..."

My mother put her hand over the receiver, a real old school move if I ever saw one. She said, "He wants us to come in and meet with him." She returned to the phone.

"No, the pleasure is all mine. Yes, thank you. Have a wonderful day. See you tomorrow."

"Meet with him? Why?" Regret crawled up the back of my neck.

"We will find out tomorrow." She said, and gave me that fake-Zen look that said, "I have been down every road, and I know it all."

It was steaming hot, especially for early May. I changed five times. I wanted to be cool and not overheated, and look good at the same time. I settled for a simple white cotton dress that had a white crocheted halter top attached and a pair of black patent leather sandals. That morning, I blew my hair straight and even put on make up. We arrived at Flower Bright early. I felt exposed and wished I had on more clothes. Mom was in her signature jeans with a white tailored shirt, a red jacket, and a giant Gucci bag, circa 1990. She had resurfaced her rich banker's wife look, even if she no longer had the rich banker. She was in the mirror all morning. Maybe she felt something over the phone and was hoping for a connection with him.

Mr. Nickerson led us into a small room with a sofa and a couple of chairs. As hard as they tried the room still looked like an odd collection of hand-me-down furniture.

Mr. Nickerson, to Mom's disappointment, was homely and wore an ill-fitting suit. I got the feeling that the agency had seen better days. He handed my mom a manila folder.

"There is someone who would like to meet you, too. Everything is in the folder. If you have any questions, please let me know. I have another engagement but the agency will facilitate any communications as long as both parties are willing. Also, please make use of the adoption registry; we encourage all our families to register. I must leave now. Please let me know if I can help in any way." He had one foot out the door and turned and said, "One last thought: you can create a folder just like the one I gave you. If others reach out, I will give them a package for you, too."

"Mom, are we registered? What others? What others, Mom? Who wants to meet us – read it, read it."

"Your birth parents, I guess. Now, lower your voice and calm yourself." She looked over at Mr. Nickerson. "Oh, Mr. Nickerson, do you mind if we stay here and go over the information?" She seemed annoyed. *No one to flirt with.*

"Not at all; help yourselves. Let the receptionist know if you would like something to drink – coffee, tea, water, or soda."

"Water would be nice; I'll let her know."

"No, please allow me."

He slipped out, quickly, like he had a bus to catch.

"Mom, what was he talking about? Who would he give my folder to? My birth parents know I am here. It must be William."

"Oh my God. I'll be damned." Her mouth was wide open. "What?"

The receptionist appeared with two bottles of water and glasses on a bamboo serving tray. From her French manicured fingers to her high heeled pumps, she was well put together.

"Ladies," she said, and put the water on the table.

"Thank you very much," my mom said, dismissing her and reading the top sheet in the folder.

"Oh my God! Sophie, it says here that you have a sister."

"Okay, maybe she is with William." My head was spinning.

"Her name is Ashferna Fitzhenry. She is about 27 and is looking for any other children that Shelly and Michael had and placed for adoption with the Flower Bright Agency. She goes on to say that Shelly and Michael are a married bi-racial couple from Chicago." She kept reading. Her boney fingers ran across the bright yellow paper that the letter was written on.

"Mom, I have a birth sister and brother! I wonder if they are together. Is there a number for them?"

"Honey, it doesn't mention William at all, anywhere."

It felt impossible, and I started to wonder who this person was. This was starting to feel like a trap or something.

"Yes, there is a number and an address. She lives on Staten Island."

"How come they didn't tell you about her sooner? Let's call her." I said.

"She's older than you are. Maybe she was already placed. When do you want to call her, today?"

"Yes, right now." I was angry with this interloper and wanted to confront her quickly so I could get back to my real search – my little brother.

"Sophie, don't you want to get your thoughts together? You only get one time to make the first contact. Let's make a list of questions and call tomorrow."

"You can't think this is on the up and up? Mom, I want to call right now. Can I use your phone?" She looked like she was in shock, but handed me her cell phone.

"Mom, it is ringing." My heart was jumping out of my chest. *My name is Sophie and I might be your sister, I said to myself. Interloper or sister, interloper or sister?*

A loud, zippy voice answered the phone. "Hello, hold the phone, I have to pee." I could hear the pee and then heard the toilet flush and what sounded like her washing her hands. I liked her instantly. Anyone who would let you hear them pee couldn't have many secrets. *Maybe she was my long-lost sister.*

"Are you sure this grapefruit diet is going to do anything but make me pee? Maybe the trips to the toilet are a secret exercise thingy? How long are we going to stay on this one, miss thing?"

"What?" I said. She had mistaken me for a diet buddy.

"Hello?"

"Hello, my name is Sophie Tracey and I am calling from the Flower Bright Adoption Agency. I think you think that we are related, like I might be your sister." I had wanted to make a joke and then say my name, but I couldn't. I could only hope that I was clear.

"Excuse me?"

"Hi, my name is Sophie Tracey, and I think you think I am your sister. I can call back." I hung up.

"Mom, Ashferna, or whatever her name is, is crazy. I should have listened to you. Let's go." My spirit began to sink. Confusion set in. We gathered our things and were about to head out when my mother's phone rang. She answered it.

"Hello. Yes. Yes. No. It's my daughter Sophie that called you." I shook my head "no" like a baby. Mom continued, "Are you Ashferna?" There was a long pause, and Mom put her finger up to her mouth and motioned for me to be quiet. "We are reading the letter and your folder that you left with Flower Bright. Right. Well, hello to you, too. My name is Synovia Tracey. That was Sophie. Right. She is twenty-two; it says here that you must be twenty-seven, that is if my math is correct. Really? Married, two kids. Really?" Mom sat down and made herself comfortable like she was speaking with an old friend. She popped open the bottled water, reached for a glass that had been sitting on the bamboo tray. She blew into the glass to get rid of any dust, and then filled it with water.

"Really, that is funny. Sophie didn't mention it yet. I understand." Mom listened and finished her water. She pointed to the phone with her free hand. "Really, we would love to meet. Let's try for Saturday. Six? That is fine. Okay Fern, thanks for calling back. We are looking forward to meeting you. Sophie, give me a pencil, quick." Mom hung up the phone and jotted down some information. "I need a drink," she said.

"Mom, don't even joke about that. What did she say? Has she met my little brother yet?"

"I didn't ask. She did say that she thought you were her neighbor Susan. They are diet buddies. And that she is sorry about the bathroom thing. She will meet us at the ferry on Saturday, after six."

"What makes you think that I wanted to meet her, Mom?

"She might know where William is, and if not you will know who she is?"

"Or who she is pretending to be. How will we know each other?"

"She wants us to wear yellow and carry little flowers."

"What?" We looked at each other for a moment. I could tell that she wanted to laugh. I wanted to tell her that Fern was starting to sound like a fruitcake. I had a sick feeling in my stomach that I would know Fern, the same way that I know my face in the mirror. The horror of seeing a mirror image of me staring back started the tears flowing.

It rained on Saturday and I had to keep my raincoat open to show off the bright yellow top. Mom had on a cool yellow hat and a yellow jacket from the eighties. I hadn't been able to eat anything all day. I had a bad feeling about Fern – a real bad feeling. *Was she going to make us pay for information about my brother?* I went back and forth trusting and hating Fern. It felt like extortion. My thinking was crazy and so was this situation.

Nothing could have prepared me for meeting Fern. She was also wearing yellow. Yellow everything like size ten shoes, a yellow dress, and yellow plastic jewelry. She was carrying a stupid little arrangement of flowers that both Mom and I forgot to buy as we rushed to get a cab to the ferry. Fern walked right up to us, and I was completely floored. She looked like me. Same skin tone, same wild unmanageable hair, only hers looked like it needed to be trimmed or something! She looked like an older me: a happier, fatter, yellow-dress, yellow-shoe-wearing version of me.

"Hello, family," she said and hugged us both. We must have looked like an amateur singing group singing for tips, and Fern was our leader with all our yellow and her flowers. We hopped in a cab and headed to a little place that Fern suggested, where we ordered martinis and appetizers. Mom had a Diet Coke.

Fern was so talkative. Damn. She told us her whole life story – starting with when her adoptive parents decided to adopt. She knew there were others, her mother told her, before she died. The irony was that her family didn't much talk about adoption, and she had more information about our birth folks than I had. And I thought that we were so open about my history and stuff.

Fern had the gift of gab. She talked so much, and her round little belly shook when she laughed, which was often. So, she talked, and Mom and I listened. I wanted to ask her about William but I didn't mind the stream of information that flowed from her lips, face, and especially her eyes. She was delighted to share herself so genuinely, and I was feeling like I had pre-judged Fern.

She was a mother of two: Madison and Jonathan. She was a part-time schoolteacher. And from what she discovered, she was placed for adoption straight from the hospital delivery room. She had decent parents – her only problem, I surmised, was that they were tea-totaling goody-two-shoes church-goers that demanded the same of Fern.

Fern said she wasn't bad off at all; it was just that she was not supposed to be human, and being sweet, clean, and pretty all the time is harder to maintain than one might think. Fern was an open book. We managed to order dinner in between the stories of Fern's life. After dinner we continued to listen to

Fern until she jumped up, swung into her yellow raincoat and announced that she had to collect her children. She and mom teased over who would pay for dinner. Fern won.

On the way home we were quiet until Mom asked, "Sophie?"

"Yes, Mom."

"What did you make of Fern?"

"She was nice enough."

"I don't remember anyone ever talking so much. It was amazing how she managed to eat her dinner. At first I thought it was nerves. No, it was Fern. Then I settled in and enjoyed all her stories."

"Mom: I made a decision tonight."

"Yes, Sophie."

"I am moving back home for good. I can't spend another second involved with Wise. He is not involved with me or my life. We stay together because it is easier than leaving."

"What are you saying?"

"I called him and told him I was meeting Fern today – and nothing."

"Nothing?"

"Nothing, Mom."

"Wow – was it something Fern said?"

"No, Mom; it was something that Wise *didn't* say. Like 'tell me what you know about her' or 'how are you doing?'"

"My program advises not to make any major changes in your life – like this. This could all be a reaction to finding your sister."

"Spare me."

"Okay – but I noticed you didn't find out about William."

"I have Fern's number, Mom."

"You might call, but I bet dollars to donuts you won't ask – she won't make room for you. Her life is full."

"Maybe you could talk to her for me then."

"And say what?"

"Ask questions; tell her about us."

"Oh right: the list of questions that I asked you to write...
Where are they? In your purse? Oh, no. Now I remember:
you didn't do it. You didn't think it was necessary."

"Mom, you said you would help. I might be strange about
this whole thing – like flipping back and forward about Fern –
but keep in mind you are my helper. So stop it."

* * * * *

After back-to-back interviews for substitute teacher gigs, I
pulled into Mom's driveway discouraged about both school and
the on-call nature of breaking into teaching. I decided to take
more of my things out of my trunk and move them permanently into the house. I was paying half the rent with Wise and
needed to get out of the lease and the relationship.

Mom had spoken with Fern, and before I could get out of
the car and put my first box down, she was all over me.

"Fern didn't know about William. She cried about having
yet another brother. She said that there must be another
brother because he was born between Fern and you. Her
mother got the call and couldn't take him. She said that he was
who she was looking for when you answered her letter. She,
unlike you, was gracious about finding a sister."

My box dropped to the ground. "I need to sit down."

"Come into the house; I'll get your things. Can you believe
this? I want to get all of you together for a reunion dinner.
Sorry, honey, right you have never met each other. Let's just
call it a get-to-know-you dinner."

And just like that there were four of us. We were an anonymous tribe of siblings. Two boys and two girls all placed for
adoption.

Mom made tea and watched me like I was about to pop or
something. She was thinking, and she was the one who popped
– after staring me down for three or four minutes.

"Mom, there must be a mistake, and Fern made it."

"I was thinking. Now hear me out," she said, almost yelling
with discovery. She reminded me of Cynthia Hagan, the

smartest girl in my seventh grade class, who never managed to put her hand down and repeated each question before she skillfully answered it. I hated her.

"If you find this other brother you will find William. Cause William was adopted by someone who had already adopted a sibling of yours. How do you like that? Well what do you think?"

"So what if this other brother is William, and Fern has her years wrong? She was a child then, Mom," I said, shutting down the Cynthia Hagan in her.

"Can you believe that Shelly had three or four children and they were all given up by her for adoption? Do you think that Shelly kept other children? See, I thought you were the only one or the first, and that there was a child after you who was being raised by another family; a family with a sibling. That was why they called me, Sophie, dear: because I had you. So, if they didn't place William with me they must have placed him with another parent who had one of Shelly's children. It was that they had a boy and that is why Shelly picked them to keep William so that both boys would be together. Otherwise she would have picked us. Right? Right?" She was smiling with relief.

Mom was jumping and pacing around like Perry Mason in those old trial shows on TV. She, my, spiritually evolving mother, missed the chasm that was full of my feelings. She looked at me impatiently waiting for some acknowledgement, some sort of pat on the head.

"Mom, you need to stop. You are making me dizzy. At least with Fern, I could follow the story." I got up and checked my car from the window.

"Sorry, honey," she said, and then disappeared into the kitchen.

I wanted my mom to help, but I couldn't jump over the boatload of feelings that held my feet stuck to the floor.

I felt like I was at that point of the roller coaster ride where you are at the tip top and about to drop, and the coaster makes that click – you wonder if it is locking your car on the track or if something is horribly broken. You scream, and no one, not even you, know which scream it is.

Gabriella M. Belfiglio

Nothing
        But
              Spaces
                    of
                        Light
                            and
                                Dark

"Every moment of light and dark is a miracle."
                                        – Walt Whitman

The collection of poems "Nothing but Spaces of Light and Dark" is a sample of my larger body of work: including poems I wrote more than a decade ago, others I have just recently finished writing, and those in between. It was not easy to make the final choices. I didn't necessarily include my favorite poems, but rather a range of work that expresses a journey of its own.

It has been a joy to create a unit of poems, like placing stepping-stones across two banks of a rough creek.

I sometimes wish I were writing a novel instead of individual poems—not that I assume it would be an easy task: far from it. I crave the continuity a novel or longer piece of prose would demand. I would love to have chapters neatly numbered, each in its correct place, instead of piles and folders full of single poems that might or might not have anything to do with one another. The space between finishing one poem and starting another often looms large. It is a little dizzying, the constant state of beginning.

Often people ask me, "What do you write about?" Each time I am left speechless. There is no subject I consider off-limits. Often what I write about is as much a surprise to me as to a reader picking up my poem for the first time. There is inspiration everywhere. Writing poetry keeps me present. It keeps me questioning everything.

Isadora Duncan once said, "If I could tell you what it meant, there would be no point in dancing it." Here's my dance.

I. Daybreak

Sun

like medicine
on this Sun-
day, like Church.

It disappears too early now
as another year
drops amber leaves.

Heads bent down
to the gold
outlined pew or

knees knelt on the
yellow-green grass
let us pray.

Starting Over

The first sun for days:
I walk into it like it will
save me.

In the mail there's a check
from my mom, her paycheck
signed over to me.
It will be the first time
in over a decade someone else
helps pay my rent.

For lunch today I have a bag
of chips – the only thing left
that's portable from my shelf
in the cabinet full of cans.

Heavy cans pushed into the gaps
between my books and clothes –
transported last minute:
mushrooms, crushed tomatoes,
mini cans with thick paste inside,
cream of broccoli soup,
and one of mandarin oranges,
that I can't bear to eat:
their promise of something

sweet and bright
waiting for me.

The first sun for days:
I walk into it like it will
save me.

Hope

The snowflakes are bigger than
Susan B. Anthony silver dollars.
They come down in torrid speed
with determination that is inspiring.
On this spring day I try to let
go—try to submit myself to
something larger that is out there,
something the snow is listening to,
and allow the thoughts that come to haunt me
fall down and melt as they hit the sidewalk.
Right now I am standing in the
cold feeling the fat drops
fall on my hair that sits on my forehead. Waiting
to catch them, I close my eyes only aware of
light and wet and infinite possibility.

Easter

After a morning of clean laundry that smells like the sun,
images of my nanna and nonno float around me.
They are smiling as we shoot out of the car and run
through the yard, where sheets the color of butter freely
ride the wind, only clothespins holding them from sky.
I jump up the steps and into my grandparents' outstretched arms.
On the porch there is iced tea and nearby
shiny aluminum cups crowded in a swarm

of colors. In the middle of the pyramid, I eye
the pink one. My nanna squeezes a lemon, always the charm,
inside as she hands it to me. The smell of dinner starts to ooze
through the holes in the screen door. Like a butterfly
I start to flutter as my stomach screams louder than an alarm.
On my face gleams a smile as bright as my new white shoes.

II. Noon

Down the Shore

The unruly ocean extends past our pocket
of the New Jersey shore, past sight.
It disappears into a blurry line
of blue, both sea and sky.

The oldest cousins spread out the threadbare
sheet, strewn with stitched baby blue bouquets.
They slick their skin with baby oil,
arrange their bodies in flat strips;
their glittery bikinis wink at the sun.

My brother and I split to find styrofoam soda cups
in the metal trash cans by the boardwalk.
We gather as many as we can carry, rushing back
through the hot sand,
build castles on the water's edge.

At the rented house,
a block past the painted merry-go-round horse,
our nanna is making it ours.
On the stove simmers

a large pot of tomato sauce,
in the palms of her hands, meatballs roll.
Neatly gathered, two white braids
stretch across her head.

Thirteen

Unwrap that miserable time:
junior high—no longer naïve
friends transforming into enemies
readying themselves.
Everyone trying to fit.

I tried—the only time.
I wore fluorescent pinks and greens,
teased my hair like Madonna.
We were budding teenagers wanting to be all grown,
though we couldn't even fill out our bras.

Suddenly girls were expected
to do more than kiss,
boys placing our hands
on their dicks.

If I knew what I know now
I wouldn't have pulled away
so quickly, scared
and ashamed—with nothing to say
my only thought: home.

I was more interested in sleepovers with my girlfriends.
Imagine us talking about everything while gently
gliding our fingers across each others' bodies—
comparing the ripples we felt when we reached

low, past our belly buttons
arriving.

Run your hands through this

> You only have to look at the Medusa straight on
> to see her. And she's not deadly. She's beautiful
> and she's laughing.
> — Hélène Cixous, "The Laugh of the Medusa"

this   head

        of   snakes

                                        come closer

          they don't   bite

this
  twist

  this
frizz

       this   rope   that   men   climb

this
    mask
      camouflage

  crown   of   fem in in it y

                         these   wild   ringlets

        curled   wands   that   charm

doors
      open

        the same ones that without these locks
                    lock in my face

this net
               web
                          pile

it's getting   **heavy**

The House Guest

Here is the Scene:

I am at my girlfriend's sister's house,
it is Memorial Day—
the American flag flaps red, white, and blue
like a warning at the front door.

The backyard is full of glee—
children splashing pool water into the hot
Florida air like fountains. Their parents
are mingling: margaritas cold in the cups
of their hands.

I am sitting on the back porch trying to remember
not to call my girlfriend *honey* or *sweetie*. I don't
dare sit next to her, even though everyone knows.
I am not the first girl
she's brought home.

Her sister introduces me to the neighbors
as *the house guest*.

I find a baby to hold and hide inside
rocking him to sleep. The weight of him
is satisfying—his balmy skin sticks to my own.

Even after his eyes have stopped fluttering,
I hold on.

I am doing ok until my girlfriend's mother
hands me the camera.
She finds me, in a room full of people,
and hands it to me.
It is a calculated move.
Will you take a family *picture for us?*
she asks me smoothly.

My girlfriend gathers amidst her
parents, her sister and brother-in-law,
the two little ones in front.

A stranger approaches me,
Here, she says reaching for the camera,
don't you want to be in the picture?
My stomach drops.
I'm not invited.
Tears surge into my eyes.

I crouch on the other side
of the pool—close to the water's edge:
shoot.

III. Twilight

A Daughter's Tale

"... how free is a woman?—
born with Eve's sin between her legs,
and inside her,
Lucifer sits on a throne of abalone shells. . ."
                    —Ai from "The Mother's Tale"

The room is full of girls
trying out the new skins of women.
I see myself ten years ago
shudder with the changes of a decade.
I hold up a book with the word feminist
in the title. Their expressions surprise me. I can
not believe this word could yield disgust
and fear in these young faces.
forgive them I think inside my head,
ask out loud: *how free is a woman?*

We can do anything we want, they claim proudly,
we don't have to hate men
don't need to burn our bras—grow long
hair under our arms. One declares: *I don't think I'm a feminist,*
but my boyfriend calls me one because I don't want kids.
I feel the subtle weight of eggs
inside of me, think: *most feminists I know are surrounded*
by children (theirs or others'). I challenge them further:

How do you respond to those that say women are the very dregs
of society, born with Eve's sin between her legs?

A quiet girl speaks up
from the back of the room.
Her hair is separated into two ponytails
curls falling over each shoulder.
She looks no older than twelve.
I think men get away with murder,
she says, *many say it is different now—*
that sexism is dead—but it's not true
men still have a larger privilege and power,
and inside her

a strength glows as bright as the moon
I am not saying all men are jerks,
just that they have more support in this world
to be who they want—without blame or judgment.
The rest of the day her face is before me wherever I go.
An image of hope.
A reminder that there is no limit
to the stories that still need to be told.
There is no ultimate truth that defines evil and good,
but many hells, and not every version has Lucifer.

The Light of the Moon

– poem for Audre Lorde

Imagining your lips—
my mouth forms words
that come like the leaves of autumn
dry   falling   and full of color

I have always been a spring person
a yellowgreen girl more day than night
skin not as dark as olives
nor as light as peaches

I have mourned the end of summer
like a lover gone—preparing my limbs
to be covered in cold neglect, the impending dark
feeling like a hole akin to a grave

But in your earth an ancient spirit rises
your words come like rain
and I find myself drenched
sink my toes deep into wet reds and browns

In the growing twilight
I move forward a little taller
less with the anticipation of joy
more with a warrior's stride of determination.

Coat for my Unborn Child

I am sewing you a coat.
The stitches are uneven
the pattern is mismatched
yet it will keep you warm.

Lately I picture you and me joined,
my stomach growing even rounder
than it does every year at my Aunt Marie's table—
after the small dishes of caponata, bowls of escarole soup,

heavy gnocchi red with sauce, stuffed artichokes—
its seam ready to burst.
Your coat has a lining of silk:
purple paisley pajamas I slept in till they tore,

linked with the frayed skirt of a movie star dress
my mother wore before I was born.
I picture her twirling—the amber pleats
rippling around her thighs.

I cannot see your face,
but your hands come to me in dreams.
Your fingers are long—tailor hands,
they pull at loose threads

reach inside soft holes
circle as the yarn unravels.
Sometimes, as you turn in and out
I see the back of your head

dark downy curls cover your ears
softer than satin.
The outside of the coat weaves
the colors of the rainbow.

I tentatively tack scraps of cloth,
more times than not pricking
the plush flesh of my own fingers—
there is blood on these fibers.

I watch other babies,
parents swallowing tiny bodies
in the midst of their own large limbs.
The babies' throats ring: *Mama.*

I look around each time
as if you were already with me.
Until then, I keep my needle threaded,
gather small pieces of cloth,

try to picture you whole.

Doing Laundry Together

The day I leave again, we go to the 24-hour laundromat—
the big one on Washington. I leave her to the sorting
of clothes, go in search of coffee. At Tom's Diner
people are grouped in twos and fours a colony of
squawking seagulls eating pancakes and eggs,
not as lucky as the others
who flew out of the city for the long weekend.
It is the end of summer and the very air is different
not just in temperature and light, but in people's
breath—a collective sigh clouds over the neighborhood.
I could walk through these streets blindfolded.
Every corner has a reminder, like a wrapped present
of somebody I have loved or hated or both.
I return with the coffee, just the way she likes it—
black one sugar. The clothes are turning in the wash.
When we woke up I lingered longer in bed than
usual, I moved my body close to her.
I could navigate through her landscape blindfolded.
But she insists there are dirty clothes I will need
mixed with hers and we leave the apartment
full of heavy bags.

IV. Midnight

This city is my lover.

I walk on her streets and let the curves carry me. The red
and green direct me, I move in and out of crowds. Down 3rd
Avenue the suits and high heels are getting out. They push
to the steps of the subway. I leave them underground
where their coats are stained black. The setting sun shines
gold into the windows. It is magic. Something good inside
these buildings that clack with the sound of beating
keys, drown with the deep monotone voices discussing
your and my life as if they knew. Fluorescent lights blaring
and coffee being carried by *that pretty new girl*
with long blond hair, *did you notice the way her ass moves*
when she walks? I cut my hair short, shake my limbs
rid of the ooze of filth that tries to stick. I walk in the shadows
past corners of people sleeping in boxes, living
off unfinished lunches left in styrofoam containers thrown away
in front of their faces. I sit on the benches in the
park on East 16th Street, watch the methadone addicts
get their next fix. This city is full of mistakes just waiting
to happen again. It hurts to keep your eyes open.
I walk her chaotic streets and the power
encompasses me. I whisper to her in earnest:
Beloved.

Close to Home

—for Stephanie and Deon

The policeman said there was no evidence
to indicate the murders were hate crimes.

When was the last time he walked out of his house
in a dress and heels, scared
of what people would do?
When did he last have to feel
that onerous weight of others' eyes on him?
Hear the hate that comes out of people's mouths
just for existing: "hey faggot
wanna suck my dick?"
How often does Sergeant Joe wonder
which bathroom to go into when he has to pee?
Tell me, did he even see *their lifeless bodies—*
pierced with at least 10 bullets each?

Stephanie wore a heart-shaped locket with a picture of
her mother, Queen, around her neck.
Queen says everything she liked
Stephanie copied: leopard patterns, scented candles,
dabs of Chanel No. 5 on her wrists and neck.
Stephanie even bought
a silver vanity table, just like her mother's.
Always now there is this subtext to Queen's words:
Why, WHY, would anyone have hated her child so much?

Stephanie thought everybody was her friend.

Notes next to the teddy bears and flowers
flag the spot they were killed. One reads:
Deon, I am glad that I had the chance to tell you
that I accepted the fact that you wanted to be who YOU
wanted to be. Love, Aunt Sharon

I picture Stephanie getting braids
woven down her back,
picking out the perfect hot pink
headband to match her nails.
I can see her inviting Deon over
to get ready together—teenagers
trying out what color lipstick looks the best.
I imagine them climbing into their newly bought
used black Camry, with tinted windows,
careful not to mess up their hair.

Half a block farther and they would have been home.

The first time

I saw Joannie,
was on a roof in Brooklyn,
suspended above buildings
stretching to reach the sky.
We were both trying to capture the same
woman. Joannie's eyes seizing
light shape form
through the frame of a camera.
My eyes prompted by desire.
There is nothing like new love.

After that, like a shadow,
beneath the blaze of sun and clouds.
Joannie kept appearing disappearing
appearing again.

The next time I saw her
was at the door of my dojo,
Joannie's long dark hair hiding
the burst of her smile.

Months later, I caught a glimpse of Joannie
dashing out of the divey bar on 5ᵗʰ avenue,
full of restless girls,
smoke sneaking out the door with her.
We both bowed our blushed cheeks
coyly aside, then took a second look.

After that, I started to see Joannie regularly
behind the large blue case
of *Fresh Fish* as we both catered
to the crowd at the farmer's market.
Her small body circled
in a faded green apron.
She sprang between
the customers and the registers—
never seeming to walk.

When my back was turned,
impishly, she'd spurt a little
closer—chirping in my ear, her
hands squeezing the soft
of my waist.

The time in a cafe off Union Square,
both of us weary after
a long day of selling fish,
she told me secrets.
Other lives she had lived.
In one, she wore lacy white,
veil and all. I've never seen
Joannie in a dress.

In another, she was still a child,
only nine years old, the city of
Saigon vanishing behind her.

The first time Joannie came to my
apartment to cook, she brought
each utensil, each ingredient,
tucked away in her
Mary Poppins bag.
She pulled out
sharpened knives
like wands—
constructing a feast
right before my eyes.
Never has tuna tasted so good.

That night, walking her
to the subway—
after she filled my tummy full of her
magic, she admitted
what I had already guessed.
Maybe if I wanted children,
Joannie told me, knowing
that determined dream of mine, her
ebony eyes flashing
possibility.

About a year later,
while I was away at school in DC,
that indelible phone call from our
mutual friend back in Brooklyn, that plays back
time and time again, found me cities away.
She uttered: *Joannie*
stated: *leukemia*
I paced back and forth
through my tiny rented room,
speechless.

The first time I visited Joannie
at Sloan-Kettering, I wasn't ready.
I had to wear a mask
round my face,
stubborn plastic gloves that
pinched the skin of my hands.
Every inch of my body fought
me, trying to reach out
to hug my friend.
No direct contact was allowed.

A jagged anger pulsed hard
through my healthy blood
the entire 204 miles back to DC.

The last time I saw Joannie,
alive it was a Thursday afternoon.
I sat in her room—the imported
hospital bed holding her
disappearing body on a slant.

Her right eye
was crusted permanently closed.
She was losing
the functions of anatomy—
this limb: immobile
this organ: collapsed
and everywhere her
blood rapidly giving up
its fight against itself.

Still, Joannie strained
to tell me she was ok.
Her still able left
hand held mine the whole time.

I asked Joannie
if she was in pain.
Tired, is what she whispered back,
Gabriella, I am always tired now.
Just like a new-born baby,
breathing took effort.

My tears came soft and steady
clouding my vision of Joannie,
as she fell asleep above the roar of
Hell's Kitchen.

In the funeral parlor
crowded with people she loved
there were the pictures she took everywhere.
Joannie's view of the world
coloring the stark white walls.

Instructions After Death

1. Save one part of the firewood of my body—
   You choose:
   hand, nipple, elbow, spleen, heart, clitoris.

2. Offer the remainder to science—
   what's still functioning, give away,
   answer someone's prayer.
   If it's too late, bring my body
   to a hospital with eager students,
   let me be touched one more time,
   eyes curious to see what's inside.

   Let them cut open, past skin,
   and like a poem in a foreign language,
   read each recognizable vein, follow
   the skinny slippery route up my thick thigh
   down my solid spine,
   make a sliver of sense of our mysterious body.

3. Burn the part you saved.
   Have song in the background,
   like at a campfire—Joni Mitchell or Nina Simone.
   If my brother is alive, rent a grand piano
   for him to play.

4. Separate the ashes into three.

5. Carry a third to Italy. Here you must
   measure out a teaspoon of the dried basil of my body
   sprinkle it into the Arno river,
   under that massive weeping willow
   there on the edge of Florence.

   With the remainder, head south.
   Keep me in your pocket.
   Walk around the streets,
   look up and down instead of left and right.
   Notice the art under your feet,
   the colors above your head.

   Talk to people along the way,
   use your eyes, your hands, the tilt of your head.
   Don't use English.
   As you walk away, say:
   sta mi bene, your fingers still reaching.

   After you find Mt. Etna growing
   out of the tiny village of Randazzo, shed the rest of me.
   There will be ash here already. Mix mine in
   with bare hands—like when you make meatballs.
   Give it a little spit in place of egg to make it stick.

6. Return to America.

7. Retrieve the second third.
   If it is winter, head to the Brooklyn Bridge.
   Here you must have a plan.

   It is not as easy as you would think to fling
   contents into the East River.
   There are cars zooming below you,
   a web of metal enclosing you: throw strong
   with a full arc of motion.

   If it is summer, take the F train to Coney Island.
   Buy something awful, like cotton candy
   or a Nathan's hot dog, or battered
   fried shrimp with more batter than shrimp.
   Maybe go on a ride or two. (I would do this
   first, however.)
   Sit in the sun, and when you are ready
   run past the mass of people, past the shallow waves,
   till you can dive into the Atlantic Ocean whole—
   empty me here.

8. With the third part of my ashes,
   go to Philadelphia, where I started.
   Find Giovanni's Room, sit by the window,
   read someone remarkable
   like Audre Lorde or Adrienne Rich.

If you find my book, read
something from there too.
Afterwards, find a private area of Fairmont Park.
And with a seed of your favorite tree,
bury me.

Acknowledgements

Gabriella M. Belfiglio

Over three years ago I placed on the small altar in my office a little scrap of paper which read: *Dear Universe, please help me find a supportive, inspirational, smart, and strong group of writers for me to be a part of.*

My request has been granted. Thank you Kim, Princene, Rita, and Olivia: I am honored to be learning and growing alongside all of you.

I have been blessed with parents who are amazing role models. Thank you, Mom and Dad, for all you have shown and given me over the years. Words don't do justice.

Julia, thank you for understanding what I am saying even when I am silent and for the comfort and reassurance I always find by your side.

I also would like to thank my extended friends and family, given and chosen. Your companionship, love, and encouragement have been invaluable. Thank you for sustaining me.

For the inspiration and guidance he has supplied in the last decade plus, I extend my deep gratitude to my teacher, Nishit Patel.

And finally, I thank Margarita for her generosity, love, unending patience, keen eye, and mostly for the balance we've discovered next to each other.

Kim D. Brandon

First I would like to thank my daughter, Darniece. I want to thank her for sharing my dream and being a perfect angel when she had to come to our writing workshops.

I would also like to thank my family – my brothers Derek and Harlan; my sisters Gale, Sylvia, and Linder; my God-mother Anita Louise; all of my wonderful nieces and nephews, in-laws, and friends – for listening to me talk on about both novels for the past few years. Their support has never diminished, and I love them for it.

A special thanks goes out to Lisel Burns, former BSEC leader, who embraced our group. She invited us to meet at the Society; she even attended a meeting or two. She also gave us opportunities to present our work to the Society.

Finally, I would like to thank everyone who has come through our writers' group and shared their work. I would especially like to thank Gabriella, Ms. Olivia Taylor, Princene, and Rita for their commitment and focus on this project. I'd like to include a special thank you to Margarita Suarez and Joel Shatzky for pulling our work together with style and for gently walking us through the printing process.

Princene Hyatt

For many years I have had the good fortune to know many kind and caring people at Brooklyn Society for Ethical Culture. In December 1998 Clergy Leader Lisel Burns invited me to participate in a community art exhibition. It was a pleasure meeting fellow artists whose work offered memorable visual feasts. Everybody loves the "alive" photographs by Annemarie Wong Mogil. Beatrice Rubin is a very warm person; her colorful artwork is a reflection of herself. Oil paintings by Blanca Machado are strong yet quiet, speaking volumes. As always, I welcomed all feedback regarding my collages.

At the opening reception of this event, Remi Gay commented that in Native American culture, one of my pieces of artwork is called a Dream Catcher. (I call it *Morning Glory*; it is featured on the cover of this book.)

Through the generosity of the Society my writing exploring my visual art began to take shape. Scheduled meetings are always reminders that there is work to be done. I thank them for providing a supportive environment and forum for our creative writing group.

Professor Joel Shatzky introduced the idea of a group publication; he has never been more than a few (nudging) feet away from our project. Many thanks to Joel. Special thanks to Margarita M. Suarez who contributed her extensive knowledge and patience to our group effort.

A special "thank you" to my sisters: group leader Kim Brandon for her valuable advice and criticism, Gabriella Belfiglio, Olivia Taylor and Rita Wilson for their feedback, support and encouragement.

Finally, I thank my good friends Chip Fears and Lauch Henry for their continuing guidance and support.

Olivia S. Taylor

The culture of the storytelling tradition in which I grew up is a treasure, which I owe to my parents and family.

I am grateful to O'Nell, Frances, Dawn, David, and all the other friends with whom I have shared stories. The platform that Brooklyn Society for Ethical Culture has provided our writers' group to read our works has been rewarding. It is a challenge and a pleasure to participate in the BSEC writers' workshops. I appreciate the work of Joel and Marg, who have assisted in bringing this collective effort to life.

Rita REB Wilson

In recognition of people who were tender and stern with voices that came at me from childhood and still resound like a drum: "Write it, just write it." You all know who you are. I appreciate your support in spirit and physically. Much thanks BSEC leader Lisel Burns (now retired) for bringing our writers together for this creative process. Lisel has been like an artist/painter, blending and creating a tapestry of people who fit for a project and add to our community.

Also, BIG THANKS to Constance Pignozzi (former Platform chair) and Nettie Paisley (Life & Ethics chair): both allowed our writers to be heard. I'm appreciative to each of them for the opportunity to express ourselves at Platform and Life and Ethics presentations.

Thanks to Damal Edmond, BSEC Administrative Director, and Eda Kapsis, Pres. of Board and Board of Trustees for allowing us a place to meet twice a month.

Sophia Askew and Annemarie Wong Mogil, respectively, you've inspired and encouraged me, that it does not matter how young or old you are, "just do it." I hope that Sophia Askew is someplace telling her story and inspiring others as she has done in the past. Thanks to Annemarie, "I'm glad we're here to talk about our stories and Julia."

Thanks to dear C. Z. Barksdale who always encourages and supports me.

Kim Brandon, Joel Shatzky, and Margarita Suarez, BIG THANKS for making this project happen.

Also, Rahgib and Rasamin, my grandchildren... Thanks for reminding me to use spell check and the dictionary.

Biographies

Photo: Joanne Scarola

Gabriella M. Belfiglio was born in Philadelphia, Pennsylvania, the youngest of four children. After graduating from Antioch College with a BA in poetry, she moved to Brooklyn, New York, which has been her permanent home ever since. She earned her MFA in poetry from American University. Gabriella is an artist, community activist, and aspiring yogini. She holds several jobs in order to keep writing a priority in her life. She teaches karate and self-defense for the Center for Anti-Violence Education, and she is part of the teaching team at Brooklyn Society for Ethical Culture's Children's Sunday Assembly. She is also a fishmonger at the Grand Army Plaza greenmarket. Her work has appeared in several journals and anthologies, including *Folio*, *The Centrifugal Eye*, the award-winning *Poetic Voices without Borders*, and most recently, *Avanti Popolo*. She can be contacted at gmbelfiglio@gmail.com.

Photo: Annemarie Wong Mogil

Kim D. Brandon was born in Baltimore, Maryland. She grew up in Brooklyn, New York, with her father Lindberg "Bird," her mother O'Nell, three brothers, and three sisters. She currently lives with her daughter, Darniece. Kim is a former Vice President from one of the top five financial institutions of New York. She is taking time off to parent and write. Kim enjoys spending time with her family and friends.

Kim considers herself as a storyteller who is putting her stories on paper. Bird was a great storyteller. As a child, she spent time in his barbershop listening to his stories while he cut hair.

She says: "My voice sometimes gets lost in the craft of writing, but just behind a misplaced semicolon; I want to give you something you can remember, something you can feel – a good laugh, a long cry, or simply the passing of a sunset long remembered."

Kim is currently working on publishing her first novel. She hopes that her work gives readers a place to pause, to relate, and to recall.

Photo: Gabriella M. Belfiglio

Princene Hyatt was a teenager just out of high school when she left her native South Carolina to claim New York City as her very own. She is absolutely sure the Big Apple has everything a curious mind could wish for. After retiring from the Department of Education, she joined the Creative Writing Group at Brooklyn Society for Ethical Culture. Her intention is to share her many life-changing experiences by writing her memoirs in the near future.

Olivia S. Taylor was born in Mobile, Alabama, in a section called "Down the Bay," along the shores of the Mobile Bay, an inlet of the Gulf of Mexico. Shortly after World War II ended, her family moved to the outskirts of town, to an area called Trinity Garden, near Rag Swamp. It was here that she came of age and finished school. She is the middle child of seven children. She moved to New York in the early 60's. She resides in Brooklyn. It is here where she has been a community organizer, parent, and teacher for almost fifty years. She founded and administered a day school from which she recently retired. Now she writes, reads, and tells short stories. She is currently working on a collection of short stories entitled *Rainbows Above and Below.*

Rita REB Wilson is a parent, educator, entrepreneur, and writer living in Brooklyn, New York. She has read her work in cafes and at ceremonies, and she has published a number of poems and articles.

As an educator she has written and produced plays, recitations, and poems for pre-school and elementary children. As a director and teacher for young children, she has been the support system to enable them to excel in elementary education, move on and advance to the next level because of her passion and devotion to the children. During Christmas, Kwanzaa, and graduation ceremonies and programs, the children render stellar performances under her direction.